Democracy and Governance in Higher Education

LRP Series: Legislating for Higher Education in Europe

VOLUME 2

1. R. in't Veld, H.-P. Füssel, G. Neave, *Relations between State and Higher Educatio*
1996 ISBN 90-411-0245-
2. J. De Groof, G. Neave, J. Švec, *Democracy and Governance in Higher Educatio*
1998 ISBN 90-411-0575-

Democracy and Governance in Higher Education

Jan De Groof
Guy Neave
Juraj Švec

Legislative Reform Programme
for Higher Education and Research
Council of Europe

KLUWER LAW INTERNATIONAL
THE HAGUE / LONDON / BOSTON

A C.I.P. Catalogue record for this book is available from the Library of Congress.

ISBN 90-411-0575-1 (HB)

Published by Kluwer Law International,
P.O. Box 85889, 2508 CN The Hague, The Netherlands.

Sold and distributed in the U.S.A. and Canada
by Kluwer Law International,
675 Massachusetts Avenue, Cambridge, MA 02139, U.S.A.

In all other countries, sold and distributed
by Kluwer Law International Centre,
P.O. Box 322, 3300 AH Dordrecht, The Netherlands.

"The authors are responsible for the choice and presentation of the facts contained in this book and for the opinions expressed therein, which are not necessarily those of the Council of Europe and do not commit the Organisation"

Cover design: Tandar, Ljubljana, Slovenia
The cover design was sponsored by the Slovenian Ministry of Education and Sport

Layout and camera-ready copy: Anne-Marie Krens, Oegstgeest, The Netherlands

Printed on acid-free paper

Printed in the Netherlands.

TABLE OF CONTENTS

FOREWORD

by Daniel Tarschys
Secretary General of the Council of Europe

The mission of the Council of Europe is defined by two great concepts: the protection of human rights and fundamental freedoms, and the advancement of democracy. Both are difficult challenges, especially – but not only – since the Organisation's great expansion to take in the post-communist societies of the eastern half of our continent.

The two goals are related but distinct. Human rights are well-defined: even their enemies know what is meant by their protection, and catalogues of core rights differ only in detail. The idea of democracy, in contrast, is as protean an idea as it is potent. Democracy is a universal value – here we side with Rousseau and Kant against Burke and Huntington. The election of the government by the people is its necessary condition, but hardly sufficient. We have been reminded recently by the implosion of Albania that a democratic constitution cannot survive without being deeply rooted in society, not only the rule of law but habits of cooperation and negotiation; here history clearly gives the win to Burke. The action of the Council of Europe to support the democratic transition therefore takes aim at a wide range of the institutions of a civil society. Significantly, the very term came to prominence in the struggles in central Europe for democracy.

Among these institutions, those providing higher education, and especially the university, have an extraordinarily symbolic character – one is tempted to say an exaggerated one, until one recalls the centrality of freedom of speech and inquiry among our fundamental human rights. The university is in origin, and to a considerable extent remains, a mediæval corporation: that is to say, a private association recognised by the state as pursuing a public purpose. This semi-public character has often appeared an anomaly to democratic and legal theorists; but it is an anomaly that should prompt better theories that recognise the value of autonomy and decentralisation even in the domain of public service. In practice, European countries, east and west, strive for the difficult balance between autonomy and accountability. It was thus natural that the first volume of the Legislative Reform Programme's book series, published in 1996, bore the title "Relations between State and higher education".

It is only a partial truth that the price of autonomy for higher education is accountability for quality. This is to make autonomy merely an instrument of rational management. But as central institutions of civil society, higher education establishments *also* have the duty to run themselves in a broadly democratic, as well as efficient, way: for one cannot educate citizens by authoritarian methods, nor stimulate free thought by coercion. Of course, education is directional, and research a competitive arena; the community of scholars, like that of sportsmen, is not one of natural equality. The governance of higher education must bring together teachers and students in a just partnership, and meet the fair expectations of other stakeholders.

The second volume of the Legislative Reform Programme's book series takes up this challenge. Its distinguished authors combine expertise in higher education policy, in education law, and experience of leadership of universities in east and west. The book is not only based on their knowledge, but on the many valuable reports provided by member countries, and the advisory missions and workshops of the Legislative Reform Programme as a whole. I commend their work to you.

Good governance is not enough for the full development of the democratic mission of the university. Access by all groups in society, lifelong opportunity, and a democratic style of learning are the hills that lie beyond good governance. I am therefore glad that the future volumes of the series will take up issues of funding, of staff, and of the status of students.

Daniel Tarschys

Daniel Tarschys

INTRODUCTION

Today, in virtually each and every democracy, education stands as the focal point in national debate. This is as true for the 'established' democracies as for their burgeoning counterparts in eastern and central Europe. Nor is higher education an exception. On the contrary, both in national debate as too in the international arena, its place in the debate is crucial.

Since the beginning of the 1980s a number of themes have dominated the landscape of higher education. Amongst them have been budget cuts, rationalisation in provision, accountability and quality control, closer links between higher education and the region and a greater alertness to changes in economic and social policy. At the institutional level, the drive towards a greater degree of latitude and autonomy has found a ready echo amongst universities and other establishments of higher education. And this, in its turn, has posed major questions about the range of responsibilities central government and administration ought to retain or to delegate.

Human ingenuity being what it is, it does not take a very great stretch of the imagination to see that many of these themes are intertwined. Change in one has repercussions upon another. Throughout this study of governance and democracy we have been especially careful to lay stress upon these interactive linkages which, of course, are far from being the same thing as a chain of causality.

The topic of governance and democracy is not to be tackled without solid reference to context. Nor can it really be analysed in a species of intellectual vacuum. Clearly, it ties in with the other themes which this series "Legislating for higher education in Europe" will attend to in the fullness of time: the relationship between the state and higher education, accountability, staff and students. In this volume, however, these dimensions are examined from the perspective of governance. It concentrates on the legislative process, on internal structures of administration and on the mechanisms of management. It explores the way in which the concept of democracy emerges in higher education, how government control is exercised and how its exercise has evolved.

The analysis of a dynamic process is always a delicate undertaking. What appears to the observer to be the 'end of the story' very often turns out to be an episode in a long-drawn-out institutional saga. "The Captains and the Kings depart" but the issue they have gathered together to settle, often assumes a life of its own. It continues to develop long after they have taken their leave. So it is with governance, with state-university relationships and with models of management. We are only too well aware that what we have investigated here represents a slice through a particular dimension of higher education at a particular moment. And given the speed at which events are taking place in Europe's higher education systems – both in the East and in the West – we are only too well aware of the provisional nature of our work.

This book is a collective undertaking. Each of us has brought his part, his disciplinary perspective, his particular experience and background to bear on this topic. We have tried to weld our very different viewpoints into a whole which, hopefully, is greater than the sum of our individual parts. Each of us, in his own manner, is deeply involved in the world of the university. All of us share an abiding loyalty to that institution, as lawyers, as historians and as medical researchers. Working together has been a source of very personal delight and enrichment and we would hope this is reflected in the fruit of our labours.

The comparative perspective is the point of departure, if not the essence, of this book. Continual comparative reference to national rules and regulations is one of the main characteristics of this investigation. Following the overview, the individual country case studies are built around a common format as a means of facilitating the comparison of individual aspects and, we would hope, as a means of pointing up where future studies may be made.

There are many conclusions to emerge from this overview. But there is one which stands out above the others. It is that a higher education strategy requires the active partnership between institutions endowed with a high degree of autonomy, and a dynamic government. Both university and government have this common feature – they serve people and they serve the community. Thus it can come as little surprise that the community requires accounts to be rendered about the ways in which institutional autonomy is used. Nor ought one to be greatly astonished when the community from time to time expresses some misgivings over the degree of rigour which government exercises in its oversight of this matter.

Because the university stands as the 'gateway to the future'[1] it bears great responsibility *vis à vis* society. This range of responsibilities, is far from diminishing. One has only to dwell on the idea, thrown up over the past ten years, that the university is morally responsible for the employability of its graduates, to appreciate the truth of this axiom. Yet, for the very reason that these responsibilities are growing – whether the universities like it or not – the need to make them both transparent and explicit – above all in a society that is both modern and democratic – remains paramount. As Derek Bok, former President of Harvard University wrote at the start of the decade, "Armed with the security of tenure and the time to study the world with care, professors would appear to have a unique opportunity to act as society's scouts to signal impending problems long before they are visible to others. Yet, rarely have members of the academy succeeded in discovering emerging issues and bringing them vividly to the attention of the public."[2]

University government ought to reflect at one and the same time the democratic ethic and the process of critical and rigorous thinking with which they have been entrusted by society. Yet, the management and the administration of the university are no longer matters exclusive to academics. How the university will develop in the future is most certainly not the exclusive concern of legislators or of professors, either. It is, however, the concern of the community. For, as one commentator recently noted, "Perhaps there

1 Clark, Burton R. (1995), *Places of Enquiry,* Berkeley/Los Angeles/London: University of California Press.

2 Bok, Derek (1990), *Universities and the future of America,* Durham: Duke University Press.

is an even greater danger if the legislation is regarded as 'belonging' to someone else."[3]

Like many of those who confide their thoughts to paper, our fondest hope is, of course, that "if our sins be scarlet, may our book be read." But we would hope, even so, that our readership goes beyond those professionally concerned and responsible for higher education.

We would also wish here to mark our indebtedness to the Secretariat of the Council of Europe, in particular to the staff of the "Legislative Reform Programme", and to Uta Börne, Catherine Montgomery, Sigita Sarafinaite, Genevieve Woods, as well as Peter Kwikkers, former programme manager of the LRP, whose dedication and enthusiasm pervades this volume in ways well beyond the obvious. Similarly, we would not wish that the international correspondants remain unthanked, unsung or unacknowledged. In fact, it is upon their labour that we have built our edifice and to the extent that it stands at all must surely be due to the solidity of the foundations on which it rests. Acknowledgement of our debts of kindness, support and help does not absolve us from assuming the burden for whatever errors of fact or interpretation this study may have perpetuated. For this, we claim full and exclusive rights – and responsibility!

Jan de Groof, Guy Neave, Juraj Švec

April 15th 1997

3 Whalley, George (1993), in *Education and the law*, Carfax no. 1, p. 6.

1

GOVERNANCE AND DEMOCRACY IN HIGHER EDUCATION

1.1 Introduction

Amongst the more enduring beliefs that contemporary society ascribes to the university, one of the most widespread must surely be that higher education places democracy on a surer footing. It is of course axiomatic that a well educated citizenry is a sure bulwark against demagogy, extremism, intolerance and hopefully against downright fraud, perjury and electoral dishonesty though these times have subjected the principle itself to unexpected strain. Higher education stands as the main route for acquiring higher learning together with the liberal and pluralistic values which go with it. It fulfils a significant role of political socialisation, though this particular function has recently come under question (Rothblatt, 1995).

1.2 Governance and democracy

Over the past quarter century, higher education in Europe has seen a large number of moves to install the principle of 'democracy' within the groves of academe. This process reached its colourful paroxysm in Paris, Berlin, Milan, Amsterdam and Stockholm over the five year period from 1968 to 1974. It brought in its wake a temporary modification to the condition and status of the Chairholders' university (*Ordinarienuniversität*), replacing it for a brief space with the equally obscure principle of the University of Group Interests (*Gruppenuniversität*). Certainly, the massification of higher education in western Europe reinforced democracy in the sense of opening up higher learning to unprecedented numbers of young people. It did not inevitably go hand in glove with the application of one man one vote in the inner affairs of university self-government.

Had it done so, much of the turmoil and acrimony which followed between 'professorial oligarchy' and the ranks of middle and junior staff – the Mittelbau of the German university – could doubtless have been avoided (Neave & Rhoades, 1987). That such tension was not avoided shows very clearly that applying the principle of democracy in one domain does not always imply its acceptability in another. Agreed, the student radicals of yesteryear, like their fellows today in the newly-liberated lands of eastern and central Europe, argued with considerable vehemence that the principle itself was indivisible. Once recognised in one domain, it ought to be extended generally and one of the areas to which it should apply was internal decision-making. Without it, participatory democracy remained without substance. Such an interpretation, however, was not always accepted with alacrity, nor was it in the area of governance, that is the procedures and principles by which an individual university conducts its internal affairs and husbandry. The basic principle of democracy as the central value running across different forms of university governance is nowadays accepted as both obvious and necessary but it is far from being unproblematic. How is it to be realised in operational detail? How should different interests and constituencies be represented? On what bodies should they figure? Should representation be confined to groups internal to the university or should it involve external stakeholders? How may it be reconciled with that other and equally essential imperative of university life, namely, the recognition of excellence? Is it compatible with the basic priority incumbent on every university, that is the advancement, to the satisfaction of the public and their authoritative representatives, of quality in teaching, learning and research?

These are central issues. Indeed, they always have been throughout the history of the universities in Europe. They come to the fore whenever society modifies its expectations *vis à vis* higher education and whenever it takes steps to develop procedures and structures to give permanent organisational expression to new or modified priorities and objectives.

These ticklish issues have to be set against our interpretation of what we understand by democracy. This, too, is neither unproblematic nor free from its historical and cultural contexts. Democracy viewed by the *Soixante huitards* has little in common – save the name – with the views advanced by the bustling adepts of the free market, ultraliberalism and globalisation. The former placed importance on collective decision-making, arraigned around the rights of different interest groups within the university to have their views taken into account. These views were explicitly opposed to harnessing higher education to the productive process. The latter emphasise the duty and responsibility of the university to uphold the right of individual choice – what she or he shall study – in keeping with the demands of the market-place. This latter interpretation shifts the prime onus on the university from acting as a collective instrument for radical political reform. Rather the ultra-liberal view of university concentrates on its place in a vaster "training system" servicing those skills which allow the individual to survive – if not to prosper – in a free economy. The university has, of course, to accommodate both. But, depending on how it balances out these doctrines, this is reflected in its inner organisation and the ways in which it seeks to meet these and other economic or social priorities. In short, concepts of democracy determine the system of governance.

1.3 Democratic participation and governance

The principle of democracy according to interest group radicals and the university interpreted as the service station to the market-place shows not only the great changes in democratic fashion. They show us the way democracy reinterprets its priorities both as regards the university and within the university.

The notion that there ought to be a direct relationship between a democratic society and university governance grounded upon the same principle has grown steadily in expression and in execution over the past two decades. The implementation of *Drittelparität* – of tripartite representation of student, administrative staff and teaching staff interests – has been a notable feature of legislation in Germany, Austria and the Netherlands, the first in the shape of the *Hochschulrahmengesetz* of 1976, the second enshrined in the *Universitätorganizationsgesetz* of the previous year and the latter in the 1970 *Wet op de Universitaire Bestuurleiding* (Frijhoff, 1992, pp.499). Though the principle of tripartite parity of representation has not necessarily taken precisely the same profile with the Swedish reforms of 1977 (Premfors,

1982), the thrust of legislative effort has lain increasingly in this direction. In effect, profound changes were introduced into governance structures in the name of 'participant democracy'. It expanded the legitimate authority of groups – some internal, others consisting of 'external personalities' – to take part in the conduct of affairs previously confined largely to academic authority. Amongst specific instances of participant democracy being introduced into the university by legislative means, one may invoke the French *Loi d'Orientation* of 1968 and its more radical successor of January 1983.

That there is convergence between democracy and the arrangements to accommodate it inside complex management systems of higher education, does not mean that historically such a convergence has always existed. Quite on the contrary, it has been remarkably absent in higher education for a very long time. Any analyst of higher education policy, who ignores the basic fact that the historic development of university governance pursued a very different path from the rise of democracy, risks a partial understanding of the fundamental significance of the past quarter century. If the full import of contemporary trends in this area are to be grasped, attention needs to be paid to the historical aspect of university governance.

1.4 Governance: a linguistic and conceptual nicety

In areas of study where intellectual boundaries are particularly fluid, as they are in higher education studies, there is a tendency to be somewhat cavalier with terminology. Terms which have a precise meaning in one setting often have their meaning changed by their transfer or application to a different context. Governance is precisely such a term. In its original form, the concept was forged by American scholarship. It applied to the ways in which administrative coordination bargained, negotiated and discharged its task at campus level. As a concept, governance served to analyse the interplay between community, position and expertise-based authority and pluralist politics (Harmon, 1992, p.1282).

The assumption within the concept of 'governance' took for granted that the individual university possessed very real and substantial powers of self determination in the use of the resources assigned to it, in the decision to raise other resources. It also presumed that the individual university controlled independently and on its own the appointment, promotion, identification, recognition and reward of academic excellence amongst its students and its staff. Thus, the supposedly plain and straightforward concept of governance contained a very specific normative presumption about the 'proper' relationship between public authorities, their representatives and the universities in which the latter were endowed with a high degree of self-government.

In its original setting, then, governance implied what recent commentators have now identified as a 'supervisory relationship' between government and university in contradistinction to the 'state control relationship' that had, for many years, been the predominant model in Europe (Neave & van Vught, 1991; for a wider application of these concepts see Neave & van Vught, 1994; see also volume 1 in this series).

1.4.1 Four models of governance

Just as this particular 'model of relationship' between government and higher education *à l'Américaine* has exercised a powerful attraction for those seeking more flexible alternatives to what was often conceived as the overmighty power of central national administration, so the terminology was taken over along with an interpretation of the model it sought to emulate. Yet, governance is far from being coterminous with management or regulation, though once settled in new circumstances, the term itself tends to be subject to subtle distortion and reinterpretation. The 'managerialisation' of 'governance' is not the least of these distortions.

Students of governance tend to distinguish between four main models:

- the collegial model,
- the bureaucratic model,
- the professional model,
- the political model.

Each model assigns a different weight to particular administrative 'styles' or ways of internal negotiation that characterise the dealings between the constituent interests within the university world. Accordingly, the collegial model underlines cooperative decision-making carried out in a non hierarchical manner in which academic staff have a significant degree of self-determination. The bureaucratic model, by contrast, places importance on formal hierarchies and on the part played by legal-rational authority. The professional model concentrates on the authority and legitimacy of experts and on the links between loose confederations of horizontally differentiated units whilst the political model examines governance in terms of political conflict between groups with contending values, views and interests (Harmon, 1992, op cit., p.1282). Modes of negotiation are only one dimension though certainly a most significant one. Negotiation, decision-making or assignment of responsibility also involve, however, different types of authority and different locations where ‘the mighty have their seats’.

1.4.2 Seats of authority

In his classic work, *The Higher Education System* (1983) Clark singled out 6 levels where authority resides. These range from the academic department as the smallest basic unit capable of discussing and executing on its own decisions reached by its members, up to the multi-site university, the province (or state), the regional or, finally, the national higher education system, others have devised a slightly different break down in authority levels (Kogan & Becher, *Process and Structure* (2nd ed., 1991). Methodological differences aside, the type of authority which predominates at one level is not necessarily the same as that which dwells above or below that level. In effect, governance systems provide the setting and procedures within which different forms of cross-cutting authority in an establishment may reach agreement on priorities, allocation of responsibility between them and, ultimately, set forth the institutional mission.

1.4.3 Types of authority

The usual convention employed to classify different types of authority present in systems of governance relies on a three way split between academic authority, enterprise-based authority and system-based authority. Each draws strength from very different sources. The way they reach accommodation in real-life characterises and in turn constitutes a given model of governance. Academic authority, according to Clark, resides in the subject disciplines – that is, in the formally defined and recognised fields of intellectual and scholarly endeavour. They are strongest at the level of the faculties and the individual base units. Academic authority emerges in various guises – as personal rulership, as guild authority or in its professional equivalent. Enterprise-based authority may permeate an individual institution (Clark, 1997) but tends to accumulate around the bodies of institutional coordination and leadership. It is primarily identified by authority vested in trustees in the United States. In Europe, it tends to derive from formal bureaucratic ties between institution and national administration. The final and most visible form of authority springs together at the level of the national system of higher education. It is composed of elements derived from bureaucratic, governmental and political authority. This, as its nature implies, resides in national administration and its specialist sub agencies. It stands as the very incarnation of system-based authority.

1.5 Referential modes of governance

In theory, the combination of levels at which a particular type of authority resides together with the source of its legitimacy should result in some 18 different profiles. Useful though it might be to locate each of the case study systems included in this volume, according to the particular governance profile from which it has emerged and in terms of the configuration and direction towards which legislation would wish it to proceed, such an exercise is at present premature. Furthermore, a recent examination of the ways in which institutional decision-making is undertaken, who takes part in it and what figures on the agenda has thrown into question the reality of some of the more established 'governance modes' and more particularly, the reality of what has been termed 'the Continental mode' (van Vught & Maassen, 1996). But until such investigations come up with alternative categories – which, as yet, they have not – it is wise to remain with established categories and most especially so when dealing with an issue as complex as governance.

Individual systems of higher education display differences both subtle and substantial in the distribution, nature and location of the various types of authority. It has been customary to refer to three particular 'governance modes' as being archetypical. These are the 'Continental', the 'United Kingdom' and the 'United States' mode. Two things should be born in mind, however, the first is that if each of these archetypes illustrates the degree of difference between modes of governance, such degrees of difference are themselves historic. They relate to the situation as it was perceived by scholars working in the mid to late 1980s. The second is that the burden of reform that has subsequently taken place will not only have altered the balance of power between central national and institutional authority, largely, by strengthening the latter, it will, in addition, have moved individual countries in different directions. The most obvious example is the United Kingdom which, over the past seven years or more has seen an unprecedented strengthening of centralised control, the setting of performance norms and indicators and performance related funding and quality maintenance.

The salient features of the 'Continental mode' of governance is the strong authority exercised both at the top and at the bottom of the higher education system. The latter emerges in the power in decision-making of faculty guilds. The former is exercised by the key role of state bureaucracy in shaping both procedure and thus practice. Historically, the degree of autonomous authority at the institutional level is relatively weak (Kivinen & Rinne, 1996). The dominant pattern in the United Kingdom has been one firmly and traditionally rooted in the strength of faculty guilds. This is tempered by what one authority has described as "a modest amount of influence from institutional trustees and administrators." (Harmon, loc. cit.). Not greatly dissimilar has been the 'governance mode' found in the United States. It concentrates authority within the individual institution. The main difference lies in the authority of academia being less than its British counterpart whereas the influence of trustees and institutional administration is, if anything, more weighty and telling (Rhoades, 1992, pp.1380-1).

Today, systems of governance are passing through a period of unprecedented and sustained turbulence. In western Europe, such turbulence is the outcome of what *faute de mieux*, may cast as the twin revolutions of democratic internal participation on the one hand and on the other, the managerial revolution with its demands for strengthened external accountability to the public interest and improved institutional efficiency (Neave, 1996). Nor are the forces of change markedly different in their impact in central and eastern Europe. There remains, as no-one would deny, an enormous difference in degree and timing. In effect, the political and economic reconstruction of higher education beyond the Oder Neisse line has perforce to be pursued simultaneously whereas in western Europe these two revisions – the democratic and the managerial – followed consecutively one after the other.

1.6 Governance: change and continuity

As in any period of root and branch upheaval, the sweep of reform makes us no less aware of the strength of continuity, a phenomenon often alluded to by frustrated would-be change-agents as 'resistance to change'. Such continuity emerges in many forms, not least the universities themselves which, as the American writer on higher education, Clark Kerr has pointed out, have retained an identifiable continuity in form and purpose seldom found in other institutions, be they states, regimes or frontiers (Kerr, 1982). Governance itself is no exception. That we still today describe the acts, values, behaviour and stances taken by the academic estate in terms of a 'guild mentality' and refer to academia in terms which hark directly back to a pattern of social organisation created in mediaeval times merely underlines the pervasive strength of continuity. Continuity invests the institution. It also applies to the ways in which the university managed itself – that is, to governance. For just as the universities antedated the rise of the modern bureaucratic state, so too did the notion of academia as a self governing, property-owning corporation with its own internal rules and practices.

Prior to the injection of participatory democracy into the governance systems of higher education in western Europe during the late 1960s and 1970s, the major changes in governance lay less in the constellation of power and authority inside the individual institution, as in the external or supraordinate levels of authority within which the university was itself seated. It is to these and to the historical development of governance systems that we now turn, and in particular to the importance of superordinate authority in shaping what, in a fine example of anachronism, may be termed governance – that is, the inner authority of the university.

1.6.1 Significance of the collegial model

In mediaeval times, superordinate authority took the form of the three powers: spiritual, temporal and learning (*Sacerdotum, Regnum et Studium*). Formally, the right to self rule exercised by the academic guild or corporation derived from the special status conferred upon the individual university by Pontifical authority.[1] Like other corporations or guilds, the mediaeval university was free-standing, self-regulating, self-financing, and later property-owning. And, once granted the right to teach the *studium generale*, generally accorded by either Pope or Emperor, the university exercised a monopoly over training for the 'professions' of law, medicine, theology. Universities occupied a species of extra territorial space, their denizens subject to sets of rules and regulations that were self devised, enforced by the scholarly community and which applied to members of that community.

Yet, the significance of the guild model was not just that it constituted a normative structure for the organisation of specialised skills, their transmission and preservation. It also constituted a way of organising academic work, defined by, and within the academic community. In short, it laid down the basis for what is commonly alluded to today as the collegial model of governance. What relationship there existed with external authority, with local patrons and, increasingly from the 16th century onward, with local rulers rather than with those twin symbols of universalism of Emperor and Pope, was largely to secure recognition for practices already implemented.

1.6.2 The rise of territorial and princely particularism

Two major influences came together gradually to extract the university from the universalist skein of superordinate authority represented in the powers

1 According to canon law a universtiy was defined as '...an institution for higher education, recognised or founded by the Pope, whose members enjoy all priveleges which are granted them by the Pope and whose ranks are recognised in all Christianity by order of the Pope.' (cf. thesis of P. de Pooter, 1994, *Statutis facultatis iuris canonici in universitatibus ecclesiasticis atque in universitatibus catholicis a Codex Iuris canonici 1917 usque ad annum 1994*, Leuven, UDSIA; also Ruegg, 1992).

spiritual and temporal of Pope and Emperor. The first was the Reformation and the division of Europe between Catholic and Protestant. In this conflict the university found itself at the forefront of the battle. Local rulers and city fathers sought the intellectual backing of the university at least and its loyalty at best. Indeed, the right to authorise the foundation of universities became one of the tests which substantiated the claim to sovereignty (Frijhoff, 1992). This transfer of ties of authority from the symbolic universalism of Pope and Emperor to the particularism of the local ruler moved the university towards a regal and territorial – rather than a universalist – identity. Granted, that identity was still primarily religious. But it also marked the first step in that long historic road that brought both university and 'national' identity into closer alignment.

The 16th century saw, then, superordinate authority redefined primarily in terms of princely particularism. It was not, strictly speaking, a relationship that one may describe in terms of university and state. The state in its modern form, grounded in a professional administrative meritocracy, did not then exist. Such ties as there were, revolved within the context of patronage, they tended to be personalised and clientelistic. From the 16th century – and more especially from the time of the Reformation onward – those clientelistic ties tended to become closer, just as the stakeholders themselves tended to multiply to include municipalities, merchants as well as princes.

1.6.3 New knowledge: an old challenge to established institutional forms

Just as the first steps in rebalancing the universalism of spiritual authority against the territorial authority of the prince were evident in the 16th and 17th centuries, so the same epoch saw the first serious challenge to the monopoly the university exercised over higher learning with the advent of new knowledge and the subsequent diversification in institutional patterns on the fringes of the university world. The new knowledge whether navigation, the military arts or accounting, saw the establishment of 'alternatives to the university': Schools of Navigation in Portugal and Spain, *Ritterschulen* in Germany, for example though here again under private initiative. Throughout the late 17th and 18th centuries, with such notable exceptions as Scotland, the Netherlands and Germany, the university came under severe pressure to renounce scholasticism and to defend its historic monopoly over the formal process of graduation. The divergence between formal knowledge taught in the university and what was seen as useful knowledge, represented by the onset of the industrial revolution, of the Enlightenment, of the rise of natural science and the attendant institutional forms alternative to the university – whether academies or learned societies – isolated the university further from the main intellectual currents of the day.

1.6.4 The 'bureaucratic revolution': reassessment

Another challenge existed, however, and it was to have profound and enduring consequences for the relationship between university and superordinate power. More especially, it was to have a seminal effect upon governance. It was to mould the basic relationship and the terms on which that relationship was to be conducted over the ensuing 250 years. The new challenge lay in the rationalisation of state administration which despots of varying degrees of enlightenment sought to introduce from the early 18th century in the case of St. Petersburg University (Verbitskaya, 1996), from the middle of the 18th century in Sweden (Svensson, 1982), and somewhat later in France and Austria (Grüber, 1982), amongst others.

Most accounts of the history of university governance dwell upon the rise of the Humboldtian and Napoleonic reforms as key events in the creation of the modern university. This interpretation can be sustained. But it is only a partial interpretation. It tends to play down the fact that the university was only one dimension in a rather broader undertaking, broader in application and for that matter, broader in time. The setting up of Berlin University, as a consequence of the Humboldt reforms of 1807 and the creation of the Imperial University by Napoleon I in 1811 may indeed mark the start of the modern university in Europe. But these events can also be viewed as particular episodes in a long drawn out restructuring of society which lasted for more than a hundred years from the mid 18th to the mid 19th century. Central in this modernisation of the state was the professionalisation of the national civil service, the drawing up of regulations and procedures, the formal setting out of knowledge, qualifications and curricular pathways required to bring about the transition of government based on personal power (*Machtstaat*) to the state based on the rule of law (*Rechtstaat*).

1.6.5 The university as a modernising force

For the first time and in an organised manner, the university found itself associated with a conscious and deliberate policy of modernising government. This, at the very least was an innovation of a major order. Public service was henceforth conditional upon the possession of formal qualifications and the monopoly of furnishing those qualifications was confirmed in the hands of the university. Thus, the first examples of the modern European university were intimately tied in with the reform of state service. Furthermore, academia itself was assimilated in its formal status to a bureaucratic rank. Despite the historical differences between individual universities, it was a step that set the academic estate firmly in the nation and within the apparatus of the state. By the same token, that feature of strong bureaucratic, administrative and governmental authority which, as we have noted, observers later came to identify as typical of the Continental mode of governance, was put in place.

1.7 Consequences of the 'bureaucratic revolution'

The advent of the bureaucratic – and meritocratic – state had three consequences of prime strategic significance upon the nature of authority exercised in the university world. It thus directly and durably shaped the nature of governance. To this general development, both Britain and the United States remained exceptions.

In the first place, the state of law superimposed at territorial level a system of oversight and control enforced through legislative enactment, ministerial decree and circular. Here are to be seen the origins of what has recently been termed the state control model of university/government relationship. This arrangement was to remain largely unchanged until its replacement by the so called supervisory model which emerged in the decade 1985 to 1995 (Neave & van Vught, 1991, 1994; see also In 't Veld, Füssel & Neave, 1996). It opened the way to the public financing of the universities via the state budget. It brought academia into the ranks of state service, thereby conferring upon it the obligation of service to the national community. Though few systems went so far as France which cast academia in the role of a state body (*le corps universitaire*) incorporation marked a further point of separation between the Anglo American concept of academia as one of the liberal professions and the European notion of its members being public servants (Neave & Rhoades, 1987). The process of incorporation – that is, bringing the university into the realm of public administration – thus marks one of the dividing lines between the United Kingdom model of governance and its Continental counterpart.

1.8 Dual hierarchies or bi-cephalous control

In the second place, bureaucratic rationalism bore down heavily upon earlier patterns of internal governance and collegiality, confining collegiality to a narrower range of activities and responsibilities within the administration of individual establishments. Academia as a self-governing guild no longer exercised exclusive responsibility for the conduct of individual establishments, and still less for the conduct of universities increasingly organised as part of a national system. This does not deny the real importance that professorial power, personal rule or collegial action continued to wield within individual establishments. As the century wore on, however, the steady reinforcement of the central government layer increased. As it did, so a dual system of oversight and control emerged with it. This dualism was not simply the product of bureaucratic power at the centre and collegial power within the individual university, the former operating via legal enactment in a top down manner with the latter acting as a vestigial form of the mediaeval self-governance emanating from bottom up. A dual chain of certification and validation, each rooted in its particular form of authority and each involving what today would pass under the general heading of 'quality control', also developed. It defined and accredited key curricular pathways leading on to careers in public service or to the ranks of academia itself. Put succinctly, the modernisation of government not only clarified the formal ties between university and central administration, it also set in place mechanisms to ensure the type of knowledge government sought to ensure its public servants possessed.

Within the administrative domain, the ties between government and university took a very specific form of a descending hierarchy penetrating into the university in the person of a permanent civil servant. His formal responsibility was to act in the name of the government, to verify expenditure, to confirm that procedures and structure within the individual establishment were in keeping with the requirements of current legislation. The German *Kanzler*, the French *Secrétaire Général*, the university director in the Scandinavian lands, or the *Regiringscommissaris* in Belgium represented – and in many instances still do so today – the direct presence of central administration within the individual university, in truth both the symbol and substance of accountability incarnate. Against this – and standing as an ascending hierarchy whose power indirectly emanated from the base units or derived directly from the individual faculties – was that other personification of varying degrees of magnificence and robed splendour, the rector or president of the university.

1.8.1 Legal frames

The third element which emerged from rationalising historic forms of governance and which was to have long term significance, lay, to use a deliberately anachronistic term, in the juridification of the university system. Nowadays, this particular term has pejorative overtones involving excessive recourse to legal procedure to resolve issues previously settled by negotiation or informal agreement. Here, however, juridification is to be understood as that part of the broader process of 'incorporation' which brought the university into the formal ambit of either administrative or Constitutional law as the main instrument for regulating the boundaries of systems of governance whilst also giving formal legal recognition to powers and areas of responsibility previously defined internally by practice, tradition and custom within and by, the academic guild. To those used to less regulated ties between government and university and especially those whose referential university systems are based on models derived from Anglo-American practice or their derivatives, juridification, the weight and minutiae of law, regulation and circular are often held to be quintessential of the Continental mode of governance.

The motives behind the legal incorporation of individual universities into the enterprise of state were, not surprisingly, many and varied. Yet, because today we are witnessing what many hold to be the relaxation of state control and its replacement by a lighter and more discrete form of supervision, it is useful to rehearse not merely why a system grounded in formal normative legislation grew up, but why it lasted for so long.

Legislation involves two very different processes. The first turns around the translation of practice into legal principle. Informal practice becomes part of the formal and normative conditions that set down and determine the conduct, responsibilities and obligations of an organisation, appointment or institution as well as its members. This, we will term 'encodification'. The second has a more radical objective. This is less to register earlier practice than to change it at the same time as setting the new conditions down in law. This we will call the process of 'modification'.

1.8.2 The task of juridification: its impact on earlier forms of self-government

Though few countries went as far as France which, in 1791 abolished the universities and in 1792 under the *Le Chapelier* law abolished guilds as self governing bodies, most were faced with a broadly similar situation *vis à vis* their universities. The inner customs which derived from the self-government of mediaeval guilds – and the concept of autonomy was not least amongst them – possessed the weight of tradition and the reality of power long before the era of enlightened 'reconstruction' swept in. The task that lawmakers had before them – and which today in both central and eastern Europe is once again the issue of the hour – was to redefine the mission and the purpose universities should fulfil. In the setting of the 'bureaucratic revolution' the prime task was how to construct a national system of publicly accountable universities in the place of the individual property-holding, self-governing corporations that had preceded them. In effect, the challenge was how to define the purpose of the university in terms of service to the national community. The creation of national diplomas represented one crucial linkage between nation state, administration and higher learning. But to set the university upon the path of serving the nation also revealed far-reaching issues about the conditions of service and responsibilities of academia itself.

1.8.3 Incorporation of academia as public servants

One of the most powerful levers in the process of incorporating the university as an institution of public service involved varying degrees of control and verification over full professorial appointment which became a matter for close oversight by central authorities in France, Prussia, Austria, Spain, Sweden and Italy, to quote but a few specific examples. Control over professorial appointment by public authority – which in Spain took the form of a public competitive national examination (Hernandez, 1992) – was crucial for a number of reasons. It ensured public due process and thus meritocratic selection as a check against the particular interests of academic clans and alliances. Equally important, however, such appointments occupied a delicate position at the point of juncture between the emerging mechanisms of accountability descending from national administration and the substantial, though curtailed, influence of the academic guild. Or, to revert directly to the issue of governance, such appointments stood at the crossing point between academic and bureaucratic authority. Irrespective of whether the procedures involved were confined to formal confirmation by government of proposals submitted by the university where the post was to be held, or whether they involved Ministers in an authentic act of choice and selection between a number of candidates, such procedures were only part of an extensive range of legislation which, in addition, set down the formal responsibilities of the full professor, in his capacity as public servant, as scholar and as scientist. The rule of law implied codifying the ties between government and university so that due process – or its violation – could be ascertained. But, it also had the task of defining the boundaries within which autonomy could be exercised as well as defining the nature of that autonomy. In the German-speaking lands the boundary between the 'public' and the 'private' lives of the university (Trow, 1978) were drawn in keeping with the Humboldtian principle of the freedom to learn and to teach, '*Lehr und Lernfreiheit*'. In Austria, the principle was stated slightly differently, '*Wissenschaft und ihr Lehre ist frei*'. Academic freedom was nevertheless defined in terms of the free quest for and the transmission of knowledge.

1.8.4 Incorporation: the consequences for academic autonomy

Such principles defined an area of responsibility over which government voluntarily exercised self restraint. At the same time, the process of incorporation into public service placed customary university practice within the setting of administrative law. The interpretation of autonomy it entailed was far more restrictive than the one it replaced. Institutional autonomy which had been the *conditio sine qua non* on which the mediaeval self government of the guild rested, and on which both individual and positional autonomy were also grounded, was now split off. Unlike in Britain which continued the tradition of corporate autonomy vested in the university through Charter or the United States where the Dartmouth judgment of 1819, conferred the guarantee of autonomy upon Trustees and upon the corporate status of the institution (Trow Martin (1993), the Continental model of governance placed the burden of both defining and upholding autonomy upon the state as interpreted through constitutional and administrative law.

1.9 Contemporary change

When set against this general backdrop, it is clear that changes made to contemporary governance systems are in essence, second order changes – that is, they provide the means of meeting a broader series of objectives themselves defined less at the institutional level so much as within the setting of national policy-making applied at systems level. Revisions to participant constituencies, to electoral procedures and to the composition of electoral colleges, the assignation of new – or alternatively, the restoration to internal organs of self government of old – responsibilities customarily exercised by academia prior to its formal subordination to party and state, may certainly be interpreted and presented as the restoration of academic self-government. And the restoration of these customary 'rights' may also be seen within the confines of that particular corporation, as anticipating the extension of the same principle to society at large. But these same initiatives may also be viewed from another perspective. They provide the university with the necessary instrumentality, procedures and discretionary powers to meet a situation which, whether viewed as economic, social or political cannot wholly be predicted – let alone met – by detailed control and oversight of national administration.

What is new in this situation and how does it impinge upon institutional governance? We have spent some time in analysing the rise of the nation state and the way it shaped, redefined and reassigned both the weight and locus of different types of authority – bureaucratic rational, personal rule and discipline-driven – that lie at the heart of different governance modes. We have traced this across the centuries and explored, in considerable detail, the effect upon changes between modes of governance of what we have termed the 'bureaucratic revolution'. This 'revolution' is in essence the creation of the modern state and its natural concomitant, a meritocratic, professional civil and public service. We justify this excursion because we are fundamentally convinced that current trends in higher education development mark the end of that long cycle which we qualified as 'the bureaucratic revolution'.

Certainly, the immediate concern of this volume is set by the ripping away of the Iron Curtain. This is an event of the first magnitude – for Europe, for higher education and, within the special focus of this study, for the governance of higher education in those countries which have reknit their natural ties with their neighbours. But governance, like the institution whose identity and tasks it defines and oversees, is profoundly historical. Previous versions of it influence what comes after, thus, for instance, the collegial model has shaped the bureaucratic model of governance. Indeed, the latter, as we have shown, emerged from the former, just as the professional model that some see as the prime feature of contemporary changes in the governance of Europe's universities, is born from its bureaucratic predecessor.

But if we are to be sensitive to the import of what is happening today in systems of governance, we ought not to confine our awareness simply to the *technicité* of these developments, though we certainly would be ill-advised to dismiss it. The longer term significance of changes in governance is only partially revealed if one confines one's attention simply to governance, management, strategic planning etc.. The events which are analysed here in the context of changes within modes of governance may be seen as a swing of history's pendulum away from the nation state as the exclusive focus of the university. Whether, by the same token, it is legitimate to interpret the counterswing as a restoration of the universal and as a reunification forged by economics to offset the territorial particularism which religious dissent put in train 400 years ago, must remain a matter of personal judgment.

1.10 New superordinate authorities

Though presented in terms of economic integration, of the globalisation of international trade and, within the narrower confines of the university, the growing bonds of international student and academic mobility, one of the most outstanding developments which cannot be without radical consequence for governance is the redefinition, once again, of superordinate authority. Since this is a change which as we have argued has always anticipated profound revisions in governance systems, that it is happening once again gives added weight to our thesis of being at the end of a long historical cycle. These new superordinate authorities emerge in the shape of the World Trade Organisation, the World Bank or, nearer home, the Commission of the European Union. Few studies in higher education have sought to ascertain the exact part this superordinate layer of decision-making has upon the setting of norms, upon systems of accreditation, higher education finance and most particularly in research funding (Kehm, 1993). Nevertheless, the influence wielded by this latter body upon individual establishments is both substantial and enduring (Neave, 1987, 1996). Indeed, the belief, often held by authorities outside the 15, that it is a normative body and that there is such an entity as a 'European system of higher education' or standard 'European practice' goes far in conferring upon it an influence which it would never officially claim for itself. Even so, the revision of the Treaty on European Union contributed to quality maintenance within member states and to mobility within the European Union. One of the explicit purposes of Articles 126 and 127 of this Treaty is to stimulate the coherence of education systems among themselves (De Groof, 1995).

1.11 Deregulation

How the Commission's influence is exercised and whether it is perceived as an extension of bureaucratic authority, of governmental authority or political authority – the prime components of what Clark has termed 'system-based' authority – have yet to be subject to the attention of scholars in higher education policy. Against the resurgence of a supranational layer of decision-making in higher education should be set that other development of the hour – the apparent loosening in the ties of control the nation state exercises over higher education. Whether justified in the name of 'deregulation', of giving free reign to 'market forces' or of restoring to institutional level a degree of self regulation that the protracted historical process of 'incorporation' had gradually reduced, one of the most influential factors in the modification of governance has been the gradual withdrawal of central administration from detailed control and supervision and its concentration upon setting out the broad strategic lines of national priorities.

Naturally, the motives that have prompted the phenomenon of the 'offloading State' (Neave, 1992) vary from system to system. They range from the ideological to the pragmatic, from the notion, taken over from neo-liberal economic theory of 'rolling back the frontiers of the State' to the empirical recognition that, in a world economy, the need to reduce both production and labour costs whilst raising the general level of skills amongst the younger generation, is the price of national survival. The central characteristic of this phenomenon is the view, as widely shared amongst politicians as it is amongst civil servants, that the pace of economic change is now so rapid and so unpredictable that the type of detailed oversight until recently exercised by government over higher education is neither functional nor appropriate. From this it follows that the basic functions of detailed control which the 'incorporation' of higher education into public service placed within the purlieu of central national administration – the detailed allocation of resources, financial, human and equipment, their optimal usage and the evaluation of the use to which they are put as too, both their effectiveness in terms of qualified student output and cost – are best handled 'at the point of delivery'. Decisions once regarded as falling within the 'systems level' or as part of the 'core functions of government' are to be relocated or delegated. Some are assigned to the regional level – the devolution of responsibility for Spain's universities to the Autonomous regions, the federalisation of Belgium or the strengthening of the role of regional authorities in Norway – are not untypical of this rationale. Other functions are handed over to the individual institution. The introduction of lump sum budgeting in France, the Netherlands and Sweden stands as a second illustration of this latter dynamic.

Delegation of responsibility, the replacement of hierarchical subordination by a concept of 'partnership' between centre and region and between region and individual establishment are the basic driving forces behind institutional self-regulation. Institutional self-regulation lies at the heart of change in governance. Such delegation has profound consequences for the particular university. It is also fraught with consequence for those within the university. New responsibilities affect the relationship between those entrusted with teaching and research as opposed to those responsible for the institution's financial health and viability. The basic challenge that the burden of increased delegated responsibility imposes on higher education is not whether the private sector can take up the financial slack which a more modest interpretation of the role of the state has created, it is rather, whether academic culture and administrative culture at the level of the individual university can work together to preserve public confidence – and demand – for higher learning.

REFERENCES

Clark, Burton R. (1983) *The Higher Education System: academic organisation in cross national perspective*. Berkeley /Los Angeles/ London: University of California Press.

Clark, Burton R. (1997) "Common Problems and Adaptive Responses in the Universities of the World: organising for change", *Higher Education Policy*, (forthcoming).

de Groof, Jan, (1995) "A few Notes on Articles 126 and 127 of the Treaty of Maastricht – Opportunities and Limitations for European education policy". The Hague: Asser Institute.

Frijhoff, W. (1992) "The Netherlands" in Burton R. Clark & Guy Neave (eds) *The Encyclopedia of Higher Education*. Oxford: Pergamon Press. Vol.i. *National Systems of Higher Education.* pp.499ff.

Frijhoff, W. (1992) "Universities 1500-1900" in Clark & Neave, *op cit*., vol. ii. *The Institutional Fabric of the higher education system.* pp.1251-1258.

Grüber, Karl-Heinz (1982) "Higher Education and the State in Austria", *European Journal of Education, vol.*17, no.3, pp.259-270.

Harmon, Grant (1992) "Introduction" in Clark & Neave op. cit., vol.ii, section iii *Governance, Administration and Finance*, pp.1279ff.

Hernandez, Angel Gonzalez (1992) "The Autonomy of Spanish universities: a problem for three powers and one issue", *Higher Education Policy*, vol.4, no.1, pp.37-4

In 't Veld, Roel Füssel, Hans-Peter & Neave, Guy (1996) *The Relations between State and higher education,* vol. 1 in the Council of Europe series *Legislating for Higher Education in Europe*, Dordrecht: Kluwer.

Kehm, Barbara (1993) *"Programmatic objectives and administrative problems of EC programmes in higher education: general features and a case study of Erasmus"* Working document, Kassel, Wissenschaftliches Zentrum für Berufs- und Hochschulforschung.

Kerr, Clark (1982) *The Uses of the University.* (3rd ed). Cambridge (Mass): Harvard University Press. p.157.

Kivinen, Osmo & Rinne, Risto (1996) "The Problem of Diversification in higher education: Counter-tendencies between divergence and convergence in the Finnish higher education system since the 1950's", in V. Lynn Meek, Leo Goedegebuure, Osmo Kivinen and Risto Rinne (eds) *The Mockers and Mocked: Comparative Perspectives on Differentiation, Convergence and Diversity in higher education.* Oxford: Pergamon Press for IAU, pp.95-116.

Kogan, Maurice & Becher, Tony (1992) *Process and structure in higher education.* (2nd ed.) London: Routledge.

Maassen P.A.M., Goedegebuure, L. & van Vught, F.A. (1996) *Inside Academia.* Utrecht: Geurts.

Neave, Guy (1987) *La Communidad Europea y la educacíon.* Madrid: Fundación Universidad Empresa.

Neave, Guy (1992) *The Teaching Nation: prospects for Teachers in the European Community.* Oxford: Pergamon Press.

Neave, Guy (1996) "Homogenisation, integration and convergence: the Cheshire Cats of Higher Education analysis", in Meek, Goedegebuure, Kivinen & Rinne *op. cit.*, pp.26-41.

Neave, Guy & Rhoades, Gary (1987) "The academic estate in Western Europe", in Burton R. Clark (ed) *The Academic Profession: national, disciplinary & institutional settings.* Berkeley/Los Angeles: University of California Press, 59 pp.211-270

Neave, Guy & van Vught, Frans (1991) *Prometheus Bound: the changing relationship between government and higher education in Western Europe*. Oxford: Pergamon Press.

Neave & van Vught (1994) *Government and Higher Education Relationships across Three Continents: the Winds of Change*. Oxford: Elsevier-Pergamon.

Premfors, Rune (1982), *The politics of higher education in a comparative perspective: France, Sweden and the United Kingdom,* Stockholm, Department of Political Science.

Rhoades, Gary (1992) "Governance Models" in Clark & Neave *loc. cit.*, pp.1376ff.

Rothblatt, Sheldon (1995) "An historical perspective on the University's Role in Social Development", in David D. Dill & Barbara Sporn (eds) *Emerging Patterns of Social Demand and University Reform: through a glass darkly*. Oxford: Pergamon Press for IAU. pp.20-53.

Ruegg, Walter (1992) *A History of the University in England.* Cambridge: Cambridge University Press.

Svensson, Lennart A. (1982) "The State and higher education: a sociological critique from Sweden", *European Journal of Education*, vol.17, no.3, pp. 295-306.

Trow, Martin (1975) "The 'public' and 'private' lives of academia", *Daedalus, vol.2*, pp.113-127.

Trow, Martin (1993), "Federalism in American higher education", in Arthur Levine (ed.), *Higher learning in America 1980-2000,* London/Baltimore.

van Vught, Frans & Maassen, Peter (1996) *Inside Academia*, Utrecht: Geurts.

Verbitskaya, L.A. (1996) "Academic freedom and university autonomy: a variety of concepts", *Higher Education Policy*, vol.9, no.4, pp.289-294.

2

HIGHER EDUCATION, THE STATE, LEGISLATIVE REFORM AND DEMOCRACY

2.1 Democracy and education reform

Over the last two centuries, the comparative analysis of European constitutions shows clearly that reform in education stands as a most sensitive pointer for monitoring social and political change. Educational reform goes hand in glove with both social and cultural advance. Yet, at the same time, reform in this domain also serves to move these changes forward both by influencing social values and, hopefully, by urging on the reconstruction of society and the economy. There is, in short, a dialectical relationship between education and social mobilisation *stricto sensu* such that periods of social upheaval serve as catalyst to change in the lecture theatre. Thus, it is that in several central and east European countries constitutional and political renovation has run in parallel with educational reconstruction.

Yet, in education few reforms of a fundamental nature will come to fruition in the absence of appropriate legislation to back them. For long, educational legislation has been seen as a suitable means of codifying and setting down practices that have evolved pragmatically over time. Furthermore, it may accelerate reform by laying out the basis of legitimacy on which the reformed system rests and, no less important, it may provide an appropriate framework for democratic values to take root – and most especially so when society itself stands at a watershed in its history. Seen from such a perspective, the instrumental role of the law underpins the democratic nature of the state and by so doing upholds basic individual values. But this same perspective also stresses the social dimension in law-making which places objectivity, legal security, stability and predictability upon social ties and societal relationships whilst eradicating arbitrariness, administrative high-handedness, the abuse use of power, subjectivity and irrationality irrespective of their origins and sources, be they political, commercial or administrative. The "Rule of Law" needs to govern the "Rule of Man". Hence, the way law is organised serves that other function, essential to a democracy, namely, the safeguarding of freedom.

2.2 Government and legislative reform

One of the major dilemmas that bedevils higher education policy is whether government in a democratic state is able to confine itself to the core tasks or to adhere to the voluntary self-restraint it has set around its own activities? This is a particularly delicate issue and especially so when government has the virtual monopoly in setting forth guidelines and has the will to forward what it construes as developments that are in the interests of society. As the Polish philosopher and historian Bronislav Geremek has noted, "The path to freedom is open but the path to democracy is uncertain." (Vanderhoeven & de Groof, 1994).

Of the more crucial tasks of government is to ensure that such principles as 'decentralisation', 'differentiation', 'democratisation' and the priority of universal, humanitarian values – principles that have been enunciated in the legislation of many countries (de Groof, 1993; 1994) – are implemented whilst ensuring institutional independence and strengthening their commitment to the principle of competition between them.

One course that suggests itself is for governments to set down within a legal framework the general political objectives of their plans for reforming higher education. Despite the heterodox nature of the suggestion, since objectives cannot normally be treated as enforceable legal norms, the formal statement of what falls under state responsibility both in the educational and in the curricular domain, may prove a useful device.

What are the advantages of this tactic? Perhaps the most marked is that all institutions of higher education become partners in the push towards democratisation thus presented. The one drawback is that the state acts both as initiator and as implementation agent and, like it or not, judge and jury in its own case! There is, however, a second disadvantage, namely that intention does not prove capability and in default of the latter, there is a very real risk of a legal vacuum ensuing, particularly so if the state itself either lacks the resources to back its will or, lacking the will, does not assign the resources it promised to the legislation it promulgated. In such a situation, getting agreement on the overall objectives of higher education would appear remote. Even so, maintaining a country's well-being is a prime responsibility of government.

2.3 Higher education legislation: three specific issues

If we turn our attention to the way in which the process of reconstructing higher education in central and eastern Europe has been carried out, three central issues emerge. These are:

- the process of consultation in setting out normative legislation,
- the reality of institutional autonomy,
- the research mission of the university.

One of the more striking developments involved in reforming higher education in some central and eastern European systems has been the drawing up of normative instruments (state educational standards) in the absence of any prior consultation with those involved in higher education. Such standards, variously referred to as minimum norms, or as models, are then implemented by higher education establishments. In some legislative enactments, such norms figure only as an appendix to the particular law, yet they subsequently assume a mandatory status. Such procedures are questionable. If they are to serve as norms, then they should figure in the main body of the legal text. Or, as an alternative, their status should be clarified and made quite explicit and unambiguous. Furthermore, it would be appropriate if any conflict between the particular regulation and the principle of institutional autonomy should be avoided and the principle of autonomy itself should be included in the law.

2.3.1 The Russian Federation: an illustration

In this context, some criticism can be made *vis à vis* the recent Federal Law on Higher and Post University Professional Education passed in 1996 by the Russian Federation. Set out in this decree is the legal basis for educational standards. It appears to go into minute detail and leaves too little room for latitude to the universities. However, it leaves too much latitude to the universities in the areas of student admissions policy, free tuition, financial support and staff salary policies. This situation is likely to lead to considerable differences between institutions, over and above those already seen between the various regions (de Groof, 1995; Farrington forthcoming; de Groof, forthcoming).

No legal cohesion is guaranteed by this new law which appears to entail a fragmentation in the steering of policies in the higher education system. In this respect, one might conclude that the various definitions contained in this law should be viewed as a standard that is intended – or aimed at – rather than rules to be immediately enforced. Thus is tradition developed, "*Gesetznorm und Gesetzwirklichkeit fallen bekanntlich nicht selten auseinander*" (Muhle, 1995). In all probability this law will have to be considered in Russia as transitional.

If funding systems do not permit institutions of higher education to freely implement their priorities for research and teaching or to draw up development plans for the future, then such autonomy as those institutions have is, at best, insubstantial. The need to gather information and experience systematically on methods of lump sum funding and finance as developed elsewhere is especially pressing. The limited possibilities for financial diversification pose a very real hindrance in other fields as well, and particularly in academic and technical staff management.

Compounding these difficulties is the often portal role of the Ministry of Finance. This has not made for an atmosphere of trust, still less of partnership, between either higher education establishments and national administration. On the one hand, there is often an absence of permanent channels of access between institutions and the Ministry. On the other hand, the Ministry of Education may only enjoy a consultative role when it comes to taking financial decisions.

2.4 Some central issues

It would be desirable for the financing of higher education establishments to be guaranteed by law, and to this end funding sources from central government, regional or municipal authorities should be provided as well as an inbuilt inflation factor for running costs. This of course raises a number of questions of general relevance for higher education in both east and west:

- are finance formulae based on estimated or actual needs?
- are registration, certification and accreditation procedures clearly set out?
- how far can the non-state sector be demand led?

It is assumed that research forms an integral part of the university's mission. This being so, in what ways do universities differ from other types of higher education establishments? In answering there are four distinguishing characteristics:

- the permanent exchange between on going research and teaching,
- the monopoly to grant academic degrees,
- the comprehensive nature of teaching programmes, of fundamental and applied research,
- the recognition of multi-disciplinarity.

That most central and east European systems of higher education are engaged in bringing together teaching and research is an encouraging and most welcomed development.

2.5 The place of comparative law

Legislating for education tends generally to reflect both a country's cultural traditions and its social and economic specificities and exceptionalisms which explains why the law varies from one country to another. Yet, comparison is both necessary and helpful, constructive and insightful and not just because one may detect an increasing sensitivity to the internationalisation of rights in education. The comparative study of educational law provides systematic and comparable analyses as well as information, the exchange of experience and, hopefully, contributes to the process of change. Like other fields involving the comparative dimension it extends the range of debate and the range of options available to the scholar, members of the legislature, government and administration with the opportunity to seek optimal solutions on the basis of tried and tested practice developed elsewhere. "Comparative law", Zweigert & Klötz noted recently, "does not simply criticise what it finds, but can also claim to show the way to a better mastery of the legal material, to deeper insights into it and then, in the end, to better law." An examination of current trends in Europe's various higher education systems suggests that differences between them appear to be less stark, in part because they are faced with similar issues and problems. The thesis that as similar economic conditions prevail so countries will tend to converge towards similar solutions, is, of course, well-known in comparative higher education as well (van Vught, 1996).

Last but not least, the comparative study of educational law contributes substantially to the quest for democratic pluralism and the guarantee of human rights which are also the main purpose of the Council of Europe. This volume may, from this perspective, be seen as helping to set in place the educational foundations of a common European home.

REFERENCES

Geremek, Bronislav quoted in Vanderhoeven, J. & de Groof, J. (1994) "The Legal Construction of Higher Education Structures", *Higher Education in Europe*, vol. XIX, no. 4, 1994, pp. 60-68.

de Groof, Jan (1993) *Comments on the Law on Education of the Russian Federation*. Leuven: Acco.

de Groof, Jan (ed) (1994) *Education Policy in Russia and its Constitutional Aspects*. Leuven: Acco.

de Groof, Jan (1995) *Federalism and Education in Russia*. Paris: OECD.

Farrington, D. (forthcoming) "The Law on higher education in the Russian Federation: funding and assessment" in Jan de Groof (ed) *Comments on the Federal Law on Higher and Post-University Professional Education,* Leuven: Acco.

Muhle, E. (1995) *Die Entsowijetisierung der russischen Hochschule, Historische Voraussetzungen, Anliegen und Verlauf der Hochschulreform in Russland seit 1985*. Bonn: Hochschulrektorenkonferenz.

van Vught, Frans (1996) "Isomorphism in higher education? Towards a theory of differentiation in diversity in higher education systems", in Meek et al., *The Mockers and Mocked. op. cit.*, pp.42ff.

Zweigert, Konrad & Klötz, Hein (1992) *Introduction to Comparative Law*. Oxford: Clarendon.

3

THE LEGAL FRAMEWORK

3.1 General characteristics of legislation: a succinct view

3.1.1 The international setting

Not a few changes in legislation are themselves a response to international trends. Work that has contributed to analysing the condition of national systems of higher education undertaken both by the Council of Europe and the Organisation for Economic Cooperation and Development in its national reviews of education, the examination of current educational statistics in the light of international indicators provided by the OECD survey on International Indicators of Education Systems, have been instrumental in putting this process in train. Governments routinely cite developments in the international arena as one of the main justifications for amending higher education legislation (de Groof, 1995a). That international developments are reflected in national legislation will doubtless strengthen the drive towards a greater coherence in Europe's education systems, in its terminology and instrumentalities at a time when a greater degree of flexibility in the administrative and financial relationships between government and higher education figures high on the political agenda (for a more detailed discussion of this see *supra* pp. 24-26).

Chapter I set out the broad framework and the long term historical dynamic that has shaped systems of governance in Europe. In this Chapter, we return to this particular issue from a slightly different perspective – that of the contemporary and legal concomitants which accompany this same process.

3.1.2 Deregulation or decentralisation?

If deregulation from an economic and ideological standpoint seeks to free institutions and individuals to pursue their interests and to maximise their personal choice, it does so from a legal perspective by seeking to reduce a vast litany of rules and regulations. Some parliaments and governments have made this objective the keystone in their education policy. Decentralisation, by contrast, seeks to assign more responsibility to regional or local authorities and governments whilst simultaneously focusing the role of central government on determining general strategic choices. This does not mean that its supervisory function is abolished, though its function of closer control is certainly modified and curtailed. Thus, decentralisation does not imply deregulation. It can, as Max Weber long ago noted, merely bring centralisation nearer home (Weber, *Wissenschaft als Beruf*).

Legal doctrine is far from unanimous in accepting the aims of deregulation, nor is deregulation immune to the equivocation of national legislators. Some, in the field of education, are even recoiling from their original enthusiasm. Deregulation does not easily lend itself to uniform implementation across all levels of the education system, though it is certainly easier to apply to higher education than it is to primary or secondary schooling. One major stumbling block across the highway to deregulation is the principle of legality. This principle obliges the legislator himself to set out the basic guidelines to educational control and regulation. He cannot off load this upon the executive, the organising authority or the educational institution.

Yet, the principle of legality requires careful handling. Not only must it observe the basic features that the constitution has set upon the state, it must also be faithful to the intentions of the legislator whilst permitting sufficient latitude for flexibility to have a place in educational policy. It is, for all that, faced with the fact that legal norms are being replaced at federal or at national level by an impressive battery of regulations and independent decisions which, in future, will fall within the purlieu of the administration in the individual institution of higher education.

Whilst it is the express intention of the legislator to confer greater autonomy and powers of self-regulation upon the individual establishment, this is offset by the obligation upon institutional administration to be publicly accountable.

Indeed, the purpose of this policy is subordinate to this latter condition. Situations such as this pose the question as to whether there is not a contradiction between the ends of deregulation and the means put in place to achieve it which often involves an even greater amount of regulation.

Yet, there is reason to believe that thinking about deregulation in education has itself moved on to a third phrase. To set the right to education as a positive law has required time and a growing arsenal of laws and regulatory enactments. One may detect a similar dynamic which moved the purely formal and theoretical right to found educational establishments of a non-state nature – often construed in certain countries as 'educational freedom' (*liberté d'enseignement*) (de Groof, 1984; also de Groof & Bray, 1996) – to the point at which such freedom had legal substance and thus the material means to implement it. The exercise of the right and the freedom to found non-state institutions is to be recommended for democracy in view of the interrelationship with other basic rights. Academic education organised by higher education institutions of a non-state nature may be said to foster objective and qualitative competition and thus stimulate research. Hence, the importance of academic pluralism in a country formerly ruled by state monopoly. Thus, it is necessary to design basic norms and criteria that are enforceable both for state as for independent universities, thereby serving the general interest.

The transition of educational law from its 19th century condition as a traditional and customary freedom towards its 20th century status as a social and cultural right was accompanied by an enlarged role of government and by an equally impressive set of legal provisions, a process which, applied to higher education, has been mentioned earlier under the concept of juridification (see *supra* pp.19-20).

Against this first phase, deregulation – that is the pruning and cutting back of a plethora of regulations and normative instruments – forms the second phase during which the withdrawal of government was counter-balanced amongst both colleges and universities by increased self-regulation – either individually or collectively (Eijlander et al. 1994; 1993). In the third phase a new equilibrium has begun to emerge. It turns around a more focused and selective control by the legislator over certain key dimensions in educational policy, a mode of oversight promulgated through general directives and implemented and executed at institutional level within the framework of the specific rules of institutional self-government. In this new setting, the legislator seeks to improve the quality and strategic relevance of central government directives whilst the task of central administration is to monitor the autonomous response of individual institutions via quality audit. It is a delicate balance, involving both a greater transparency and clarity in the core regulations, functions and responsibilities of the centre as well as their close meshing with the detailed regulations operating at institutional level. The principal task of central national administration is to ascertain whether the core goals, their strategic thrust and application have been met by those who 'bear responsibility for scientific and scholarly education'. Such an arrangement reflects that basic principle which lies at the heart of educational policy, namely co-responsibility.

3.1.3 Legal continuity and the unity of legislation?

The dynamic that is necessary for the law to evolve often has its price and that price is legislative fragmentation. Often, laws and decrees promulgated one year are modified the next and the legislator finds himself reduced thereby to mere casuistry. The emergence of substantial difficulties demand further modification. Or, as a further possibility, major changes to the original intent are inserted. Education policy abounds with such corrections and revisions – the definition of study cycles, the amalgamation of university and non university institutions, measures of rationalisation and changes to programme structures – and they have direct consequence for governance. If the drive by higher education institutions to differentiate between courses and resources as a way of responding to 'market-driven' change continues – and the view of those working at the cutting edge is that it will not merely continue but gather additional impetus (Clark, 1995; 1997) – then the fragmentation in the mission and task of higher education could well add a further and hitherto unsuspected dimension to legislative fragmentation.

Generally speaking, however, laws are modified:

- to take account of case-law in jurisprudence whether national or European,

- to meet the wishes of the administration in particular institutions or to fall in with the requirements of those having influence and authority at the seat of power,
- or to provide leverage, reward or punishment to back initiatives taken by government.

Some might see such flexibility as evidence of legislative dynamism, but not all are agreed on such a view "*L'erreur sur le caractère dynamique du droit vient de la succession rapide des lois.*" (Ripert, 1955). The danger of such spasmodic and continuous adaptations is that they are paid for by an absence of unity in legislation. Thus "Laws are being sent out into the world every other day in which modifications to be modified are made to the modified modifications." (de Groof, 1995b). It is no easy thing for the legislator to ensure stability – that is, coherence in the legislation – whilst upholding the law's dynamic accommodation to changes in society.

3.1.4 The general good or private interests?

The balancing of these two complementary but often contending conditions has particular significance when it comes to granting broader scope to institutional autonomy. It is one of the fundamental principles of negotiating legal enactments that, if consensus should be sought with the interested parties, the general interest takes precedent. Thus, extending the range of activities that come under institutional self-regulation – or autonomy – is by no means the same thing as 'promoting private interests' or reinforcing corporate privilege, that is, the interests of one particular constituency within higher education – say academic staff alone – to the detriment of the remainder.

In the first place, "The State authorities (shall) therefore always balance their own interests on the basis of the advice received" (van der Vlies, 1991), and reach their decision on the basis of what is best for the common good. Whilst establishments of higher education are often closely involved in drafting their own internal regulations, it is clear that institutions ought not to be in a position of determining their content in advance. Such a manner of proceeding would be tantamount to public authorities endorsing 'corporate interests'. In effect, though corporate interests have their place, they are receivable only to the extent that they fall in with the general interest. Nor is the general interest to be taken into consideration solely at the moment of negotiating the range of responsibilities to be assigned to a given institution of higher education. The latter are set up, in some cases funded and in all instances require recognition by the appropriate national administration, and whilst many may see themselves as 'havens of self-management' their obligation to render public account in return for official backing, remains. Thus, the notion of 'privatisation' cannot be seen as coterminous with the suspension of the basic obligation to be answerable for the responsibilities granted them. As we have already pointed out in certain western European systems of higher education the interests of the academic corporation alone have been extended to embrace other interest groups, non academic staff, administration, students and other 'consumers' (see *supra* pp.6-8). Since these groups have acknowledged rights, they enshrine a concept of accountability which is both internal and, in the case of 'external personalities', external to the establishment and thus to the public. We shall return to this theme later.

3.2 International covenants relating to higher education

Through the legal instruments that define its mission and govern its administration and management, higher education is firmly rooted within the nation state. To be sure, the strengthening of international ties, the links of joint research, of staff and student exchanges together with those powerful forces in the economy which shape nations and, by extension their systems of higher education have over the past decade exerted pressures for change and innovation. These pressures are no less today. How is this drive to transcend national frontiers reflected in international law as it touches upon higher education? Is there a coherence in international law which itself transcends national legislation and different juridical norms?

Whilst some international treaties deal explicitly with the right to education in general, there are those – though they are not many – which have bearing on higher education specifically.

Article 26 of the Universal Declaration of Human rights (10 December, 1948), states that "*Everyone has the right to education. Education shall be free, at least in the elementary and fundamental stages.*" As regards higher education, it says, "... *higher education shall be equally accessible to all on the basis of merit.*" From this, it is self evident that higher education is not necessarily free and that access to it is dependent on demonstrating 'merit', though the latter term remains undefined. For its part, the European Commission for Human Rights (ECHR) has declared, in a decision of 16 May, 1977 (No. 6598/74, not edited) that access to higher education or to particular types of colleges may be subordinated to the possession of another diploma, to success in the entrance examination or to other objective criteria. Likewise, in a further decision (9 December, 1980 No.8844/80) the ECHR stated that reasonable progress in studies already started should be a condition for their continuation.

An especially important definition was provided in Article 13 of the International Covenant on Economic, Social and Cultural Rights (19 December, 1966) Paragraph 2 stipulated that "*Higher Education shall be made equally accessible to all, on the basis of capacity, by every appropriate means, and in particular by the progressive introduction of free education.*" Clearly, the statement did not require that higher education should be free but rather that its eventual free nature should be forwarded progressively. Furthermore, the insistence on 'capacity' suggests that entry to higher education does not extend to everyone. Thus, until such a guarantee effectively exists, the less well-off members of society will continue to face unjust discrimination.

3.3 Statutory features of higher education institutions

The ideological, ethical or philosophical composition of education provided by central authorities is usually set out, directly or indirectly, by the constitution, by positive legislation or, as a third possibility, in keeping with the general legal theory governing services to the public. Some national regulations guarantee the 'ethically neutral' nature of state education by requiring certain mandatory conditions attached to the qualifications held by teachers.

At the same time, national administration subsidises and recognises establishments set up by private interests, by local authorities (municipalities, communes, counties), assigns grants – the size of which varies depending on the particular country – to the organising networks which have met the necessary prior conditions as set down in law. Such grants are for equipment, to offset running costs or in support of staff salaries.

In many instances, this guaranteed underwriting is accorded once the right to 'salary support' attains the status of a 'subjective right' that is, a right that may be requested from the courts once the statutory conditions have been met. In this way, the funding of educational institutions not directly dependent on central national authority is subject neither to parliament nor to the vagaries of party political majorities. The right to support is then acquired automatically on fulfilment of the statutory requirements. Seen from this perspective, the state's obligation to found its own educational establishments is balanced by its duty to support 'types of education recognised as valid outside state education' and to subsidise their staff.

International conventions and national constitutions subscribe to the right for educational provision to be made on the basis of a particular ideological view or pedagogical methodology. Private associations in turn, have their own bye-laws, their requirements of commitment to a particular ethic when recruiting staff and, in a certain measure, oversee the application of such rules. The state's obligation, in keeping with the right for all to receive education, is to provide education for all even those who do not adhere to a particular ethical standpoint. Between state education on the one hand and private education on the other, are other public authorities whose status does not have to be the same as that endorsed by a country's central authorities.

Complex arrangements such as these are themselves pointers to the fact that the boundaries between private and public law are becoming less distinct. And some voices have been raised in support of abolishing the national status in education. In other countries, the line between statutory and contractual conditions of employment has become so fine that the idea has been mooted to do away with the formal public servant status of teachers. Including non-public education within the ambit of public law allows the argument to be made that the former also contribute to the common weal. They award degrees recognised in civil law, they undertake the function of what has been termed the organic public service. Non-public education, it is argued, acts as a functional public service. Their qualifications confer the right to exercise particular professions and the education they provide constitutes an undoubted public benefit.

3.4 The application of the general principles of justice

There is a certain advantage to be had by making non-public institutions of higher education subject to public law. Not the least is that there can no longer be any doubt that the general principles of justice and due process in administration also apply to them and, more specifically, those relating to the observance of due care (the requirement to substantiate decisions and uphold the principle of equality), the casting aside of the rejection of authority, the principle of proportionality, together with that of surety in law and confidentiality.

In applying these principles, one of the first tasks involves ascertaining how far the discretionary power invested in the appropriate educational authority is legitimate, particularly in the areas of personnel management, budget allocation and distribution, and research project management. Certainly, administrators involved in these decisions will have to show observance of due care and due process. In addition to subjecting them to careful scrutiny for the strict legality of their decisions, it is clear that those responsible for these functions will no longer be able to take refuge behind the discretionary powers they once held.

In public law, there is an abundance of precedent and case-law dealing with the exercise of discretionary powers. To this is now added the idea that the legality of decisions should be supplemented by marginal testing as an extra lever in verifying an institution's policy and its execution. The wider the range of discretionary powers, the more necessary an 'audit of appropriate procedures' the purpose of which would be to detect possible conflicts with the public interest. Such procedures of verification are directed not merely at protecting the institution from itself but also at protecting a broader set of interests. If the general interest is not tied to the general principles of justice, it is irremediably damaged.

3.5 The principle of subsidiarity

The principle of subsidiarity has been laid down in statutes and decision-making instruments and in particular in Article 3B of the Treaty on the European Union. The Article states:

> "The Community shall act within the limits of the powers conferred upon it by this Treaty and of the objectives assigned to it therein. In areas which do not fall within its exclusive competence, the Community shall take action, in accordance with the principle of subsidiarity only if and so far as the objectives of the proposed action cannot be sufficiently achieved by the member States and can therefore, by reason of the scale of the proposed action, be better achieved by the Community. Any action by the Community shall not go beyond what is necessary to achieve the objective of this Treaty."

Clearly, though it is set out, the principle of subsidiarity is far from being a novel concept. But there are few cases where national legislation acknowledges the principle *expressis verbis*. Belgium is one and does so in Article 24 – formerly article 17 – of its constitution. In countries where federal structures site educational affairs with the nonfederal members, it applies implicitly.

Though the majority of European countries neither mention subsidiarity in their legal texts nor show evidence of a structured application, it is held that increasing adherence to the principle is observable as a matter of political necessity. In essence, subsidiarity consists of conferring only such responsibilities to an organisationally superior unit as cannot be fulfilled sufficiently at the lower level.

This way of working has important consequences particularly in the relationship between the state and higher education institutions. This principle first delegates to the institutions tasks formerly carried out at government level. Second, such a delegation of tasks bears upon institutional autonomy and upon the exercise of freedom in education.

The principle of subsidiarity does not imply that universities and other institutions of higher education within this legal framework can operate with entire freedom. Their participation in educational policy-making obliges them to assume their own responsibilities. Their own statutes and bye-laws should not show either lacunae or contradictions with legislation promulgated by government. It is even arguable that there is a duty to cooperate between different institutions of higher education in order to create a certain degree of homogeneity.

Nevertheless, subsidiarity does not mean that governments have to take reluctance alone into account. The principle also encloses the criteria of both efficiency and proportionality. If a particular higher education institution is unable or unwilling to cooperate in order to secure a certain level of convergency – which in the setting of the European Union will become of increasing significance – government may always have recourse to those measures it deems necessary to guarantee quality.

REFERENCES

Clark, Burton R. (1995) *Places of Inquiry: research and advanced education in modern universities*. Berkeley/Los Angeles/London: University of California Press.

Clark, Burton R. (1997) Common Problems and Adaptive Responses in the Universities of the World: organising for change, *Higher Education Policy*, (forthcoming).

de Groof, Jan (1984) *Droit à l'instruction et liberté d'enseignement*. Bruxelles: Acco.

de Groof, Jan (ed) (1994) *Subsidiarity and Education: aspects of comparative educational law*. Leuven: Uitgeverij Acco.

de Groof, Jan (1995a) *The Overall Importance of Educational Law*. Paris: Unesco.

de Groof, Jan (ed) (1995b) *The Legal Status of Teachers in Europe; mobility and education*. Leuven:

de Groof, Jan & Bray E. (eds) (1996) *Education under the New Constitution in South Africa*. Leuven: Acco.

Eijlander, Ph. et al. (1993) *Overheid en zelfregulering*. Zwolle: Centrum voor wetgevingsvraagstukken.

Eijlander Ph. (1994) *Wetgever en de maat van de tijd*. Zwolle: Centrum voor wetgevingsvraagstukken.

Ripert, G. (1955) *Les Forces créatrices du Droit*. Paris: Librairie générale de droit et de jurisprudence.

Van der Vlies, I.C. (1991) *Handboek Wetgeving*. Zwolle: Tjeenk Willink.

C. Wright Mills & H. Gerth (1964) *From Max Weber, essays in sociology*. Oxford University Press

4

DEFINING THE UNIVERSITY'S MISSION

4.1 Introduction

For as long as the history of the university has been recorded, demands to define the university's mission have been never-ending, as a recent study of the universities in mediaeval Europe by the Flemish historian, Hilde de Ridder Simoens, has shown (de Ridder Simoens, 1992). What the value of higher learning for the individual? Can the university not afford to take an ethical stance on issues which face society?

Questions such as these about the task and function of the university are receiving answers, circumspect though they are, from those systems of higher education which, in eastern and central Europe, are in full transition towards democracy. In this chapter, we deal with the ways in which the university's mission is being shaped and carried out.

In defining the task of the university, law-makers are seeking to ensure a certain degree of continuity. This they do by limiting themselves to compiling lists of institutions that qualify as university institutions. In some countries, the attribution of the title 'university' is subject to legal protection.

Yet, there are glimmerings of change, in keeping with changes already observable in society at large and in keeping with a certain degree of agreement within the university world itself. The university is seen as going beyond the traditional dichotomy of an institution for educating the highly qualified versus an academy for scientific research. To include service to the community as a third function over and above scholarly research and teaching appears suspiciously like a redundancy. Teaching and research are after all amongst the most fundamental services that society receives from higher education. Nevertheless, there is a view amongst law-makers that this function needs to be included.

Yet, an adequate definition of 'service' is far from obvious given the multiple aspects involved. What one can say is that by including it, one emphasises the very different type of relationship between university and society that flows from its figuring as a third and integral element to both teaching and research (de Groof & Peeters, 1993-4).

4.2 Determining the mission of the university

One of the generic characteristics of higher education across Europe is the very precise end of the university sector by contrast to other sectors in higher education and in the nature of the differentiation in the tasks before it, be they academic or professional. (This is not what sociologists or historians would say. The current trend is towards blurring boundaries and differentiation between establishments). For long it has been part of the university's established mission to conduct scholarly and scientific research and to dispense learning on a scientific, rational basis. In effect, this entails learning grounded in the most recent findings of research which itself stands as a disinterested quest for new insights and knowledge in all fields of human endeavour. Its purpose is to permit the independent advance and practice of science, scholarship and research or the practical application of such knowledge. Community service is an addition to the first of these two tasks.

As a totality, the university discharges these three core functions. It serves as an institution which, on behalf of society, is actively engaged in prosecuting scientific and scholarly research, teaching and learning to the highest level whilst providing to the community both scientific and academic service and support.

Scholarly research is the university's prime core responsibility. It plays a central and vital part in the education of students, in the training of researchers (Clark, 1993, 1995) and in the transmission and preservation of fundamental knowledge. There is a view, though it is not without challenge even in established systems of higher education in western Europe (Kogan & Henckel, 1983), which believes that, save for the setting out of society's broad priorities for research, government should not interfere in the conduct of research. It remains a fact, however, that research, whether disinterested or applied, is the path to the future and it ought to occupy a position of undisputed primacy within the university system. Whether it is really possible to find an enduring balance between fundamental research and its more goal- or- mission-oriented equivalent will remain subject to debate. But responsibility in these areas is not limited to the university alone. Those interests which, outside the university, have a stake in determining science research policies need to remain aware that the tension between demands that are recognised and the knowledge that comes from disinterested research is a necessary condition for the development of both.

Universities together with national research councils, wield the prime responsibility for allocation of research funds between different fields of enquiry and investigation. They may do this via the internal research funding element that forms part of the individual university's budget. And in this regard it is highly desirable that they make known their own priorities for distributing such funds between different research fields. Nor should particular disciplines be systematically excluded from the support which underpins free, disinterested investigation.

Providing high level academic and scholarly education, intimately grounded in the interplay between active research and teaching, is the second core responsibility of the university. In a society which is itself in constant change, the argument, made long ago by Wilhelm von Humboldt about the desirability of training through research finds its contemporary echo. Indeed, the transfer of research-generated new knowledge and technique to the minds of students may well be the most important form of knowledge transfer (Clark, 1995 p.15). As a noted scholar in the field of comparative higher education has recently written, "Approaching the twenty-first century, the intellectual moment favours even more than in the recent past the universities that best integrate research activity and research training with teaching and study." (ibid.).

In practice, however, this – the second of the university's missions – is observed more in the breech, despite all that we may learn from the very notable exceptions. We now face a situation in which one must indeed question how far 'academic education' can in reality be distinguished from 'education at an academic level' and most especially so with the advent of 'professionally oriented' courses within the university.

The final area of responsibility that falls to the university is the rendering of expert and specialist services to the community. Such services are protean in their form and variety: health care provision in teaching hospitals, expert analysis and advice to government or to private interests, help in the technical management of certain social services, in the organisation of scholarly dialogue and, last but not least, an independent and critical assessment of issues central to society.

4.3 Universities and the knowledge society of tomorrow

The three missions that have been laid out here can, naturally, be interpreted as a straightforward updating of the traditional responsibilities of the university as they have been defined and refined over the years by the academic community. Yet the real challenge lies not so much in the missions themselves as in the context of social and economic change to which higher education both contributes and by which it is itself shaped. But this in turn begs the question as to what are likely to be the driving forces behind such social and industrial mobilisation? An interesting glimpse is given in the forward to the European Commission's White Paper on Education and Training, published in 1995, entitled *Teaching and Learning: towards the Learning Society*. It is an optimistic interpretation not entirely devoid of a certain technocratic utopianism:

> "The internationalisation of the economy, the information society and scientific and technological progress, the impact of these events can be seen every day. Within enterprises they are driving the development of new types of work... These changes are not incidental, but herald the society of tomorrow... In this context, education and training clearly play a central role... there will be a wide-ranging debate involving all those with a key interest in education and training. They will have one and the same objective: to prepare Europeans to pass smoothly to a society based upon the acquisition

of skills, where one continues to learn and to teach through life, in other words, a learning society."

If society in Europe is fast approaching the point at which the economy, hitherto based on capital intensive and labour intensive production, gives way before an economy based on the production and sale of knowledge and services, then the university as one organisation whose production has been based on precisely this commodity, ought to enjoy a strategic position of immense significance. But this too is highly problematical. Whether the university will continue to enjoy such centrality or will do so in structures that are recognisably similar to, and bear a recognisable relationship with, today's university, is a matter on which many have voiced increasing disquiet. Though the key to the learning society is often held to be research and research based training, there are incontrovertible signs that these functions are no longer the exclusivity of the university. In certain key areas associated with technological development, these functions are settling elsewhere; from the research based firm to the firm which trains its own research personnel is a short step that some have already taken (Eurich, 1985). Thus, it does not necessarily follow that because the prime characteristic of post-industrial society will reside in its skills of symbolic manipulation, that the 'learning society' will of necessity foregather in the same institutional settings that history has associated with high level learning in the past.

4.4 Universities and the labour market

It is amongst the more commonly held views that economic competition on a global scale will place a special premium on developing what technospeak calls 'human resources' which is in reality the type of skills the individual citizen acquires and the techniques which permit those who employ them to get the best returns in raised productivity, lowered cost and greater profit. Much has been written about the need to develop cooperative work styles, to equip the individual to face up to labour markets that are culturally diverse and technically interdependent. In structural terms, it is very clear that jobs for the unskilled will rapidly disappear. Those seeking entry to the labour market will need to master skills that are closely linked with and generated by symbolic knowledge. And those wishing to remain in that labour market will, it is believed, need regularly to update their knowledge if only to avoid redundancy or to retain their value *vis à vis* against a rising generation which in turn, will possess more recent knowledge and certainly will be cheaper.

In a market-driven economy, it is beholden on higher education to meet the skills demands coming from employers and passed to the world of learning via student consumerdom. Under such impulses, higher education is driven to develop systems of education and training that are more flexible and more open ended, largely out of the conviction that a broader educational experience fosters a greater adaptability by the individual to change that is both inevitable and unpredictable. Information technology profoundly alters the structure, content and means of access to knowledge. For many people, the type of labour market that appears to be emerging from this new industrial base places a particular premium on a broad general education. Thus, even training of a highly professional nature should include elements that, until recently, were primarily associated with the humanities: language skills, ability to communicate effectively, historical insight, alongside such abilities as handling information technology, a good grounding in computer science, a grasp of management and marketing and above all, the ability to seek out information that is appropriate and relevant to the task in hand. In fine, what industry and firms appear to need are high level generalists.

The drive towards specialisation, most marked at the undergraduate level, is not without its dangers. At a time of massive acceleration in the pace of change involved in restructuring the economy, irrespective of whether that restructuring takes place within a market economy or consists of the transition from a command economy to its free market successor, the risk of mismatch between the skills students possess and those needed, is considerable. Such tremendous waste in human resources, not to mention the social tensions such a situation generates, are never tolerable though they are often tolerated as the lesser of hopefully passing evils. In some systems, particularly in central and eastern Europe, attempts have been made to reduce graduate unemployment in this period of transition by retaining vestiges of earlier practice through controlling student input and output. Whilst this policy might be justified in certain limited instances, and one thinks here of highly specialised programmes largely of a technical nature specifically geared to industrial demands, generally speaking such a stance is in contradiction with the principle of a free labour market. It also runs the risk of freezing the content of knowledge taught within the framework of an earlier age, by cutting the university off from the need to innovate in keeping with market-driven change.

It goes without saying that if flexibility, adjustment and innovation are characteristics that the market demands of students, they are also features that ought not be left aside by institutions of higher education. But if institutions in their turn are to meet what appear to be society's expectations considerable revision is called for in the way institutional policy is formulated, discussed and determined which returns us foursquare to the issue of institutional structures, responsibilities and procedures for internal decision-making – that is, to governance. Key to this process of self-regulation is self-evaluation, not only with respect to what the university does and how it does it – which has to do with curriculum structure, degree of specialisation involved and the degree of specialisation required – but also with the way in which what universities do is perceived by those who deem they have in interest in the institution, be they students, parents, sponsors, patrons or benefactors.

If these myriad and expanding 'constituencies' have an undoubted interest in being regularly and clearly informed about the goals, policies and achievements of higher education, be it the individual institution or the national system as a whole, it does not follow that their concerns are wholly met by presenting such 'accounts' as exclusively economic in nature (Trow, 1996). The university does not live from industry alone, even though an increasing share of its resources may come from that source. Universities are also part of the nation's cultural patrimony, its historical memory and very often the founthead for political renewal and a revitalised sense of national self-awareness. In the words used in the Magna Charta Universitatum Europearum, which in 1988, marked 800 years of the university in Europe, "... The University is an autonomous institution which produces and transmits culture in a critical way, through research and education."

REFERENCES

Clark, Burton R. (1993) *The Research Foundations of Graduate Education: Germany, Britain, France, Japan, United States*. Berkeley/Los Angeles/ London: University of California Press.

Clark, Burton R. (1995) *Places of Inquiry: research and advanced education in modern universities*. Berkeley/Los Angeles/London: University of California Press.

de Groof, Jan & Peeters, B. (1993-4) "De Universteit: dienstverlening bij uitstek", *Tijdschrift voor Onderwijsrecht en Onderwijsbeleid*, Nr.4.

EC (1995) *Teaching and Learning: towards the Learning Society (White Paper on Education and Training)*. Bruxelles: Commission of the European Union.

Eurich, Nell (1985) *Corporate Classrooms: the Learning Business*. Princeton: Carnegie Foundation for the Advancement of Teaching.

Kogan, Maurice & Henckel, Mary (1983) *Government and Research: the Rothschild experiment in a government department*. London: Heinemann Educational Books.

Rüegg, Walter (1992) "Themes" in Hilde de Ridder Simoens *History of the Universities in Europe. Vol.i Universities in the Middle Ages*. Cambridge: Cambridge University Press.

Trow, Martin (1996) "Trust, markets and accountability in higher education: a comparative perspective", *Higher Education Policy*, vol.9, no.4, pp.309-324.

5

THE PLACE OF ENLIGHTENED SELF-GOVERNMENT

5.1 Introduction

For more than a decade in western Europe, higher education has been going through very substantial changes in internal governance. However, as we pointed out in the first Chapter, it is possible to view this transition in a longer term perspective once one accepts that governance is not exclusively to do with the introduction of new management techniques alone. If one steps back from this narrow 'managerialist' view which equates reform in governance simply with technical innovation in the instruments available for determining institutional priorities and if one adds either a political or an historical perspective, as we have done earlier, then changes in governance involve a rather more complex series of issues, not least of which is who is to take part in the agenda that such bright new instruments and techniques make possible? As we have seen, governance also involves redefining those constituencies and interests, both external as well as internal to the particular establishment, which may take part in institutional decision-making. If one endorses this latter and wider definition, it is self evident that the more specifically 'managerial' revolution – the introduction of strategic planning, the setting in place of mechanisms and procedures for institutional self-assessment (Bauer, 1988) and the elaboration of more sophisticated indicators of cost control, performance evaluation, the paraphernalia for estimating academic productivity and institutional efficiency – represents a second phase in this Europe-wide saga.

5.1.1 Basic pragmatism

Concentrating on the managerial component within governance, two aspects immediately stand out. They are not so much the emphasis on the withdrawal of central administration to the commanding heights of strategic planning at system level, nor yet the drive to deregulate – or to 'set free' the pent up forces of institutional enterprise and initiative. They are, rather, the basic empiricism which has driven this reform forward and the truly amazing speed at which pragmatic innovations have assumed all the weight of established legitimacy. The managerial revolution in western Europe began as a pragmatic response by governments – amongst which the British and the Dutch stood in the lead – to reduce public expenditure on the one hand, and, on the other, in keeping with the aging of the population, to redistribute public expenditure towards the older age groups. Task concentration and reviews of financial efficiency, which were the first steps in what has subsequently been reinterpreted as evidence of strategic intent behind the managerial revolution in both the Netherlands and Britain – to cite but two instances. It stood as pragmatic and short term measures to force greater efficiency from higher education at a time when its resources were being forcibly cut back. Only later was the ideological element of reducing the power of the central state, the reinterpretation of higher education as 'market driven' as opposed to social demand led, opening higher education up to 'market forces' together with the gradually emerging concept of deregulation, grafted on as a fully-fledged policy to this otherwise fragile stem.

5.1.2 Amazing haste

The second aspect is no less worthy of note particularly so in the context of reconstructing higher education in central and eastern Europe. Revisions and refinements to the instrumentality and techniques available to university management, got under way in western Europe around the mid 1980s and have, naturally, accelerated since then. In effect, measures which stood at the very least in their systems of origin as provisional, whose appropriateness had yet fully to be ascertained, and whose earliest glimmerings could at best be traced only to the mid 1980s in western Europe, were presented after the fall of the Berlin wall as proven, accepted, and established practice, as a template on which reconstruction of higher education in the newly self-liberated lands should be based. It is difficult to find a more outstanding example of faith, hope and consultancy conferring so solid a retrospective credibility on changes which in their systems of origin were in process of becoming.

In an earlier Chapter, we summarised the basic categories and components that set aside one type of authority within institutions of higher education from another (see Chapter 1, pp. 9-13). We also examined the levels within higher education systems at which different types of authority tended to concentrate. We set out three archetypical governance modes and introduced an historical interpretation to the long term dynamic which has underpinned what may be seen as the 'Continental' mode of governance.

Whatever one terms this particular process – deregulation, '*de-étatisation*' or 'privatisation', the dynamic in higher education systems at the closing years of the 20th century is seen as sweeping universities towards greater institutional autonomy, towards greater structural and organisational differentiation (Clark, 1997) which are themselves necessary conditions for competition to take root and for academic entrepreneurship to flourish. Such a reinforcement of the powers and responsibilities exercised at the institutional level is naturally accompanied by changes in the role and function of national administration. Scholars use a variable terminology to described this latter process. Some see it in terms of moving away from 'the State control' model of higher education government relationship, towards a more 'supervisory' role. Others describe this same process in terms of a revision in the administrative style which involves replacing 'direct and constant intervention' by institutional self-regulation. Yet, a third group of writers uses the concept of the move from 'state control', via decree, circular and the detailed and constant use of oversight, towards the so-called 'evaluative State' (Neave, 1988) in which occasional but regular evaluation, publicly available, sometimes tied to performance based financing, is substituted. This approach, often identified with what is termed 'remote steering' by central government as opposed to minutely stipulated control, sets great store on the evaluative or shepherding role of national Ministries than on their regulative or punitive role (Peterson, 1996).

5.1.3 New divisions of academic and administrative labour

It is trite to say that the task of higher education in modern society is becoming more complex just as it is to say that the demands society places upon it multiply. These complexities – and they emerge in such areas as the growing diversity of ability, career plans and age range of students, right through to the establishment of joint industrial R&D ventures with regional firms and the development of international outreach – have to be taken into account. They require new forms of collaboration, negotiation and agreement as much between the university and the growing range of external ventures that often accumulate around it physically – of which science parks are a good example – as they do within the institution between academic staff, managers of projects, institutional administration and leadership. Just as academia is driven forward by the accumulation of knowledge, by the proliferation of specialities and the emergence of new sub fields, so institutional administration is subject to a similar division of labour. Activities once informally handled by enthusiastic teachers or researchers in their spare time, soon become formalised, command resources and open up administrative and managerial career lines. In earlier times, student exchange, to take one example, was handled within the department. Nowadays, this function, often formalised and carrying a budget line of its own, constitutes an institute-wide sub unit or even division. When projects become a means of raising additional income, the function of 'project manager' to oversee a programme's finances and non-substantive daily routine – in short, to ensure its efficient workings – swiftly acquires a new found importance.

5.1.4 Towards new bureaucracy?

Clearly, as the range of responsibility the individual institution is asked to assume increases and as other functions – human resources management, institutional evaluation, internal quality assessment, income generation and strategic planning – are added to the customary tasks of financial allocation, curriculum development, a particular premium is placed upon the further professionalisation of administration. And tasks that once were exercised within departments – that is, in the area where personal rulership and discipline-generated authority hold sway – become formalised and professionalised, so they move over to those levels in the institution where bureaucratic authority dwells or entrepreneurial authority has its being. Such a process involves redrawing the boundaries between those types of authority that shape governance systems and the balance of power amongst the constituent interests which go to make them up. They affect the weight accorded to academia and the influence wielded in decision-making by administration. From this the question arises whether deregulation will result in greater power to administration – a development some have qualified as a confiscated revolution – or whether, on the contrary, it will result in the restoration of the power of the academic guild?

5.2 The right to education: its consequences for governance

Seen from the perspective of those organising education, the notion of the freedom of education has three specific senses: the freedom of establishment, the freedom of philosophical orientation and the freedom to organise. In this volume we are concerned with the last. The granting of a margin of independence to higher education institutions has, as we have insisted earlier, a long history. The granting of academic freedom which, depending on the particular country involved, may variously be traced back to the 18th century, acknowledges that those engaged in scholarship should have the liberty to determine both the content and the methods to be used in their inquiries.

In this general context, the role of the law-maker is to draw up the general legal framework within which higher education is set. This framework encompasses higher education administration in its entirety. It includes the study programmes available, access, the awarding of certificates and distinctions that mark the successful completion of a recognised course of study. It extends to financing higher education, to the payment of academic staff, the financial support to the individual student, embraces the formal titles held by the different ranks within the academic estate, sets out the basic structure of the higher education system, defines the administrative provision of institutions and, last but not least, also lays down the conditions under which the principle of participation is applied to the management domain.

Depending on national circumstance, the planning of higher education and the formulation of research policy often falls under the competence of more than one Ministry. But irrespective of whether this responsibility is exercised exclusively or jointly, the role of government is not confined to coordinating such freedom. It also conditions the way in which academic freedom comes into being both at the regional or institutional level. Such regulations, as set it out, apply to non-public (non-state or 'free') institutions and, to the degree that such establishments follow the conditions demanded of institutions engaged in public service, they receive government subsidies and their degree certifications carry similar privileges to public sector universities and colleges.

Moreover, the government may also encourage and, where it deems appropriate, limit competition. Promoting cross-institutional or cross-sectoral co-operation, defining the distribution of academic work, and evaluating specialist research and teaching units in the light of their performance according to objective indicators, and requiring that they work together are amongst the tasks of national administration as its duty to promote the public interests in education.

5.3 Different spheres of authority: patterns of change

In the ties between central government and higher education institutions, the question, "Who regulates what?" receives a different answer in different countries. Beneath this variation, the degree of uniformity which detailed regulation imposes on higher education appears to be moving towards a certain flexibility. In the move towards deregulation, the law-maker voluntarily limits himself to developing minimum requirements in such areas as study programmes, managerial structure, staff policy and planning. Questions of resource distribution or the observance of procedural issues may be assigned to administration working at institutional level. In effect, central government now tends to operate in an *a posteriori* manner. It verifies whether the objectives set out have been attained, whether they fulfil the minimal requirements as stipulated and whether the procedure that brought them about is in keeping with the law.

5.4 Administrative freedom: potential and limits

The balance of responsibilities emerges with particular clarity in the field of administrative freedom of higher education establishments. Whilst it may be viewed as an element included in the freedom to organise, administrative freedom is greater for non-state – or non-public-institutions. It may extended to the make-up of the executive council as well as the nature of the authority exercised by a formally legal entity. How far administrative freedom can carry a restrictive burden depends on the legally recognised identity of the non-public institution and the specificity of its mission. In the case of public institutions, it is usual for the mandate and responsibilities of the various administrative and governing bodies to be laid down formally by law since it is the community itself which constitutes the organising authority (de Groof, 1985, 1989).

Furthermore, the matching of bodies with administrative responsibility within universities, whether public or private, requires a set of general legal normative enactments. The less specific the latter, the greater the latitude for institutions to set up their own bye-laws and regulations. This holds good as much for the governing board that sets general academic policy as it does in the case of committees with more limited executive powers within the faculties, sections, departments or institutes or for the internal division of authority itself. That said, wide ranging delegation of powers does not obviate the overall responsibility of the appropriate authority to act for the establishment as a whole.

Thus, for example, whether responsibility for appointment and nomination of staff falls under the purlieu of the faculty, or expenditure under the department is set out in the organisational chart and in the internal regulation of each university. On the other hand, guideline on staff recruitment and promotion, budgetary allocation criteria at departmental level and the signing of research contracts fall under the responsibility of the governing board, that is, of the whole academic community.

Government may also apply sanctions against the university in the event that internal audit is itself insufficient. Here the joint responsibility of central government and university authorities is crucial.

Thus, regardless of whether decentralised or not, the model implied in administrative freedom in no way diminishes the ultimate responsibility of university authorities to the government and thus to the nation. University authorities have charge over coordinating institutional policy, over the observance of internal rules and regulations, over quality control and the auditing of financial transactions.

But the authority of the governing board does not mean the absence of authority by government. The government may invoke legal regulations as well as the necessity for the university to abide by its own bye-laws, to observe the general principles of good management, and to justify its decisions. In short, the obligation of accountability retains its basic strength.

5.5 Participation

5.5.1 Participation as a moral and positive right

Promoting the public interest also requires that the government organise systematically the means of consulting the universities, building, where possible, consensus around the mission of the university in general and that of individual establishments. Such a consultative mechanism may reside in the rectors' conference, an inter-university council or be seated in other consultative committees. The legal basis of this mechanism is contained mainly in positive law, though sometimes the right to participation is enforced *vis à vis* the competent authorities on grounds of its being a moral right vested in the consumer of education. Still, that educational establishments show great reluctance to concede the right of access to information to students and staff to the same extent as this exists on the shop-floor and in industry, is a cause for dismay.

5.5.2 Staff rights: individual and collective

There is, in the university, however, a certain tradition of users and 'clients' being involved in the conduct of administration and management issues. This tradition can be traced back to 13th century Italy, more particularly to the University of Bologna where, for a short period, students engaged and paid academic staff (Rüegg, 1992). As has been pointed out in the introductory Chapter, the participatory impulse of the 1970s was considered to be a powerful means of democratising higher education and, as time passed and managerialism became in vogue, it was also subsequently held to be conducive to the efficient functioning and transparency in administration.

Within the limits permitted by legal enactment, that universities enjoy self-regulation is offset by the governing council seeking the advice and views of professionals, by its drawing on the expertise within its ranks and by giving ear to members of the academic community. Yet there is a view that has gained ground which argues that the 'social goal' of the university corporation calls for the involvement of the main constituencies. Education and rational arguments are the university's basic task. Those affected by administrative decisions ought to be able to make their views known on this basis to the appropriate decision-making body and to extend, where appropriate, discussion to others in the academic community.

The representation of interests may, of course, take many forms right up to and including joint management and co-responsibility. But the moment that students take part in the deliberations of faculty, department or governing council, they have gone beyond the role of interest group and assume a part of the overall responsibility for the institution since they have, at that point, become part of the common weal.

5.5.3 Participation: a vital element in institutional autonomy

It would seem judicious, as governments delegate part of the responsibility that has been incumbent upon them down to the institutional level and increase thereby the scope of self-regulation of the individual institution, that the latter should take steps to set in place a decision-making system to involve all parties with a potential interest in the institution's development – and thus its policies. Whether such interests should be endowed with the capacity to take decisions, as opposed to influencing their outcome, remains a delicate issue.

5.5.3.1 Who should participate?

There is much to be said for student participation, irrespective of whether this is justified in the name of a university version of consumer rights or justified on the pragmatic grounds that it is better to have students comfortably inside – rather than riotously assembled outside – the doors of the senate house. And whilst there is considerable advantage in including the representatives of a younger generation, there is the other and no less powerful argument which drives in the same direction; that the student body itself is changing. Over the past decade, increasing numbers of adult – even retirees – have followed the path of higher learning. It is somewhat misplaced to believe that the responsibilities they exercise as full citizens should be suspended and that they should return to a species of semi-tutelage simply on account of their wish to pursue learning. Arguments made on grounds of the need to listen to the views of the rising generation are persuasive, especially as the academic estate is itself becoming distinctly grey. They are, however, not a wit less powerful to the generation that has risen and which may bring a solid experience of society beyond the groves of academe to enrich them.

Furthermore, alumni should not be forgotten, though whether their nostalgia can be tapped to the same degree as their American counterparts, appears at present remote. Still, some universities in Europe do have this provision – British universities in the form of the convocation and the Portuguese with a similar body reserved for past graduates (CRE, 1986, 1987). Finally, there is the question of 'external personalities' whose presence on French university councils is provided for in the *Loi d'Orientation* of 1984, to cite one example. They furnish a valuable source of impartial judgment, advice and links with the community, whether local, regional or national.

5.5.3.2 Which model of participation to choose?

In higher education policy just as in men's fashions, there is nothing so absurd as believing that other peoples' reach-me-downs will provide one with a snug fit! Bearing in mind such a stricture, the choice of a model of participation is no small challenge. Much depends on the current condition of higher education, the interest groups present and their readiness to be involved and, last but not least, the nation's particular historic circumstances. However, as one looks at participation systems generally, two tendencies stand out. The first revolves around those which call for authentic and genuine participation on a given organ of university government: senate, general council, university council. A sub-variation on this model involves participation in advisory groups the conclusions of which are passed upwards and on to the point where the decision is reached. The second is rather more informal and may be seen less in terms of participation than that far less precise but often no less influential process of 'taking soundings'. Whilst the former are official, and resemble what one British government specialist who worked on educational pressure groups, termed 'legitimate' groupings, the second are more nebulous. Their status tends towards the subterranean.

5.6 Similarities and differences in Europe

The general rubric of participation covers many groups, academic staff, students of all ages, and other interests often alluded to – erroneously – as stakeholders. Strictly speaking, stakeholders are those who have a stake – or a part – in a venture, usually secured by dint of money. Nowadays, this term has been extended to such an extent that it has become an omnium gatherum – a residual category – composed of neither staff, students nor employees of the university.

From what emerges from the country reports, if all higher education systems of the Council of Europe member states recognise the principle of participation, there is a not wholly unexpected degree of difference and variation in the form it takes. In the United Kingdom where the universities have long enjoyed a very high degree of institutional autonomy and self-government, participation in the formal governing bodies of universities – the council, the senate or the court in the older universities or the board of governors, the academic board in the case of universities who attained this status after 1992, these bodies are involved in crucial aspects of decision-making. The council, for example, is responsible for university finance, investments and the management of plant and buildings. It also exercises oversight in the areas of teaching and research. The senate has responsibility for the academic work of the university, including course approval, the recognition of new degree programmes and the conferment of degree titles.

5.6.1 Lithuania: a case study

There are also systems of higher education where, if the academic staff enjoys considerable rights in theory, practice does not reflect them. Such is the situation in Lithuania, though it could be argued that such a condition exists in most countries where there is a tradition of strong intervention by the central state. Let us look more closely for a moment at the Lithuanian case. Ostensibly, universities enjoy full independence in distributing financial resources, though these flow from the state budget. Universities must follow rules set down by parliament and other laws and regulations. Universities appear to have no latitude to seek out sources of backing other than from the state. As for participation on governing bodies, it extends only to members of academic staff. Only in the student parliament are students represented. The powers of the student parliament are consultative, both at the departmental council level and at the level of the council of the institution and, then only in student affairs. Save the presence of parliamentarians and members of the Ministry of Education, no outside *Prominente*, notable or individual is formally part of the decision-making process either in a consultative or personal capacity. When one turns one's attention to the responsibilities of these bodies, they appear confined to internal regulation. Thus, the academic council elects the rector, evaluates faculties and other similar units.

Between these two extremes in the continuum of participation, power and responsibilities discharged by bodies of institutional governance, a host of different arrangements is to be found. For example, in Switzerland and Austria, no legal basis or any other regulation provides for the participation of interest groups of a social, political or economic nature. Certainly such groups exist and try to make themselves felt which in Austria they do successfully, though their participation is informal. Yet students as opposed to groups do enjoy full legal membership of certain councils (faculty council, convent) and even take part in the selection of academic staff.

REFERENCES

Bauer, Marianne (1988) "Evaluation in Swedish higher education: recent trends and the outlines of a model", *European Journal of Education*, vol.23, nos.1-2, pp.25-36.

Clark, Burton R. (1997) "Common Problems and Adaptive Responses in the Universities of the World: organising for change", *Higher Education Policy*, (forthcoming).

CRE (1983) "On the perils and rewards of boldness", *CRE Information, No.62*, 2nd quarter 1983.

CRE (1986) "European University Systems part i", *CRE Bulletin No.75*, (Standing Conference of Presidents, Rectors and Vice-Chancellors of the European Universities) 3rd quarter 1986. Geneva: 1986 Conférence des Recteurs Européens. 140pp.

CRE (1987) "European University Systems part ii", *CRE Bulletin No.77*, 1st quarter 1987. Geneva: 1987 Conférence des Recteurs Européens. 136pp.

de Groof, Jan (1985) *Les pouvoirs publics et l'enseignement subventionné*. Bruxelles: Cepess.

de Groof, Jan (1989) *La Révision de la constitution de 1988 et l'enseignement en Belgique*. Bruxelles: Cepess.

Kogan, Maurice with Tim Packwood (1975) *Educational Policy-making: a study of interest groups and Parliament*. London: George Allen & Unwin.

Neave, Guy (1988) "On the cultivation of Quality, Efficiency and Enterprise: an overview of recent trends in higher education in Western Europe 1986-1988", *European Journal of Education*, vol.23, nos.1-2, pp.7-24.

Peterson, Marvin W. (1996) "Images of University Structure, governance and leadership: adaptive strategies for the new Environment", in David Dill & Barbara Sporn (eds) *Emerging Patterns of social demand and university reform: through a glass darkly, op. cit.*.

Rüegg, Walter (1992) "Themes", in Hilde de Ridder Simoens *History of the Universities in Europe*. Vol.i *Universities in the Middle Ages*. Cambridge: Cambridge University Press.

6

UNIVERSITY STRUCTURES AND INSTITUTIONAL AUTONOMY

6.1 Education and research

Across the university landscape a whole host of different arrangements for organising higher education are to be found. In some, the traditional pattern organised around the professorial Chair, itself bonded into highly specialised areas of teaching and research, still flourishes. In others, the basic pattern has moved on and the university is organised into departments, more closely reflecting the definition and alignment around academic disciplines. A third variation builds less around broadly defined disciplines but rather around specialist sub-sets within disciplines – the *Fachbereiche* or *Vakgroepen* of the German and Dutch universities.

The fragmentation of academic disciplines into smaller teaching and research units – or even their recombination grouped around 'Schools of Study', found in certain innovating British universities, is perhaps the most deeply-laid and unavoidable development in today's universities, following as it often does, the basic dynamic in related areas of knowledge (Clark, 1995). The ebb and flow within the various fields and sub fields that go to make up a discipline, fragments large units and brings about the merger of smaller ones. And since this pattern of movement is determined by the way the particular field of research evolves in the light of the findings made in it, it is a dynamic not easily controlled by administration, be it institutional or national. Indeed, the acceleration of knowledge which lies at the heart of the university enterprise, is one of the major uncontrollable factors of that undertaking.

To be sure, above this seething layer of teaching, research, creativity and discovery, the university tends still to retain the time honoured faculty structure. The faculty, in many respects, is the crossing point where one type of authority deriving from repute, excellence and the personal influence of the scholar in his speciality meets the authority that derives from the law, from government and the formal responsibilities that both have defined as falling to institutional administration and leadership. Thus, when we turn our attention to bureaucratic authority we find that the faculty, by and large, is responsible for the coordination and organisation of degree programmes, the upkeep of quality, academic staffing and, to a certain extent, the allocation of resources. In contrast to the shifting intellectual boundaries that characterise academic organisation below the faculty level, the latter tend to cleave to the classical divisions in the structure of knowledge. The faculties of law, psychology, politics, history, languages, medicine, engineering to mention but a few, retain both an administrative and an historical continuity, despite the intellectual dynamism that continues to alter their content.

Yet even the faculty model shows variation. Thus it is that certain higher education systems split their universities into three faculty conglomerates – human sciences, exact sciences and the medical and biological sciences. Others will opt for a rather different profile, the arts, social sciences, natural sciences, engineering and the medical sciences. For many, the essential generic feature of the university is the presence within a single establishment of several faculties, though it has to be recognised that there are other definitions as well and that certain countries, irrespective of the reasons that have prompted them to take this stance, have substantial numbers of universities in which a single faculty predominates, France is one (Neave & Edelstein, 1993). In others, once influenced by the Soviet model of higher education, the vestiges of highly specialised universities, concentrated around one or two cognitively-related faculties, are still to be seen (Darvas, forthcoming).

Faculties dissolve down into subject groups in pyramid fashion. In turn, subject groups can be further subdivided into centres, departments or institutes which tie individuals more closely together around a common area of intellectual commitment and endeavour, and at the same time, serve to tie research to teaching. Finally, anchored to the nexus of centres and departments, though extending beyond them, are the highways along which scholarly exchange moves back and forth. These are the research networks.

These latter always have had supreme importance as the lifeblood of the university. Today, when research is seen as the basic, saleable commodity, information society's equivalent to the coin of the realm, it is difficult indeed to underestimate their place in moulding the innovative and enterprising university. In some universities, the income derived from competitive tendering for research contracts from the private sector exceeds both the internal research funds that government assigns the university as part of its annual budget and that which is awarded by research councils and other Ministry sources. The capacity of research units to generate additional non-government income and the flexibility needed to do this have important repercussions on the relationship between institution and research group. In some cases, the need to maintain this capability has brought about the setting up of groupings legally separate from the university, either as non-profit making bodies or as university based firms. The latter is especially appealing when payment of intellectual property rights on behalf of members of the university is involved. Clearly, it is in the interest of all, the university not least, to maintain these links. At the same time, the university company formula allows more latitude in retaining the principle of accountability to central institutional administration.

6.2 Autonomy

6.2.1 Definitions

The concept of institutional autonomy (see vol. 1 in this series) implies that the university enjoys freedom from government regulation in respect of the internal organisation of the university, its governance, the internal distribution of financial resources, in the generation of income from non-public sources, the recruitment of its staff, conditions of study and finally, the freedom to conduct teaching and research. Put succinctly, institutional autonomy is that condition which permits an institution of higher education to govern itself without external interference. Such is the theory. In practice, no higher education system is wholly free from external control. Furthermore, institutional autonomy is not a constant over time. It is, rather, a boundary condition between university, government and society which is capable of being modified, redefined and having new conditions enforced as a price of its continuation (Tapper & Salter, 1995).

That institutional autonomy is 'conditional' – that is, it is dependent on, and its extent determined by, an institution's fulfilling certain previously defined criteria of cost, output or performance measured in some other manner – is one of the most significant revisions to this age-old concept that recent policies in certain western European countries have introduced (Neave & van Vught, 1991). When we analyse the reality of institutional autonomy in the light of cost-driven priorities, it is evident that the expansion in the range of responsibilities assigned away from central administration down to the individual establishment, whilst adding to the sphere of activities in which institutional self-regulation operates, is also conditioned by a parallel strengthening of the principle of accountability, performance assessment and audit. Institutional autonomy has never meant an absence of law. Universities are answerable to general legal instruments, be they national constitutions, constitutional or administrative laws and decrees as well as to that portion of the law which deals specifically with higher education.

Even though autonomy is neither a monolithic whole, nor like the Republic, is it indivisible, there is today a tendency which seeks to distinguish between the different aspects contained in this overall notion. If the idea of 'conditional autonomy' has been applied to describe changes in the relationship between government and higher education in western Europe over the past ten years, so other sub-categories have also arisen. One of the more interesting is the distinction between 'substantive autonomy',' procedural autonomy' and what certain legal writers have termed 'organic autonomy'. Since they have direct bearing on both the range of activities which fall under the purlieu of the institution and their nature, it is useful to spell them out.

Substantive autonomy is the right of a university to determine its own study programmes and their goals. Procedural autonomy involves the right of a university to determine the means it shall devote to fulfil priorities agreed upon beforehand and assigned to it as part of national policy. Organic autonomy recognises the right of institutions of higher education to determine their own academic organisation, whether it is to be based on faculties and departments, schools, institutes, professional areas etc..

The drive towards decentralisation of decision-making away from central administration down to the individual university and the gathering momentum of deregulation that accompanied it, certainly extended the range of academic work which fell into the domain of institutional freedom (Wasser, 1995) and was very often accompanied by significant change in institutional status. In the non-state sector of Belgian universities, the Catholic University of Leuven and the University of Brussels acquired corporative status. In the state sector, the Universities of Gent and Liège were endowed with greater administrative autonomy with respect to internal budget distribution, the presentation of accounts and in staffing policy. Under the terms of the 1993 University Organisation Law, Austrian universities obtained more extensive self-government, acquired new structures of management to improve internal efficiency and powers of internal budget allocation. Similar initiatives are visible in the Higher Education Acts passed in Finland (1986) Denmark (1992) and Sweden (1993). All of them involved a considerable degree of decentralisation whilst, at the same time, adding to the functions that came under institutional governance. Of these various initiatives, amongst the most sophisticated emerged in the Netherlands. Here, the key concept revolved around the idea of 'remote steering' which assigned the formulation of national strategy to central government whilst conferring a wide degree of latitude in determining how this strategy would be fulfilled by the individual university. Cross sector planning, between university and non-university institutions was introduced by aggregating different disciplines into nine sectors. Not only was this thought to increase flexibility in subject provision, but also flexibility in meeting student demand. Both were designed to improve the employability and appropriate qualifications amongst Dutch graduates.

The path towards institutional autonomy amongst the universities of central and eastern Europe differs in several respects from its western counterpart. In the aftermath of the collapse of the ancien regime and the political changes injected by the Velvet Revolution, much weight was laid upon securing what were rightly regarded as basic academic freedoms, and particularly institutional autonomy. Such rights were very rapidly incorporated into new higher education laws. But if conducted in terms that drew heavily upon the vocabulary and terminology of western 'managerialism' as symbolic of the break between a command economy and its free-market successor, the basic impulse was primarily political in focus. This is scarcely surprising since the political symbolism of western managerialism, with its emphasis on individual free choice, as against collective obligation, reflected the very different circumstances that prevailed. But just as the academic estate justified restoring institutional autonomy in the name of bringing in the trappings of the free market, so the government employed similar terms of accountability and efficiency to reassert the right of central administration to correct some of the more exaggerated forms of autonomy.

6.2.2 Towards a more 'modest' state

Thus, the vocabulary of a liberating managerialism fuelled political rhetoric. Its rationale was invoked by both academia and government in support of their respective cases – academia calling for institutional liberty as a means of nurturing individual freedom and efficiency whilst governments justified a revived hold over higher education by invoking accountability and managerial efficiency. But the use of managerialist terms to conduct a political dialogue between universities and public authorities as part of the redrawing of the boundaries of responsibility between the two, is no less evident in western Europe. The general consensus is that as government withdraws from detailed oversight of higher education and concentrates on elaborating strategy, so it leaves the means by which the nation's goals for higher education are to be achieved as decisions to be taken within the individual university in the light of the latter's particular and specific circumstances. Irrespective of whether this development is construed as 'corporative rationality' applied to higher education or as the fostering of 'entrepreneurial management', one cannot avoid the question whether the rhetoric of deregulation and enhanced self-regulation reflects any reality, other than the wish fulfilment of Ministries or the intent of legislators?

Behind the concept of the 'modest state' (Crozier, 1987) on the one hand, and the more responsible university on the other, lies a species of zero sum game that says "The more deregulated or modest the part of national administration in the workings of higher education policy, the greater the degree of institutional autonomy". And conversely, that by increasing institutional discretion, latitude, initiative the greater the effective scope of institutional autonomy. But it does not of necessity follow that as national administration offloads certain aspects of detailed control away from the centre, that the 'periphery' automatically benefits from an enhanced degree of self-government. Much depends on the conditions that accompany the centre's acquisition of 'modesty'.

A close examination of the areas from which governments appear to be reducing their commitments suggests that these areas correspond to what may be termed 'process control'. Briefly stated, process control as its name implies, concentrates on controlling the processes of higher education as opposed to the 'product'. Process control accordingly, focuses on the curriculum balance, the disciplinary profile, the distribution of students between disciplines, in short, the conditions, means and resources which form the 'product' of higher education. The latter involves student output, their qualifications and certified abilities, research projects tendered for and completed, publications, patents taken out etc. (Neave & van Vught, 1991 pp.251-252). Once we distinguish between these two domains, we obtain a more nuanced interpretation of the reality of institutional autonomy. Effectively, in such countries as Finland, the Netherlands, Norway and Sweden, reducing intervention in the daily activity of institutions is largely focused on the area of process control. It does not always extend to product control.

Enough evidence exists to suggest first, that increased institutional autonomy is largely grounded in the withdrawal from exercising close control over process but, second – and this is vital to our argument – that institutional self-regulation in the process domain is itself dependent on success and good performance in the area of 'product control'. The rise of *a posteriori* financing, performance monitoring and, last but not least, the flourishing quality assessment industry points to the fact that, greater institutional autonomy in the process domain is not always reflected by a similar latitude in the product domain. Indeed, the price to be paid for enhanced self-regulation in the process domain appears to be closer surveillance over institutional performance judged within the sphere of the product domain (Neave & van Vught, 1991 loc. cit.; and de Groof, 1995). It is a nice calculus indeed that would allow the individual university to determine whether the gains in process autonomy are worth the losses in product autonomy.

There is, finally, another way of interpreting deregulation, that is less in the terms of the particular processes freed or scrutinised, as by the level within the higher education system at which functions previously under central surveillance are relocated. In this connection, the rise of specialised 'agencies of public purpose' (Trow, 1996, pp.71ff) in the fields of quality assessment, validation and accreditation, is especially noteworthy. It is a moot point whether such agencies form part of central administration for often their status emphasises formal independence from Ministry or Funding Council. By the same token, however, their significance as a part of bureaucratic authority functioning nation-wide cannot be denied either. It remains to be seen whether such functional agencies, despite their formal independence or their indirect ties with the Ministry, do not constitute a powerful countervailing weight to the centrifugal forces that deregulation appears to support. (See *infra* Ch.8, pp.71ff).

6.2.3 Three dimensions to autonomy in governance

6.2.3.1 The legal perspective on autonomy

The legal perspective on autonomy as opposed to either the sociological or the historical, subscribes to a number of definitions of university autonomy. One is to see autonomy in terms of independence from the state. Another stresses the principle of *Selbsverwaltung* or 'self-administration.' In exploring the more specifically legal dimensions to this concept we will focus on:

- external autonomy,
- organic autonomy,
- administrative autonomy.

6.2.3.1.1 External autonomy

External autonomy is a criterion preeminently formal. If the decision to found a university was taken by a private individual – or group of private individuals – then the university will stand as an independent legal personality as it may also be if the status of an 'organising power' is either conferred upon it or transferred to it, by law. In several countries, however, the university stands as an 'administrative service' of the state.

This criterion is not hard and fast. 'Free'- that is non-state – universities may become subject to general university legislation once they accept government subsidies or once their diplomas are recognised officially. In contrast to this is the recent change in French higher education which extends the right of a public service to enter into contractual agreements (contractualisation) with partners in the private sector.

6.2.3.1.2 Organic autonomy

Organic autonomy confers upon the university the capacity to determine its own internal forms of academic organisation. State universities, for the most part, have an identical arrangement across all establishments within the sector of public universities. Free (non-state) universities follow the provisions laid down in their Act of Foundation or Deed of Incorporation. In this latter instance, organic autonomy derives from the constitutional right to found educational establishments outside the public sector.

There are, however, certain developments the importance of which merit attention. Public universities are under the obligation to conform to the laws, decrees, governmental circulars and statutes which touch upon their internal academic organisation. However, provided the university remains within the general guidelines, the thrust of this legislation is increasingly to allow the possibility of individual variations between establishments. Yet, it can be argued that both administrative and academic organisation should become more uniform, irrespective of the legal status, public or private, of the establishment, the better to facilitate *entre autres*, international exchange and student mobility.

The specific identity of an institution of higher education is set down in its Charter or founding Statutes. Neither the specific identity nor the degree of administrative autonomy a university enjoys prevent government from requiring that it implement certain procedures – for example, setting down internal regulations governing disciplinary proceedings, disputes over examinations or public tendering – measures justified in the name of clarity in decision-making.

6.2.3.1.3 Administrative autonomy

Administrative autonomy or, autonomy grounded in institutional self-coordination is the touchstone of institutional independence. Under this rubric come freedom to choose priorities and to decide *vis à vis* duties and opportunities. It also embraces the power to set complementary detailed procedures for institutional administration, budgetary control and personnel policy. Such discretionary powers are limited on a first level by the Charter or by government legislation and at a second level by the regulations issued by administrative instances in the execution of their powers. The exercise of this particular dimension within institutional autonomy is clearest when applied to staffing policy, the organisation of teaching and research and in finance, budget and management.

a Staff

The largest single heading in the university budget are personnel costs. Within the sphere of staff policy – over and above the issue of salaries, pension rights and social security – a division of responsibility between national administration and institutional management, is to be found. The career structure, conditions of appointment and the salary structure within each rank are often laid down at the national level, as too are sickness benefits, vacation allowances etc..

Yet, freedom for an institution to appoint its staff is crucial. How far it has this power and in what form is subject to considerable difference and various procedures exist – recommendations to appoint with confirmation remaining in the hands of national authorities, the right to appoint only to non-tenured posts or to lower levels within the ranks of non academic personnel. In the case of higher education systems based on a central national appointments procedure, that central authorities bear in mind the interests and priorities of the institution where the appointment shall be taken up, has much to recommend it.

b Teaching and Research

Though there are notable exceptions, the subjects offered by universities are often confined to the areas of study for which they have obtained validation, recognition or accreditation from central government and that the corresponding diplomas to which such courses lead, are likewise recognised. Furthermore, such validation also ties in with legislation on the financing both of institutions and of particular courses. The state can set down norms for estimating the numbers of students to be accepted and even the numbers themselves as a condition for granting public funding. How far universities are free to offer courses that do not benefit from government subsidies, is a matter of variation between countries.

Amongst the normative regulations laid down by central authority which surround teaching are length of study time, the number of credits, course points required, conditions governing transfer between courses and registration procedures, course programmes etc.. In addition, each university lays down its own regulations for courses and examinations, determines the teaching programme, timetable, the method of assessment and criteria for evaluating individual student performance.

c Management of administration and finance

Despite the noise and clamour that has accompanied the introduction of the idea of 'market-driven' higher education and despite outstanding examples of individual universities attracting quite massive funding and support from the private sector, for the greater part of Europe's universities reliance on public funding remains the rule. Income from student registration fees, investments, gifts and legacies as a percentage of total yearly expenditure, tends to be meagre indeed. Moreover, certain countries do not permit registration fees to exceed what is set down by law, primarily to avoid the accusation of sacrificing the talented but less well-off and infringing thereby the basic principles of equity and merit. And those that have tried and permitted the interested parties to be consulted, are not always successful (Hendrichova, in press).

One of the prime tasks of national framework legislation, as it applies to higher education, is to seek to strike a balance between budgetary continuity for the institution as a whole as against its intellectual freedom *vis à vis* the state as prime paymaster. Some have argued that institutional management should have greater discretion in the internal allocation of funding within the university on the grounds that those in the institution are better placed to know what its specific needs are likely to be. If the university is to meet the changing needs of the labour market and of student 'consumerdom', develop those academic fields that it deems worthy of strengthening or, alternatively, to reduce those for which demand is weak, it needs the powers to manage the income assigned it, whether from public or from private sources. This is a strong argument. It contradicts neither the principle nor the requirements set out by government and by financial regulation, that both demand accounts be rendered for the use of public monies.

No public funding authority will base higher education finance on the issuing of blank cheques. Universities are answerable for their funding and the governing council must show without peradventure that the institution falls fully in with the public standards and requirements of financial rectitude. Furthermore, governments can insist on an internal audit, just as the institution has itself to show how quality control bears out its own policy and priorities. Yet, the calls for a species of conditional budgetary freedom are mounting. Under such an arrangement, legislation would lay down the rights, obligations and duties incumbent on both government and institution for the good husbandry of public funds. Added to this would be the proviso that in the case of the institution's own assets and its own income the principle of freedom to follow its own priorities should hold valid. Two strictures exist, however. Several countries regulate the use of an institution's self-generated funds, often on the grounds first, that such funds are used to top out basic running costs and second, because the prime source of an institution's internal funds is the state budget. This situation often arises as a result of carrying forward operational surpluses that stem from public subsidy to fund future expenditure.

Since the budgetary cycle is annual, so is the presenting of accounts. Several states, however, apply a multi-annual planning cycle in university affairs and require therefore that institutions present budgetary headings and line items according to a similar format.

6.3 Academic freedom

If these three elements within academic autonomy pose crucial issues for the future, and for the responsibilities laid upon systems of institutional governance, there remains one final principle which has been and ought continually to be the central value that both justifies and makes possible innovation and organised creativity. That principle is academic freedom – the central and pervasive principle of academic work (Barnett, 1990).

The principle of academic freedom can be defined as the freedom for the members of the academic community – that is teachers, students and scholars – to follow their own scholarly enquiries and are thereby not be dependent on political, philosophical or epistemological opinions though their own opinions may lead them in this direction.

Defined thus, academic freedom can be regarded as an application of the right to the free holding of opinions and the freedom to express those opinions but specifically applied to the individual position of researcher, professor or student. These rights to the free holding of opinions and the free expression of opinion are expressly included in all human rights treaties. Nor are these freedoms missing from democratic constitutions. Hence it may, at first sight, appear superfluous expressly to incorporate the right to academic freedom in a treaty, constitution or even in an ordinary law. Yet, an examination of the constitutions and legislation on higher education of the member states of the Council of Europe shows us that 'academic freedom' often enjoys legal or constitutional protection.

Thus, there are countries which entrench 'academic freedom' in their constitutions. Such is the case in Austria, Belarus, Bulgaria, Estonia, Finland, Germany, Lithuania, Romania, Slovenia, Spain, and Turkey amongst others. In this list it so happens that some of these countries which give constitutional right to academic freedom are 'young' or 'new' democracies. And, it is very likely that this development can be explained as a swing of the pendulum against authoritarian regimes and the accompanying absence of academic freedom under which the world of higher learning laboured for so long.

If we turn our attention to those countries where no constitutional protection is formally afforded to academic freedom, we see that they fall into two sub groups. On the one hand are those afforded legal protection to academic freedom in their educational legislation. Amongst them are Bulgaria, Denmark, France, Greece, Hungary, Latvia, the Netherlands and Slovakia. On the other, stand those which make no mention of this basic right. This is not to say that in such cases, academic freedom is a concept without value, meaning or significance. On the contrary, it is looked upon as a key and unalienable quality of university education. Two examples will serve to illustrate this situation. The first is the Netherlands, the second the United Kingdom. In the case of the former: "There are two freedoms of importance: the freedom of education, which is guaranteed in the Constitution and the freedom of scholarship which is not explicitly guaranteed in the Constitution. The latter has been shaped in the long tradition of academic life within the universities." And the latter instance stands perhaps as one of the most complete expressions of this unwritten but powerful concept: "The government is effectively prohibited from intervening in matters of higher education. Higher Education Institutions are independent, self-governing bodies and responsible for their own financial, administrative and academic affairs."

Thus, academic freedom guarantees the liberty of those engaged in higher learning to teach, research and to express opinions in the areas for which they are qualified and the advancement of which they are professionally committed and to do so without fear that such considered views will make them answerable for *délit d'opinion*. An alternative interpretation, more in keeping with the Germanic legal tradition, regards academic freedom as the exemption in the area of academic endeavour and scholarship from government instructions and intervention.

Whatever the particular legal setting in which it is located, academic freedom remains the fundamental philosophical premise on which the transmission of established knowledge and the generation of new knowledge are grounded. It is, in short, held to be the optimal condition for the advancement of knowledge, for underpinning the pursuit of excellence and the application of human creativity to matters of concern to the various communities, scholarly and economic, industrial and social, which have a stake in higher learning (van Ginkel, 1995).

In an institution of higher education endowed with institutional autonomy, academic freedom is protected by law and guaranteed by individual governments. Nowhere, however, is academic freedom explicitly mentioned in international treaties, though there are plenty of declarations and resolutions issued by non governmental organisations and which have the force of moral suasion, though formally speaking, none have that of international law.

6.4 University autonomy

In this Chapter we have examined the various interpretations of autonomy, its legal underpinning and the operational consequences of different definitions for the functions assigned to both national administration and to the institutional level. We have explored some of the assumptions that lie behind the current notion of deregulation and the implications that arise from the reassignment of what may be termed some of the 'core functions' – finance, access, certification, accreditation, staffing policy – of this complex organisation. In the course of this analysis, we have noted how the unprecedented mobilisation of higher education across Europe has brought into question some of the more established notions about autonomy – the rise of conditional autonomy as a key instrument of policy in certain western systems of higher education being one. The two interdependent but operationally very different concepts of 'process' autonomy and 'product' autonomy stand as further illustrations to the often radical modifications that this cherished emblem of organised learning has undergone.

From one point of view, it is perhaps surprising that there is no single concept of 'university autonomy' shared across the member states of the Council of Europe. After all, university autonomy is an ideal much sought after and one which has endured even after 'the captains and kings' have departed, some voluntarily, others hooting and struggling. But if we remember that university autonomy is seated in society and endorsed by society's authoritative representatives, that it reflects both a nation and its culture as well, then that very variety, difference and variation reflect the myriad of ways in which one concept can be valued and realised. Like the notion of democracy itself, the central idea leads on to many interpretations and a multitude of ways by which one may move towards its fullest expression.

6.5 Commonalities and differences in Europe

These differences emerge very strongly when one peruses the country case studies in this volume and the commitment to the central principle of autonomy itself is no less evident. Though the drive to enlarge the scope of institutional initiative and self-regulation in higher education stands as a generally agreed upon priority, the notion of institutional autonomy as an earnest of democratisation in higher education is particularly noteworthy in the newly self-liberated lands of central and eastern Europe. Indeed, institutional autonomy is exactly seen and in the precise etymology of that term as having the function of a political catalyst – that is, it precipitates change in other areas of the social fabric. The successful implementation of this principle in higher education – though clearly, as we have noted, its forms will vary – is looked upon as a prior condition for its broader application. Such a conviction is evident in Albania, Belarus, the Czech Republic, Latvia, Lithuania, the Russian Federation and Slovenia. No less worthy of attention is the explicit incorporation of the principle of institutional autonomy in higher education legislation or even, in the case of Slovenia, its writing into the constitution. In other European states, this is most unusual. Naturally, they too share the view that enhanced self-steering by higher education institutions is an important development. But, it is often expressed in a different legislative context. In Austria, for instance, it is considered as accompanying the freedom of scholarship and teaching (*Wißenschaft und ihre Lehre*) and is not expressly mentioned. Enlarging the scope of institutional autonomy is associated less with revitalising the nation's political culture so much as improving a series of technical instruments in terms of overhauling the mandate of governing bodies, of extending the principle of staff and student participation in decision-making and involving the financial independence of universities.

Money is not merely the sinew of war, as the Emperor Napoleon I once remarked. It is also the fulcrum point on which greater institutional autonomy turns. And, as we have remarked earlier, there is a widely held view which believes that greater institutional initiative is largely conditioned by reducing the degree of constraint imposed by over-centralised systems of university finance. This may indeed be the case. Either way, it is worthwhile paying attention to some of the shared features that characterise the public financing of higher education.

For many decades, higher education has been greatly dependent on government funding and resourcing. If the state provides, it is not to be disputed that the monies granted for education and research should be accounted for and that proper statement be made of the results and achievements such largesse has permitted. But methods of control and procedures of both accounting and accountability (and they are very far from being the same thing) (Trow, 1996) are very far from being uniform. Some may be accommodating, others may insist on the extremes of rigour. Nor, to add further complication, are the sources and agencies from which such funding flows the same across the nations. The same applies to the bodies which control and verify accounts.

6.6 Financial control

The financial control of higher education is often separate from the exercise of general oversight which falls into the purlieu of the Ministry of Education, sometimes of Science, others of Research. Financial control tends to be exercised elsewhere in central government. In Austria, the verification of university accounts is fulfilled by the Court of Audit (*Rechnungshof*), established by constitutional law. On the other hand, in the Russian Federation it is less the Minister of Education who has a dominant role in control and management so much as the State Commission of Higher Education, not forgetting the Minister of Finance.

Increasingly, higher education is being exhorted not to live by government funding alone. Whether this objective can be met depends on whether universities are authorised to seek sources of revenue other than those derived from public expenditure and again, on whether universities can acquire property on their own behalf. Not untypical of the changes introduced in this area are the revisions to Austrian practice. Up to 1987, Austrian universities were empowered to accept donations, inheritances and legacies. External contracts with firms and other outside bodies could be signed. However, the money thus earned was considered to be the property of the Republic. For the university to claw such sums back from the Ministry of Finance involved procedures that were complicated and protracted. It was, in effect, a procedure that did not set great price on incentives for entrepreneurial behaviour, neither by individuals, nor by institutions. In 1987, this situation was rectified and henceforth gifts, donations, contract-generated income are deemed the property of the university that has deserved or earned them. Such sources of income are held separate from the federal budget and are administered by the university corporation.

REFERENCES

Barnett, Ronald, (1990) *The Idea of Higher Education*. Milton Keynes: Open University Press for SRHE. pp.136-148.

Clark, Burton R. (1983) *The Higher Education System: academic organisation in cross national perspective*. Berkeley/Los Angeles/London: University of California Press.

Clark, Burton R. (1995) *Places of Inquiry: research and advanced education in modern universities*. Berkeley/Los Angeles/London: University of California Press.

Crozier, Michel (1987) *L'Etat moderne, stratégie pour un autre changement,* Paris, Fayard Darvas, Petr (forthcoming) "Hungary" in Clark and Neave (eds), *The encyclopedia of higher education,* 2nd edition, Oxford.

de Groof, Jan (1995) *Personeelsbeleid aan de Vlaamse Universiteiten*. Dordrecht: Kluwer Rechtswetenschappen.

Hendrichova, Jana (forthcoming) "Diversification of tertiary education: the Czech experience in an international perspective", *Higher Education Policy*.

Neave, Guy & van Vught, Frans (1991) *Prometheus Bound: op cit.*.

Neave, Guy & Edelstein, Richard (1993) "France", in Burton R. Clark (ed) *The Research Foundations of Graduate Education: Germany, Britain, France, United States, Japan.* Berkeley/Los Angeles/London: University of California Press. pp.159-220.

Tapper, E. R. & Salter B. G. (1995) "The Changing Idea of University Autonomy", *Studies in Higher Education,* vol.20, no.1. pp.59-72.

Thune, Christian (1994) "Setting up the Danish Center", in Alma Craft (ed) *International Developments in Assessing Quality in Higher Education.* London: The Falmer Press. pp.67ff.

Trow, Martin (1985) "Comparative Reflections on leadership in higher education", *European Journal of Education,* vol.20. nos.2-3, pp.143-159.

Trow, Martin (1996) "Trust, markets and accountability in higher education: a comparative perspective", *Higher Education Policy*, vol.9, no.4, pp.309-324.

van Ginkel, Hans (1995) "The University in 2050: the organisation of innovation and creativity", *Higher Education Policy*, vol.8, no.4, pp.14 – 18.

Wasser, Henry (1995) "Redefining Autonomy of Universities", *Higher Education Policy*, vol.8, no.3, pp.15-17.

7

UNIVERSITY GOVERNANCE: COMPARATIVE PERSPECTIVES ON A QUESTION OF BALANCE

7.1 Structure, governance and rules: long-term influences in higher education policy

No country's history is the same as its neighbours', and, since the university is one expression of the nation's historic memory, it can come as no surprise that structure, practice and procedures show a similar diversity across national systems of higher education (Neave & van Vught, 1991, pp.x-xi). Nevertheless, scholarship which is often about imposing order, detecting patterns, identifying trends and forging categories to make sense of a bewildering world, has set archetypical status on four traditions as a means to describe the relationship between government and higher education. These have already been explored in volume 1 of this series (In 't Veld, Füssel & Neave, 1996, p.46). In this Chapter, we focus on the question of governance within the general perspective of the national system as a whole and upon the noteworthy differences between them. As a preliminary to the more detailed analysis, we return briefly to the four referential systems in European higher education. Subsequently, we examine four models of governance, which if slightly different from those outlined in the first Chapter, are basic categories. These four models reflect not merely the changes in conceptualisation that has taken place in the area of governance over the past four years largely as a result of the 'managerial revolution', they also reflect a slightly different disciplinary perspective. This perspective lies in the field of government studies, whereas the categories we used to explore the historic dimension of systems of institutional governance hailed in the main, from organisational sociology.

The way nations organise their higher education systems and the policy that guides their development is often presented in terms of four referential systems: the Napoleonic model (France), the Humboldtian model (Germany), the market-driven model (the United States) and what some, though by no means all, would term the Newman model of higher education, after the 19th century Catholic divine, Cardinal John Newman, which is equated with Great Britain. The essential characteristics of the first are held to be the overwhelmingly public character of the universities, a strong interventionary style of government (Premfors, 1980; Palmer, 1985) which was expressed in close control over financing, over academic appointments, a weak definition of institutional autonomy, the organisation of research apart from the university and the use of legal instruments to standardise curriculum innovation and development. The second is marked by a high degree of academic independence from government, by a highly developed system of internal self-regulation, by the integration of research with teaching together with a strong basic research capacity (Gellert, 1993) and by a system of staff appointment that is internally initiated. The third ideal type, that of the market driven system typified by the United States, places stress on meeting external demands from society, openness, research that tends towards the applied end of the spectrum, a high degree of managerialism, a strong executive role of the president and a training which if it preserves the tradition of liberal education at the undergraduate level, is both market and research driven at the graduate level (Clark, 1997). The salient features that once were long part of university education in Britain may similarly be summed up as an attachment to elite education, a highly developed stratification within and between universities, polytechnics and colleges and a concept of personal development of students in addition to their intellectual training. Most marked, though that to has altered out of all recognition, has been the very high degree of institutional autonomy and independence from government intervention.

Most systems of higher education in Europe can be classified around features derived from at least two – sometimes, three – of these 'idealised types', though the relative importance of the components may well differ. Thus, for instance, Spain (ICED Report, 1987; de Miguel et al 1991) and Italy (Moscati, 1991; Martinelli, 1992) possess characteristics once shared with France in the degree of power accruing to the centre and in the heavy reliance on legislative and ministerial circular to govern higher education.

The Humboldtian 'tradition' has been particularly pervasive in the German-speaking world and up to the 1960s, in Sweden. It has been especially powerful in influencing the notion that teaching should be combined with fundamental research – a basic feature of the modern university – and in this dimension has had an influence both on British and most especially American universities, though the structures through which the latter two countries assimilated the research imperative were very different from the original template (Gellert, 1993; Clark, 1995).

There is, naturally, equal variation in the patterns that emerge from systems of governance (Kogan, 1994, pp.12-32). A recent analysis revealed four basic models:

- the collegial,
- the managerial,
- the market,
- the social utility model.

A certain degree of overlap is detectable with respect to some of the categories in this analytical framework and that employed in Chapter I, (p.9) particularly in the case of the first of these four, the collegial model of governance. Since the collegial model is certainly the most ancient form of governance and some would say, the most open, no great harm is inflicted if its characteristics are rehearsed once again.

7.1.1 The collegial model

The presence of the Collegial model of governance is especially developed amongst those systems of higher education where the values of institutional autonomy go hand in hand with a limited concept of the place of the state. Collegial style governance rests on the presumption that it is legitimate for academia to insist on the individual freedom to teach and to research and to do so in accordance with the values, expectations and rigour set within the various academic disciplines which, in turn, constitute the university's *raison d'être*. The notion of collegiality is essentially internalist and expresses the notion of the supremacy of academic endeavour over the means and techniques of husbandry and administration whose purpose is to facilitate and support the advancement of knowledge and its effective transmission. Thus, it is at one and the same time, both a principle governing the relationship and behaviour between individuals just as it is a statement about the way power is distributed and decisions reached within the institution by members of the academic community.

Over the years, the recognition of this principle has emerged in structural form through the various bodies with internal decision-making powers, powers that are endowed with legal status and with formally defined competence and responsibilities. The formal nomenclature of these bodies is legion. Some systems of higher education acknowledge the right of faculty members to decide on academic appointments, to define both curriculum and content, to set both examinations and standards of student performance for the award of diplomas. Others set a superordinate body over the academic senate. Whether governing council, council or board of trustees, such bodies are concerned with the allocation and control over resources as well as relations with the external community. The collegial model was basically consensually based, an organism given over to collective decision-making amongst peers whose responsibilities were not limited to teaching and research, but also included administration.

7.1.2 The managerial model

In many respects, the 'managerial model' of governance began to take shape with the incorporation of the university into public service and was thus a natural outcome of what was termed in Chapter 1, the 'bureaucratic revolution'. The century-long saga of 'incorporation' formalised the status of academia as public servants, superimposed, rationalised and coordinated procedures for academic appointments, placed responsibility for the recognition of courses and diploma titles upon the State and, as time passed, drew up formal conditions for financing higher learning. In effect, this early version of 'state managerialism' defined the general conditions of 'academic work' and, *grosso modo*, set forth a division of labour characterised by its bipolar distribution of power between state administration and academic oligarchy (Clark, 1983). This, however, is not the orthodox interpretation of the managerial model.

The essence of the managerial model of governance is a functional division between those who define, plan and oversee the tasks to be carried out and those whose duties are so defined that theirs is the responsibility to execute the tasks assigned. The managerial model implies then the presence of a strong functional hierarchy which, if it does not always take the form of 'line management', nevertheless limits the range of decisions to be dealt by the collegium and confines them to professional administration and 'leadership'. The latter has the power to demand answerability from their subordinates and the terms of their answerability are set out in legal provision and enactment of national application. Institutional autonomy, thus, applies to a narrower range of activities.

7.1.3 The market model

Universities have always had the task of making highly qualified and trained individuals available to society. And insofar as those individuals have the opportunity freely to negotiate the conditions of their employment and advancement, the university has supplied a 'free market'. Certainly, universities are influenced by 'market conditions' to the extent that they permit the individual to choose his or her field of study and that individual does so in function of his or her career plans. Historically, the largest single sector of the graduate labour market, whether in east or west, has been in that sector economists qualify as the 'fixed price' labour market – that is public service and teaching. In other words, the demand exerted by students lay in a sector of the market where the educational requirements – as too the career prospects – were fixed by law and predictable. The rise of the so called 'market model' of governance stems from the collapse of the 'public sector labour market' both in eastern and western Europe and the need for higher education to provide expertise to a 'market' in which conditions of employment are under great flux and the skills requirement of which has rarely been foreseeable in other than the short term.

The market model of governance arises from the shift of higher education's major outlets from the public to the private sector of 'free economies'. Likewise, many of the instruments and techniques of administration – quality assessment, total quality management, criteria of performance, notions of accounting and techniques for ascertaining financial viability derive and are taken over, from private sector industry. The prime feature of a 'free market' is competition and the insertion of this value into higher education is the prime lever in moving governance structures over to the 'market model'. Yet, in many respects, the market model amplifies developments already visible in the managerial model. Competition between institutions for money, repute and status places a further premium on the managerial rationalisation of tasks and responsibilities and most particularly so now that the survival of a university becomes dependent on the strength of its ties with external society. And this is reflected in the nature of basic tasks of governance. These are less to do with accounting to a 'privileged interlocutor' – central national authority – than with how to attune what were once regarded by the collegial model as the prime purpose of university – teaching and research – and which are now construed as services aggressively to be presented to the outside world.

Since the university has now to negotiate with multiple external interests, funding sources and perhaps, benefactors, the role of internal leadership, the strategic and increasingly autonomous decision-making capacity of an institution, becomes crucial. But this is a highly complex process, and the rationalisation of tasks and responsibility drives towards an even more pronounced stratification of functions, between those involving strategy, internal control, verification, evaluation and assessment of institutional achievement and those which turn around producing the basic human product – abilities, talent and skills. This tripartite differentiation of functions places considerable reliance upon a highly specialised administration whose importance in the general running of a university increases with the hour. Whether the 'market model' heralds the subordination of academic endeavour before the gathering weight of administration and, from there leads on to the reduction of the once-proud professorial oligarchy and academic community to the condition of 'intellectual workers' is a situation that, doubtless, many would wish to avoid. There is, however, a lesson to be learnt from these developments. The market model has the potential to show that cutting loose from the ties of public service certainly extends the boundaries of institutional self-determination. But, it does not follow automatically and ineluctably that power within the institution reverts to the academic community. Thus, institutional autonomy, when one looks at the operational consequences of its reinforcement, is very far from being a surrogate for academic self-determination, *stricto sensu*.

7.1.4 The social utility model

At present, the 'market model' of governance is the focus of an attention so virtually universal that it can perhaps be qualified as higher education's counterpart in a secular age, to the millennial visions and religious revivals that from time to time flared up in days of great uncertainty and dire distress. Higher education is not simply an outpost of the private sector, its responsibilities go wider and involve priorities other than production for sale and profit. Just as it is possible to see certain elements in that mode of governance which we have attributed to 'managerialism' as being firmly rooted in the history of that institution, so it is just as possible to see the 'social utility' model in a similar historical light. Indeed, the Humboldtian and Napoleonic reforms, coming as they did at a time of defeat and war, are excellent illustrations of the central importance of the university's role as an agent of social cohesion (Neave, 1992a). Today's functional, equivalent of this priority, is seen in rather different terms, but remains essentially the same: namely, the integration into national life of non autochthonous communities on the one hand and, on the other, as part of that broader, complementary issue, to wit the preventing, at a time of immense economic upheaval, of social exclusion and the marginalisation of the younger generation.

This places a rather different perspective on the responsibilities that lie before the university – between economic efficiency and individual enterprise and its moral obligation to contribute to upholding the living standards and quality of life of communities, defined spatially, by origin or by age. Whereas the market model lays stress on revitalising governance structures as a means to improving the quality of output, qualification and abilities appropriate to economic demands, in short upon individual opportunity, the social utility model directs the newly released efficiency in the institution towards expanding access and extending equity in society.

These four models of governance are, as is any model, ideals. They represent a quintessential summation from a reality of immense complexity and variation. Obviously, whilst they reflect an aggregated reality and allow us a better grasp over what is happening, it would be amazing indeed, if their characteristics were wholly united in any one establishment. Yet, these four models are not simply variations on the way institutions deal with – or, in certain instances, are authorised to deal with – their internal agenda. They may also be seen as successive stages in the evolution of institutional governance itself. In other words, they may also be considered as steps in the dynamic behind the changing rationale of governance itself and the structures, organisational patterns and mandated bodies through which governance is conducted.

7.2 Higher education, governance and differentiation

If there is one basic driving force that underpins all models – save perhaps the collegial – it is differentiation and task rationalisation. As the scope of responsibilities the university assumes becomes broader and at the same time, more vital for individual establishment's survival, so we see functions, previously part of – say, the departmental agenda – becoming self-standing specialities located elsewhere – within faculty or institutional administration. Research fund administration may be one example. The drive to differentiation stands as another all pervasive development in higher education systems seeking to cope with the equally pervasive value of market-regulated competition. Differentiation in tasks is not confined, however, within the bounds of individual institutions as they move along the path of rationalisation that takes them from collegium to managerial onwards to the market model of governance.

7.2.1 Policies of structural segmentation

Differentiation is generic to higher education. It emerges at all levels of decision-making and bears down upon all types of higher education. And, because differentiation – whether expressed in terms of public repute and resources, whether earned by competitive tendering or assigned by public budget – defines an institution's position publicly, it is a most weighty influence and shapes an institution's strategy and internal priorities. It also has to be taken into account when defining the type of academic and administrative organisation required for priorities and goals to be fulfilled. In short, the presence of differentiation, not only amplifies itself, it is a most powerful factor in determining the appropriateness of a given type of governance structure – or variations upon it – to service the institution's purpose.

Current doctrines of higher education development look towards the market to determine the fate and fortune of a university – that is, effectively, to 'pick winners' and 'leave losers' to benign neglect – which is itself a devastatingly effective and practical form of differentiation. But if today differentiation comes from 'the market', it has not always been thus. For many years, national legislation dealing with universities in certain European countries – Germany, France and Italy come to mind – insisted on the formally equal status between universities. There was, in contrast to Britain, no official stratification between institutions of the same type. Nevertheless, governments have both upheld and supported another form of institutional differentiation – between the university *stricto sensu* and institutions of higher education of a non-university status.

This policy which got under way in Britain and France in the mid 1960s (Pratt & Burgess, 1974; Doumenc & Gilly, 1977) extended to Germany by 1972 (Kehm & Teichler, 1992), underwent a second stage in the late 1980s in Finland (Kivinen & Rinne, 1996) and by the early 1990s had been taken up in Austria and the Czech Republic (Leitner, 1996; Sebkova, 1996). Originally viewed as a strategy of institutional diversification, its rationale did not primarily involve changes in governance, though as the non-university sector matured, significant variations did emerge (Robinson, 1972). Rather, the creation of the British polytechnics, the French university institutes of technology and the German Fachhochschulen sprang from the need on the one hand to increase the numbers of higher technicians and middle level management in the private sector and, on the other, to introduce into higher education a training capable of meeting the short term needs of the economy, as against the university which was held to supply the more predictable long-term requirements. Less optimistic spirits have interpreted these developments more as a strategy of deflection, to move increasing numbers of students away from the university as the prospect of mass higher education loomed. The features that distinguished the non university sector were its generally shorter length of studies, though this did not uniformly apply either in Belgium or in Britain, its lower cost – largely as a result of excising research from its task – and its explicit vocational orientation.

Over the ensuing two decades, the growth of enrolments in the non university sector was substantial and in some cases, far more rapid than its university counterpart (Furth, 1992). The policy of sectoral differentiation which, in effect, short cycle higher education represents, is interesting from several points of view. If it was regarded as creating a sector complementary to the university, it was also seen as one which, because of its close contact with private sector industry, would rapidly assimilate and implement demands for qualifications and abilities that the university was apparently less capable of supplying. Such a capacity to innovate would, it was felt, not only attract more students, it would also oblige the university, if the latter was to retain a modicum of prestige, to become similarly adventurous. In effect, inter-sectoral competition for students was thought to bring about general change throughout the system of higher education. There is some evidence to suggest this hope was partially born out (Furth, 1992).

7.2.2 Structural segmentation and patterns of governance

More important from the standpoint of governance structures was the explicit commitment to developing ties with firms in the immediate locality, a local commitment that many universities had abandoned in the drive to mass higher education. In France, the stipulation that 'external personalities' should figure on the *conseil d'administration*, two years before the passing of the 1968 Higher Education Guideline Law which introduced the same principle to the universities, was a major innovation. In Britain, polytechnics came under municipal responsibility. Their internal management closely followed the administrative pattern found in local education authorities. Essentially, this pattern involved a reversal of the collegial relationship long established in university between academia and administration. In British polytechnics, the latter ensured major coordination through a system of line management in which heads of departments were primarily nominated as administrators rather than as teachers with academic standing. Thus was the supremacy of academia stood on its head, a situation that anticipated what was to happen in British universities by some two decades.

The British binary policy was not the only example of changes in established patterns of governance following in the wake of structural differentiation between sectors. Equally noteworthy were developments in Sweden grouped around the higher education reforms of 1977 (Premfors, 1980). The Swedish reforms differed markedly from the prevalent trend inasmuch as they gave rise to an integrated higher education system – a comprehensive university to match the comprehensive school – thereby superseding the traditional division between university and non-university establishments. The creation of seven regional universities with links to outlying colleges went hand in hand with very substantial reforms in governance. The main innovatory thrust lay in, first, assigning the financial responsibility for short courses and courses related to local industry to regional authorities; and second in what one student of Swedish public administration qualified as the abolition of "academic self-government in the sense that the members of various boards of the institutions were to be recruited from all kinds of staff." (Lane, 1992, pp.692-693). The regional coordinating boards were abolished as part of the 1986 reforms on the grounds that they constituted an intolerable 'bureaucratisation' of governance. Still, outside representation on institutional governing boards has continued to grow. Six members out of a total of eleven were drawn from outside academia according to the terms of the 1987 reform (Lane, 1992, ibid.).

7.3 Hidden governance and external influence

Clearly, the closer one looks at changes in governance, one consistent feature, independent of the particular model which circumstance and progress may favour, is the very radical alteration in constituencies, participants or interest groups involved in steering an establishment and most especially, the rise of 'external constituencies' and 'personalities'.

There is a convention which, in Anglo-American literature, insists on calling these entities 'stakeholders', an amusing conceit which assimilates, unwittingly one hopes, higher learning with horse-racing, greyhounds and flash coves in loud check suits! There is one difficulty with this denomination. It does not really draw the line between those who have a real stake (i.e. money, donations, investments, gifts of ancestors' wealth etc.) from those whose part generously includes the metaphorical, moral or temporal in the sense of giving one's time to the institution. Yet these are very different creatures, with very different liens and interests above all when it concerns external stakeholders "other than those governing the institution".

A distinction may be drawn between stakeholders representing politics or administration on the one hand and interest groups on the other. A further subdivision amongst the former would break out those representing central government as against regional or local authorities whilst the interest groups would require account to be taken of whether the interests represented were employers, ex-graduates, employees or trades unions.

The presence of outside interests on university decision-making bodies takes many forms. In Belgium and Austria, no such external interest groups exist, though that does not mean to say that approval for certain types of decisions must be sought from external instances and especially the Federal Minister of Science, Research and the Arts. In Spain external interests of employers, civil society in general and trades unions are brought together in the *consejo social* of each university (ICED,1987; Garcia Garrido, 1992), though they may not have taken part in decisions involving academic affairs *stricto sensu*. In some instances, external interests take direct part in decision-making. In Slovenia, parliament draws up and determines the higher education 'master plan' which includes teaching programmes (Kump, forthcoming). Whilst no stakeholders formally participate other than those governing the establishment in Denmark, there is some suggestion that influence is exercised from without, though no exact indication is given in the case study.

Direct participation of external interests does not appear to weigh very heavily in the balance. But what of interests that fulfil a consultative and advisory capacity? Here, we need to distinguish between national consultative bodies on the one hand and on the other committees of advice operating within the establishment. The former fall most certainly into that category of organisations often called 'intermediary bodies' which occupy the ground between the Ministry of (Higher) Education and national administration and the individual university. Intermediary bodies, as we shall see later, cover a multitude of functions, possess highly differentiated powers and wield varied degrees of legitimacy and influence (Neave, 1992b). Institutional arrangements in Latvia provide for an advisory body – the so called convent of advisers. Similar provision is to be seen in Austrian universities – the advisory board – and in the Spanish consejo social. The former acts as a link with industry and the local community. With a membership composed of civil servants, businessmen, employers and employees, ex graduates as well as representatives from central or local government, it assists the university in such matters as long term forecasting, evaluation, internal allocation of resources and the election of the rector. In Norway, an important advisory role is assumed by the trades unions.

7.3.1 External verification

External influence is a somewhat imprecise concept and for that reason leaves a considerable margin for different implicit interpretations. However, the line between verification and regulation is clear. Regulation involves direct external intervention in the affairs of an institution as permitted by law within terms and conditions promulgated by instruments having the force of law. The main purpose of regulation is to ensure that measures taken by an institution are in keeping with the formal procedural requirements thus stipulated. Verification, by contrast, though it too may be endowed with legal backing, is carried out by external agencies or 'bodies of public purpose' (Trow, 1985) acting on behalf of, or reporting to public authority. Their results, though not primarily intended for institutional consumption, may nevertheless exercise an important indirect effect on the way an institution conducts its affairs, particularly when monetary resources are involved.

The distinction between outside influence following on regulatory activities and that attendant upon procedures of verification is neatly illustrated by referring to Denmark. There, the regulatory domain has been strengthened with the creation of a Centre for Quality Assurance and Evaluation. The Centre's evaluations inform the Minister of Education on institutional course and programme provision. The Minister may intervene either to limit the number of courses offered, or to set a ceiling on the number of student entrants to particular courses should such courses not meet the standards and conditions set out by ministerial circular. For its part, the parliament has put the National Audit Office of Denmark to verify institutional accounts. *Autres pays, autres moeurs*. In Norway, establishments are answerable directly to the Ministry of Education, Research and Church for the full range of their activities. In Slovenia, a rather closer exercise of oversight operates in research which is monitored by the Ministry of Science and Technology and which the same Ministry may also 'steer' by budgetary means. Financial auditing comes under the ambit of the Ministry of Finance.

There are countries which see direct pro-active control as incompatible with institutional autonomy. Thus, for example, the Bulgarian Higher Education Act 1995 does not permit control to be exercised either by the Council of Ministers or by the Ministers of Education. Judicial control of the actions of the governing council is all the Act provides for. Yet again, there are countries – Switzerland and the United Kingdom being among them – which stoutly assert there is no place for external influence in either decision-making, or in proffering advice.

7.4 The changing place of government

The place of government in higher education, as too the relationship between itself and the universities, has been altered out of all recognition in the course of the past decade and a half in Europe, central, east and west (Neave & van Vught, 1991). Higher education in general and the universities in particular have, with one or two notable exceptions, seen the scope of activities over which they may take the substantive decision, grow spectacularly. To a considerable degree, they now determine the general content of their courses. They have, to all intents and purposes, independence in the appointment of staff – teaching, research, administrative and technical, in assessing their achievements, not to mention a greater discretion in the internal allocation of recurrent expenditure.

That said, government support for higher education and research is not limited to determining the system's formal structure. It also extends to content and quality. The recognition that higher education and research are the gateways to the future has led governments to enlarging the domain over which universities may act on their own behalf and that with increased efficiency in cost and in the use of human resources. However, central authorities remain the main paymaster and continue to exercise general oversight for the proper use of public monies.

Furthermore, government responsibility is still engaged *vis à vis* the central purpose of higher education and research. Succinctly stated, government has to ensure that the academic community has a complete set of provisions which:

- meet the individual needs for high-quality education and research, in keeping with the individual's intellectual and physical abilities and irrespective of the students' income or that of their families of origin,
- meet society's demand both quantitative and qualitative, for university graduates,
- continually meet society's need for scholarly knowledge and insights *lato sensu* and as they bear upon the findings of fundamental research.
- with the knowledge thus acquired, enable the academic community to place itself permanently at the service of the community, for the greater benefit of that community in the widest meaning of the term (Tweede, 1990, p.19).

7.5 Content and quality

To carry out this general purpose, the government funds universities, recognises their degrees, diplomas and certificates, sets out regulations for rationalisation and planning, advances scholarly research, identifies hindrances and shortcomings, assists universities in forwarding an international commitment and presence and safeguards the quality of teaching and research. Government also seeks to ensure that public funds are used optimally and efficiently. In short, governments retain a 'supervisory' or 'facilitatory' role both in defining the duties of academia and, by extension, in operationalising academic freedom. The government's new role places especial weight on accountability and budget control and to this end, specific legal instruments have been devised.

7.6 A Flemish exemplar

To illustrate this process, we will draw upon a hypothetical example of a university in the Flemish Community of Belgium. Three points merit attention:

- the annual budget sets out income and expenditure charged to the state's operating budget. It also contains an itemised summary of all income and expenditure, income and expenditure on student welfare as well as research grants and research expenditure,

- the government retains the authority to examine a university's budget in order to ascertain whether it corresponds to the requirements stipulated by, or pursuant to, the appropriate legislation or ministerial decree. It verifies that the finances of the university are viable from a long term perspective. It examines the balancing of the university's budget, checks to see that the number of staff authorised has not been exceeded and that investment as planned is in keeping with the institutional investment plan. Finally, the government examines the budget to ascertain its compliance with formal procedures for budgetary presentation,

- should these conditions not be met, legislation specifies the measures to which government may have recourse. In such an eventuality, central authorities may begin a procedure which, in first instance, requests the university to modify its budget. Should the university's response be deemed insufficient, monthly payments from central authority can be rescheduled. Other measures are ruled out on grounds that personnel costs account for 80 percent of an institution's budget. It is, of course, always possible to roll on to the following financial year monies remaining unspent in the current year.

Given that salaries account for more than 80 percent of operating grants, universities in the Flemish Community, along with their budget are also required to submit a financial plan for the coming five years. The investment plan sets out proposals for financial restructuring and their means of implementation as well as the financial reserves available. Until government approval of this financial plan is forthcoming, no staff appointments or recruitments paid from operating funds may be made (de Groof, 1992-3).

By such procedures, government strikes a balance between the institution's legal safeguards and the authorities' oversight. In presenting its annual accounts, the university discloses all sources of income and expenditure, liabilities and assets including those resulting from its own capital resources. In addition, rules of presentation, finely spelt out, ensure that the way financial management and performance are set out, allows easy verification of the uses to which government grants were put.

Some countries have specific supervisory agencies. They can lodge an appeal to the government against decisions reached by university administration or its delegated committees in those instances where such decisions infringe legislation, ministerial decree or pose a threat to the university's financial health. A successful appeal may result in the original decision being overturned. In the case of public universities, it may be accompanied by a total or partial suspension of payments. Other countries employ a system by which major heads of expenditure require prior examination and approval.

7.7 Balancing government policy and institutional personnel policy

In many of Europe's higher education systems, one may interpret the action of law-makers as an attempt to balance out a policy which, despite opposition, remains by and large centralist in operation, in contrast to the more extreme forms of devolutionist temptation which press for the relinquishment of all centralised authority. In this area of tension and conflicting interest, the issue of the management of human resources and personnel policy is crucial. It is crucial for the self evident reason that knowledge, its creation, application and transmission which are the central purposes of the university, wholly repose on people. What will be the limits and characteristics of a personnel policy that has sufficient flexibility both to meet society's demands (see Tweede Kamer, *supra*, p. 107) to secure the enthusiastic backing of institutions and that of the academic community, are matters to which both the legislator and case-law will have much to contribute.

7.7.1 Quality, qualifications and personnel

Just as human resources and personnel lie at the heart of the enterprising university and the innovative university, so does research of high quality. On it rests the reputation for excellence, the institution's position across the various labour markets to which it contributes and on which it draws (Höltta, 1995), its command of resources and its attractiveness to students. No higher education system has ever been without the means of ascertaining and demonstrating its quality (Neave, 1994, pp.115-132). But whether the ways which it does so are perceived as appropriate – and by whom – are very different matters.

Qualifications and the type of knowledge long valued by public service, enshrined in the various degrees and diplomas that confer upon the individual eligibility to sit the competitive examinations which lead onto the 'glittering prizes', are far from receiving similar valuation from industry, commerce and those who consider themselves as the nation's forgers of wealth. That the legislator and governments have gradually urged this issue to the forefront of the policy agenda and that, for the past five years or more, quality in higher education has thrown up a host of national agencies reflects only this: the need to realign and restate this basic function in terms which the private sector values and holds as relevant.

7.7.2 Recent developments

At present, the thrust towards a more detailed and sensitive system of quality control takes it in a number of directions. One of these moves inward to the institutional level. It turns around a permanent but regularly activated system of assessment and reporting back on both teaching and research undertaken within basic units and by individuals. A second direction moves outward towards specialised agencies, sometimes located outside the Ministry responsible for higher education, sometimes reporting directly to it. In Europe, the use of external, international reviewers at both levels is an interesting and significant development (Maassen, Brennan and Westerheijden, 1994).

Powerful though this lever is and however beneficial the effect that self-evaluation has had upon institutional cohesion, it remains very much a moot point whether quality control spurs reform on. Certainly, it may serve, depending on the items included for assessment, to foster greater mobility, improve teaching through merit awards, and focus attention on career planning. As a tool to shape human resource policy at the level of the particular establishment and as an instrument for maintaining independence so long as the results are positive, its effects have been substantial.

7.7.3 The legal framework

Beyond the institutional level and penetrating down to it is the legal framework, set down by government and the latter's regulatory role. Its existence implies that governments too should not hesitate to implement a substantial degree of quality control which, if it includes chastisement, ought not to exclude incentives. Quality management, it may be argued, falls fully into the function of that surveillance and oversight normally associated with funding and general compliance with law and procedure at institutional level. Quality management has been raised as the fundamental principle of good administration. Such an exalted status does not alter either the discretionary nature of the legal authority that institutional management wields, nor does it alter the supervisory authority of government as established in law. Indeed, one may contend that the legislator did not regard the government's oversight as limited to monitoring the compliance with the formality of administrative procedure or its counterpart with respect to budgetary decisions. Since personnel policy cannot be left to the discretion of individual administration, therefore the government's authority in the matter remains intact.

The application of general principles of justice in the domain of personnel policy falls equally under the purlieu of the organising power or central national authority. Employees have a right to both clarity and certainty in respect of their legal status and condition. This means that the conditions of employment ought to a certain extent, to enjoy the protection of the organising or appropriate national authorities. In the general area of quality management, it is proper and reasonable that, in return for conceding greater discretionary authority and greater latitude in allocating public resources, the government should make consequent demands on the way quality in higher education is stated, assessed and presented.

7.8 Cross-institutional comparison

That the legislator attaches sanctions and penalties – as we have noted earlier in connection with suspending the payment of subsidies to non compliance with procedure, plus the public nature of the results – shows the weight of importance the legislator lays both on the government's right to take initiatives and to the accountability incumbent on each establishment. If government is to exercise its authority in respect of quality assessment, then procedures and provisions will have to be drawn up that permit comparison across institutions and within types of institutions. And, if this should show that individual establishments have failed to meet their legal obligations, then the government will be forced to act for it is inconceivable that the government would permit the administrators of individual universities the choice of whether or not to carry out the government's demand for quality in personnel.

REFERENCES

Clark, Burton R. (1983) *The higher education system: academic organisation in cross national perspective.* Berkeley/Los Angeles/London: University of California Press.

Clark, Burton R. (1995) *Places of Inquiry: research and advanced education in modern universities.* Berkeley/Los Angeles/London: University of California Press.

Clark, Burton R. (1997) "Common Problems and Adaptive Responses in the Universities of the World: organising for change", *Higher Education Policy*, (forthcoming).

de Groof, Jan (1992-3) "De gewijzigde regelgeving voor de universiteiten in de Vlaamse Gemeenschap", *Tijdschrift voor Onderwijsrecht en Onderwijsbeleid*, Nr.1.

de Miguel, Mario, Mora, José-Ginés & Rodriguez, Sebastián (eds) (1991) *La Evaluación de las Institutiones universitarias.* Madrid: Consejo de Universidades.

Doumenc, Michel & Gilly, Jean-Pierre (1977) *Les IUTs: ouverture et idéologie*, Paris: Editions du Cerf.

Furth, Dorothea (1992) "Short cycle higher education", in Clark & Neave, *The Encyclopedia...* Vol.ii. *The Institutional Fabric of the higher education system.* pp.1217 ff.

Garcia Garrido, José-Luis (1992) "Spain" in Clark & Neave, *The Encyclopedia*, Vol.i. *National Systems of Higher Education.* pp.663-673.

Gellert, Claudius (1993) "Germany", in Burton R. Clark (ed) *The Research Foundations of Graduate Education: Germany, Britain, France, United States, Japan.* Berkeley/Los Angeles/London: University of California Press.

Höltta, Seppo (1995) *Towards the self-regulative University.* Joensuu: University of Joensuu Publications in Social Sciences, no.23.

International Council for Educational Development (1987) *La Reforma Universitaria española: evaluación e informe.* Madrid: Consejo de Universidades.

In 't Veld, Roel Füssel, Hans-Peter & Neave, Guy (1996) *The Relations between State and higher education,* vol. 1 in the Council of Europe series *Legislating for higher education in Europe.* Dordrecht: Kluwer.

Kehm, Barbara & Teichler, Ulrich (1992) "Federal Republic of Germany", in Clark and Neave (eds) *Encyclopedia op. cit.,* vol. i. *National systems of Higher Education,* pp.240-259.

Kivinen, Osmo & Rinne, Risto (1996) "The Problem of Diversification in higher education: Counter-tendencies between divergence and convergence in the Finnish higher education system since the 1950s", in V. Lynn Meek, Leo Goedegebuure, Osmo Kivinen and Risto Rinne (eds) *The Mockers and Mocked: comparative perspectives on Differentiation, Convergence and Diversity in higher education.* Oxford: Pergamon Press for IAU.

Kogan, Maurice et al. (1994) "The Changing Framework for the academic profession", in *Staffing Higher Education: meeting new challenges.* London: Jessica Kingsley. pp.12-32.

Kump, Sonja (forthcoming) "Slovenia", in Clark & Neave (eds) *The Encyclopedia* (2nd ed)

Lane, Jan-Erik (1992) "Sweden", in Clark & Neave (eds) *The Encyclopedia...* vol.i, *National systems of higher education*, pp.692-693.

Leitner, Erik (1996) "Unequal competition: access to universities and Fachhochschulen in Austria between open door and selectivity", *European Journal of Education*, vol.31, no.3, pp.259-272.

Maassen, P. A. M, Brennan, J. & Westerheijden, Don (1994) *Changing Contexts of Quality Assessment: recent trends in Western European higher education.* Utrecht: Lemma.

Martinelli, A. (1992) "Italy", in Clark & Neave (eds) The Encyclopedia of Higher Education, vol.i. *National Systems of Higher Education.* pp.355-368.

Moscati, Roberto (1991) "Italy", in Neave & van Vught *Prometheus Bound, op. cit.*.

Neave, Guy (1992a) "War and educational reconstruction in Belgium, France and the Netherlands, 1940-1947", in Roy Lowe (ed) *Education and the Second World War.* London: Falmer Press. pp.84-127.

Neave, Guy (1992b) "On bodies vile and bodies beautiful: the role of 'buffer' institutions between university and state", *Higher Education Policy,* vol.5, no.3, pp.10-14.

Neave, Guy (1995) "The Politics of quality; developments in higher education in Western Europe 1992-1994" *European Journal of Education,* vol.29, no.2 June, pp.115-134.

Neave & van Vught (1991) *Prometheus Bound: op cit.*.

Palmer, R. G. (1985) *The Improvement of Humanity: Education and the French Revolution.* Princeton: Princeton University Press.

Pratt, John & Burgess, Tyrell (1974) *The Polytechnics: a report.* London: Pitmans.

Premfors, Rune I.T. (1980) *The Politics of Higher Education in a Comparative Perspective: France, Sweden and the United Kingdom.* Stockholm: Department of Political Science.

Premfors, Rune I.T. (1981) "National policy styles and higher education in France, Sweden and the United Kingdom", *European Journal of Education*, vol.16, no.2, pp.253-262.

Robinson, Eric (1972) *Polytechnics: the people's university.* Harmondsworth (Mddx): Penguin Education Special.

Sebkova, Helena (1996) "Access to higher education in the Czech Republic", *European Journal of Education,* vol.31, no.3, pp.273-289.

Tweede Kamer (1990) "Explanatory Memorandum on the Dutch Higher Education and Scientific Research Act", *Lower House of the Dutch Parliament, session 1988-1989*, p.19.

Trow, Martin (1985) "Comparative Reflections on leadership in higher education", *European Journal of Education,* vol.20. nos.2-3, pp.143-159.

8

QUALITY AND EVALUATION

8.1 Quality

In the turbulent policy of higher education, evaluating the quality of the services universities provide has become an overriding priority. Yet quality, as the students of *Zen and the Art of Motorcycle Maintenance* will recall, does not easily lend itself to definition. Indeed, the fate of the writer of that work suggests that the challenge of definition leads on to temporary insanity! The proliferating literature on quality distinguishes between three interlinked categories which are usually subsumed within the overall term. They are: quality management, quality assessment and quality control. Within this general frame, it is agreed that only through a complex approach – and a no less complex methodology – can a university handle the issues posed. A university can attain an acceptable level of quality once human resources, budget, teaching, research, organisation and management are brought together in such a way as to achieve the establishment's goals. In turn, assessment of quality is feasible only when the complete and overall performance of the university is taken into account. From this it follows that this same global approach applies in the matter of institutional evaluation.

In any programme of evaluation or assessment involving quality, the objective – namely the improvement of quality in a particular establishment – should be explicitly stated and universities should take an active part in the whole evaluation process. As a means to get the institution thinking about its own role, purpose and goals, to encourage academia to ask questions about the quality of its own performance and the ways of improving it, few techniques are more powerful than self-evaluation. And recourse to external evaluation may give a further bite and focus to any exercise of quality assessment.

Clearly, the exercise of quality assessment should be grounded in legally established procedures and it is as well to include the following elements: aims directed towards improvements; scope to cover teaching, research, service to society, institutional management; focus which concentrates on input, process and output; and lastly, method, which may be objective, that is, institutional evaluation based on stipulated performance indicators, or subjective in nature. The latter draws upon peer review, visitation committees etc..

8.2 Evaluation and institutional autonomy

Evaluation is an analytical process which, when applied to quality should have as its goal to measure, to demonstrate and eventually to raise the level at which any function in the university is carried out. Evaluating higher education is a logical consequence of that institution's autonomy and for that reason evaluation is deeply embedded in the intellectual fabric and traditional behaviour of the academic community. Evaluation and the techniques on which it relies, are nowadays applied across an institution. Previously, however, the basic techniques, their application and indeed the development of evaluation itself were confined to within the academic community and more particularly within the organised bodies of knowledge around which the university revolved, namely the disciplines. Evaluation, as a recognised procedure for identifying excellence and merit, creativity and originality, was sited within the varying internal and disciplinary cultures (Becher, 1989) that constitute the heart of academic life. It operated according to the canons of scholarship by which the masters of disciplines regulate the production of new knowledge – that is, primarily, research. Self-judgment, the opinion of peers are, both actually and historically are not only a powerful means of organising cohesion between individuals working on a specific domain and thus giving that domain and those individuals a shared intellectual identity. Nor, for that matter, are evaluation schemes entirely pragmatic instruments for assigning reward, though that certainly has and remains one of their outcomes. Evaluation and its outcomes, repute – good or shameful – prestige – acknowledged or absent – stand as an integral part of that uncontrollable dynamic behind knowledge and its growth (see *supra* pp. 42) which has brought us to the foothills of the 'knowledge society'. But it is also an integral part – if not the coping-stone – on which academic authority, standing in one's speciality, personal rule and authority are built. And this form of authority, as we have suggested earlier, is not only a key element in governance, its relationship with administration is basic in determining the nature of the governance exercised within the institution – whether collegial, managerial or market oriented – or, as an alternative way of classification, collegial, bureaucratic or professional (see *supra* pp. 9ff.).

In effect, when we talk about evaluation in connection with the quality of institutional achievement, we are talking at one and the same time about a practice long regarded as essential in the transformation of science and scholarship to becoming objective knowledge as opposed to their earlier status as revealed knowledge. But we also touch upon very new dimensions that have been added to the essentially internalist, discipline-bounded function that evaluation assumed in the past and which represent a very real change in, as well as an extension to the scope of application of, this function. Broadening its scope of application and the shift of evaluation from being solely discipline-oriented towards an administrative function applied across the institution as a whole, has been the main burden of many government initiatives over the past decade or so. As a result, techniques used by academia to assess both quality of research projects and, by the same logic, the attribution of research funds were, in the name of greater transparency and responsiveness to the market, progressively extended to teaching and from there, to institutional performance. In fine, a procedure that lay at the base of academic authority was now firmly relocated in those levels of decision-making associated with bureaucratic authority within the institution or 'systems authority' within the nation.

Evaluation as a way to check up on performance, is a key instrument in the development of that mode of policy-making often called 'remote steering'. It replaces verification of procedure with evaluation of how far objectives – whether national or institutional – have been attained. Quality evaluation serves as a powerful lever indeed in shifting institutional attention from what was earlier termed 'process' autonomy to 'product' autonomy (see *supra* pp. 79ff.). There is, however, another dimension involved. Since it too has considerable relevance of a political, ideological and contextual nature, it is as well to set quality and evaluation within it. Much of the weight of regulation is the outcome of defining and refining procedures involved in both system and institutional control by central national administration. Such procedures have, over the years, acquired considerable heaviness not only in the detail but also in the effort needed to fulfil them. Their replacement by 'objectives', however, and the insistence by governments on the application of evaluation techniques standardised across institutions, are central elements, which whilst they are focused on the specific area of higher education, also tie in with the broader political agenda of 'deregulation'.

8.2.1 Developing evaluation methodology

In this study, we have had many occasions to remark on the diversity and differences that make up Europe's higher education landscape. That it should also be a characteristic of national evaluation systems, their varying criteria, quantitative and qualitative can, surely astound no-one. Performance indicators are empirical – data either qualitative or quantitative that should point out how far an institution's goals have been achieved (Sizer, 1992, pp.156-161). How these indicators are incorporated into the routine of the national system and its institutional units, will largely follow the custom of national administration. Some will be set out in national legislation and ministerial decree and are conceived as part of an interactive flow of information between national administration and individual establishment. Indicators enable the former to ascertain general progress towards attaining national goals. They allow the latter to verify how far their particular institutional plan either meets – or departs from – national strategy on the one hand or how far it corresponds to demands from a rapidly evolving social and economic context on the other.

At a national level and at the level of the institution, evaluation may follow one of two approaches – though rarely both at the same time. The first concentrates on the institution as a complete unit of analysis. The second focuses on a single facet, discipline or activity – for instance, teaching and research conducted within a particular field of study. Discipline based evaluations move steadily across the different establishments of a similar type, status or within the same sector – i.e. between universities or between similar non-university institutes, as the case may be (Staropoli, 1991; Neave, 1996).

8.2.2 The European dimension to quality management

A number of western European countries are active in developing new procedures, standards and mechanisms for quality management. Some entail changes in the legislation applied to higher education. Others draw their inspiration from international examples and contacts. To illustrate this particularly dynamic area we will draw on the experience, *inter alia*, of the United Kingdom, the Netherlands and France.

8.2.2.1 Britain

In the (then) non-university sector of the United Kingdom quality, control since the mid 1960s was exercised by the Council for National Academic Awards (CNAA) (Brennan, 1990). It should be noted, however, that this system was exceptional in its time, particularly in its procedures and also in its mandate which applied not at all to the universities. The universities continued with a long established system, involving what was essentially a provisional and tutelary period of probation exercised over the degree courses of newly established universities by those establishments long in place and with both repute and experience in successfully upholding standards.

The CNAA in effect ensured the quality of institutions in the municipal sector and was set up to ensure that their mission, first conceived as radically different from that of the universities, (see *supra* Chapter 7, pp. 102), was adhered to. Nominated by government, its prime responsibility was the validation of degree level courses – or their equivalents – a process in which it drew upon representatives from the liberal professions, from industry and from the established universities. Unlike the universities *stricto sensu*, the municipal sector came under the purlieu of Her Majesty's Inspectorate of Schools whilst its funding issued from the (then) Department of Education and Science rather than from the Treasury (Ministry of Finance).

Abolished in 1991-2 after the publication of the 1991 White Paper on Higher Education and the promulgation of the Further and Higher Education Act of 1992, the CNAA was replaced by a number of new agencies which came to occupy the terrain of quality assessment. In 1991, the Committee of Vice Chancellors and Principals, representing what were to be known as the "old universities", set up the Academic Audit Unit, essentially a body to ascertain the uniformity of methodology and items involved in institutional self-assessment. Parallel to this stood the Higher Education Quality Council into which the Academic Audit Unit was later assimilated. In the area of funding, three regional Higher Education Funding Councils were established, one each for England, Scotland and Wales and they in their turn have created Quality Assessment Committees (Green, 1994). The task of the latter is to assign funds on the basis of quality assessment exercises carried out by the individual institution of higher education. The British arrangement to date displays a certain bicephalic character. Higher education is audited by one agency – the Higher Education Quality Council and assessed by another, the regional Higher Education Funding Councils.

8.2.2.2 The Netherlands

Until 1985, quality assessment in the Netherlands revolved around research funding, a situation which, if not unusual, was radically revised in that year by the memorandum entitled Higher Education Autonomy and Quality (HOAK). Under the new arrangement, responsibility was split between a university umbrella body – the Association for Cooperating Dutch Universities (VSNU) and the governments official arm, the Higher Education Inspectorate. Under this arrangement, quality audit fell under the responsibility of the former whilst the latter was assigned the duty of carrying out 'meta-evaluations' – in effect, evaluating the audit and following up the results of the assessment (Vroejnsteyn,1995).

Quality evaluation in the Netherlands passes through four stages. These are:

- self-assessment of the institution via a dialogue between all members of the academic community, students included,
- peer review carried out by a Visitation Committee which is published by the VSNU,

- a 'meta evaluation' conducted by the Higher Education Inspectorate,
- presentation to the government of the completed evaluation report.

In extreme situations, the government may proceed against an institution either by cutting off funds from a particular study programme or, doubtless rarer by far, by increasing them.

8.2.2.3 France

If, outwardly, quality assessment in France appears to be more centralised and thus in keeping with the historic features of governance in that country, the long term strategy tends very definitely towards strengthening institutional initiative and enterprise (Neave, 1996). The Higher Education Guideline Law, promulgated in 1985, made provision for the establishment of a National Evaluation Committee (Cazenave, 1990; Staropoli, 1987). Formally speaking, the Committee is a governmental agency, however, it has the unique feature of reporting directly to the president of the Republic, a condition which guarantees its independence *vis à vis* the Ministry of Education and other executive bodies. Its seventeen members are also appointed directly by the head of state. The methodology employed is based on institutional self-assessment with the judicious use of visitation committees and a final report drawn up by the Committee after consultation with the institution under review. The chairman of the CNE at the end of his five year mandate, presents a summary of the major developments over his period in office in the light of the reports and assessments carried by the CNE during the same period. It is presented to the president, published and, to judge from the public reception of the first two, widely commented upon.

The CNE over the twelve years of its existence has completed the first round of institutional assessment. All institutes of higher education in the country have been reviewed. The second round, which began in 1994, focuses more on the evaluation of disciplinary fields and in particular, their contribution to regional and local development.

In the majority of western European systems of higher education, procedures of self-evaluation both at faculty and institutional levels, are carried out by quality assessment committees. These committees are headed either by vice-rectors, vice-presidents or members of academic staff, nominated by the institution's academic leader. Their task is continuously to operate quality control over teaching, research and community service – where it is relevant – by monitoring information that can serve as performance indicators and subjecting them to computer processing and analysis. This continuous updating has the advantage of being able to summon up appropriate data as and when needed for external audit.

It is to be recommended that self-assessment, peer review, preparation and presentation of templates for such evaluation should be written into major legislation dealing with higher education.

8.3 Accreditation

The concepts of accountability and quality assessment are formally institutionalised and their logistical base set out in the system of accreditation. Accreditation – that is, state or public recognition accorded by an authoritative body – and quality assessment – that is, evaluation – serve different ends and thus demand different procedures. The accreditation of a newly-founded university or a newly-developed study programme is a very different matter from assessing existing institutions and well-established programmes, though clearly both are the final responsibility of the state. Put succinctly, accreditation is a process by which an external agency – or accreditation committee – judges the conditions, levels of attainment and the resources necessary for such levels of performance to be maintained in relation either to one or more specified study programmes or for an institution in its entirety. The agency, its servants or nominees acting on its behalf and in its name, compares resources provided and conditions of study in the institution under scrutiny against a series of formally defined norms, standards or procedural requirements which, depending on the particular legislative style of the country, may be set down in law or possess by other means, the weight of 'normal good practice'.

The salient feature of accreditation – which is also known as validation in some countries – is the application of standards external to the institution under examination. Thus, when accreditation involves a programme to be certified as having a quality appropriate for undergraduate or for postgraduate education, the standards to be set are determined by professionals who themselves are acknowledged as leading exponents or practitioners in the same specialised area as the one under investigation. Obviously in the case of institutional accreditation, the range of norms, standards and levels of expected performance to be covered is far wider. The criteria may extend to general quality of academic staff, their experience and qualifications, basic organisational requirements, size of library, provision of space and equipment, ability to service and maintain the same, management capacity, a sound financial position etc..

8.4 Four stages in quality assurance

Four stages in quality assurance can be distinguished. These are:

- self-evaluation and self-improvement at institutional or faculty level,
- external quality assessment by independent – where appropriate international – peers the objective of which is to raise quality but which does not involve either accreditation or decisions involving financial allocation,
- accreditation (state or public authority recognition) of institutions or study programmes to admit students, to receive public funds or to award diplomas leading to publicly recognised occupations. Only at this level should the withdrawal of funds or recognition of diplomas be admitted,
- the opening or closure of study programmes in the light of national need or interest.

As in the case of evaluation, the basic principles governing accreditation and its procedures, the requirements demanded formally of institutions and the powers together with the responsibilities of government should be set down clearly in the laws relating to higher education.

8.5 The purposes of accreditation

In essence, the purposes of accreditation are:

- to foster excellence in higher education through laying down criteria and guidelines that ensure the highest quality, effectiveness and efficiency in teaching, research and services made available to the nation,

- to encourage institutions in the improvement of their operations by means of continuous self-evaluation and strategic planning,

- to furnish evidence that an institution or a specific study programme demands and achieves a stipulated level of quality that is clearly defined whilst commanding conditions and resources such that the objectives which it has set itself may be met,

- to assist the institution in developing and improving its own programmes,

- to endeavour to protect institutions against encroachments that place in jeopardy the effectiveness of the institution to fulfil its educational and social mission or its academic freedom.

Whether nominated by state authorities, by the council of universities – or its equivalent – or whether functioning as an autonomous non-governmental agency, the accreditation commission, bearing in mind the results of self-evaluation, the conclusions of the peer review, the report of a visitation committee and the replies of the interested institution, may decide whether to grant, to deny, to withhold or to reaffirm, accredited status.

REFERENCES

Becher, R.A. (1989) *Academic Tribes and Territories: intellectual enquiry and the cultures of disciplines.* Milton Keynes: Open University for SRHE.

Brennan, John (1990) "Quality assessment in the Public Sector in Great Britain", in Leo Goedegebuure, Peter Maassen & Don F. Westerheijden (eds) *Peer Review and Performance Indicators.* Utrecht: Lemma.

Cazenave, Philippe (1990) "France", in H. R. Kells (eds) *The Development of Performance Indicators for Eleven Countries.* Paris: OECD.

Green, Diana (1994) *What is Quality in Higher Education?* Milton Keynes: Open University Press for SRHE.

Neave, Guy (1996) "The Evaluation of the higher education system in France," in Robert Cowen (ed) *World Yearbook of Education 1996 The Evaluation of Systems of Higher Education.* London: Kogan Page. pp.66-81.

Sizer, John (1990) "Funding Councils and performance indicators in Quality Assessment in the United Kingdom" in Leo Goedegebuure, Peter Maassen, & Don F. Westerheijden (eds) *Peer Review and Performance Indicators: quality assessment in British and Dutch Higher Education.* Utrecht: Lemma.

Sizer, John (1992) "Performance indicators in government-higher education relationships: lessons for government", *Higher Education Management*, vol.4, pp.156-160.

Sizer, John (1995) "Teaching Quality Assessment in higher education institutions in Scotland: the Staff Development Aspects of Scottish Higher Education Funding Council Quality Assessment framework", *Higher Education Policy*, vol.8, no.2, pp.50-51.

Staropoli, André (1987) "The French Comité National d'Evaluation", *European Journal of Education*, vol.22, no.3.

Staropoli, André (1991) "Evaluation policy and techniques in France" in T.W. Banda et al. (eds) *Proceedings of the Third International Conference on Assessing Quality in Higher Education.* Knoxville [Tennessee]: Center for Assessment Research and Development.

Vroejnsteyn, Ton (1995) Improvement and Accountability: *navigating between Scylla and Caribdys:* Guide for External Quality Assessment in Higher Education. London: Jessica Kingsley.

Westerheijden, Don F., Brennan, John & Maassen, Peter (eds) (1994) *Changing Contexts of Quality Assessment: recent trends in Western European Higher Education.* Utrecht: Lemma.

9

MANAGING THE AUTONOMOUS UNIVERSITY

> *"And I say unto one 'Come', 'and he cometh and to another, 'Go'. And he goeth. For I am a man having authority".*
>
> St Matthew, Ch 8, verse 9.

9.1 Introduction

The university is a complex organisation which has to accommodate a vast range of tasks, cross-cutting interests, demands and obligations, some of them imposed by law, others that arise from the usual friction which comes with large numbers of people working on widely different projects in the same surroundings. Managing an institution which has variously been described in such dire terms as 'monadic chaos' (Lane, 1981) 'organised anarchy' (March & Olssen) 'bottom heavy' – that is, the considerable influence residing with the base units, departments etc. – is a redoubtable challenge. In principle, management is the application of rationality to work, so that the task in hand is accomplished in the most efficient way by those whose skills best suit them for the task they have been assigned. Management implies a rational division between those who determine mission and policy, those who plan and oversee the execution of that policy and finally those who deliver the goods, services or products according to the terms and under the conditions set out by the two hierarchically superior levels. In the task of organising and steering collective endeavour, Europe's universities, however, have developed other forms of decision-making. Some of them, as we pointed out in Chapter 1, are of considerable antiquity. They command great loyalty and immense symbolic value in the academic community. Collegial forms of governance figure prominently here.

But the press of economic change, of society's expectation that higher education will provide the qualifications, skills and abilities it needs, has imposed a growing conditionality upon the university. If society is prepared to support higher education, it is on society's own terms. And these terms are, nowadays, rarely without strings. In return for backing and resources, society and its representatives demand greater efficiency, often exactly stipulated in terms of lower unit costs, fewer students dropping out, better preparation for employment and, above all, that the university now account regularly and publicly for the resources confided to it, how they have been used and what they have achieved.

Factors such as these have profoundly altered the objectives, assumptions and balance which characterised the more historic forms of organisation by which an institution 'manages itself'. Such priorities have, as we have had cause to note earlier, given rise to alternate arrangements which carry with them each a different concept of the university's mission. These alternate forms – whether described as 'the managerial model', 'the market model' or the 'social utility model' – involve significant revisions in the balance of power between academia, administration and leadership in the internal governance of the university (see for instance Chapter 7, pp. 25-100).

9.2 Managerialism as a philosophy of university governance

The introduction of quality, efficiency and the cultivation of enterprise (Neave, 1988) as the axial points in higher education policy and thus as objectives for institutional development, entered into the world of Britain's universities in 1981. The origins of what was then described as the 'new managerialism' (Shils & Daalder, 1981) do not coincide precisely with the cuts in the university budget of that year. Nevertheless, those cuts effectively ushered in a new era in the relationship between government and universities. Managerialism, according to the American analyst of public policy, Martin Trow, "...as understood by central government in Britain is a substitute for a relationship of trust between government and universities, trust in the ability of institutions of higher education to broadly govern themselves. The chosen mechanisms... are assessments of the 'quality' of the teaching and research done in universities, carried out by committees and individuals appointed by the central funding agency and linked directly to funding." (Trow, 1994, pp.11-18).

It is arguable, however, that the importance of managerialism certainly lay in its introducing into academia criteria of productivity and indicators of efficiency which hailed in goodly part from commercial practice rather than from disciplinary cultures. But its importance did not lie solely in the loss of confidence so much as in the deep philosophic pessimism the introduction of such techniques implied. By linking institutional performance directly to funding and setting in place a battery of performance and assessment indicators, the British government not only showed it no longer subscribed to the 'trust and confidence' that, hitherto had been the essence of the relationship with the universities (Templeman, 1982), it also denied a fundamental premise which had long informed the British concept of university self-management. This premise rested on an abiding view that academia, despite its independence, was nevertheless capable of according its own interests to those of the nation. Put another way, the unparalleled degree of institutional autonomy and unprecedented range of responsibilities which fell to each British university – and they extended to the internal allocation of public finance, the admission of students, the recruitment and appointment of academic staff, the setting of study programmes, of their content and the award of degrees and diplomas – reflected an optimistic philosophy. This optimism was not just that the academic community should be master in its own house but that it was capable out of its own volition of acting in the name of the public good.

It was, however, precisely this historic 'voluntarism' which came under fire. In effect, managerialism in Britain rested on the conviction in government circles (Kogan & Kogan, 1983) that academia was not able to act out of 'inner motivation' or, on its own accord, recognise the national interest. It was capable only of defending its own narrow and corporatist concerns. To counter these corporatist interests, however, required the introduction of explicit penalty, of negative incentives. This was a policy which, however much dictated by the financial pressures of the moment, nevertheless rested on a pessimistic interpretation of the nature of '*homo academicus*'. Without material constraint and without the constant oversight that close techniques of individual and institutional scrutiny provided and which were to be explicitly managed from the centre through agencies of public purpose, academia would remain unheeding – if not out-rightly indifferent – to the new social and economic ethic not to mention the operational consequences for higher education that market forces incarnated.

It is one of the more outstanding paradoxes in British style 'hard managerialism' that it involves systematic constraint upon the universities to accomplish the move towards a higher education system driven by 'free' competition and market forces. It is no less of a paradox that competition as the new referential principle, was injected through central administration acting as a species of pseudo-market (Williams, 1995) to generate competition between institutions for funds and student places, where in reality little existed. It is perhaps less surprising that in doing so the power and place of 'systems authority' should become immensely strengthened despite the public rhetoric and doctrine of 'rolling back the frontiers of the state'. From the standpoint of the universities, truth to tell the injection of market forces went hand in hand with the rolling forward of those self-same frontiers. And, as the various agencies of quality assessment moved into their stride, so an orgy of elaborating formal procedures, issuing forms and circulating questionnaires engulfed higher education.

In Britain, despite the exceptional developments of the past decade, the introduction of change at institutional level tends rarely to be carried out by legislative decree. Rather it still relies, to a considerable extent, on the decisions of individual establishments or is a product of understandings reached between institutional leadership working through their national body, the Committee of Vice Chancellors and Principals. The emergence of managerialism owed as much to this traditional mechanism of accommodation as it did to the weight of government fiat. In short, its advent resulted from developments at two levels. The first of these two currents worked upon the national level. As we have seen, it introduced national standardised procedures for quality assessment and quality audit. The second current operated at the institutional level and focused on particular functions. One may distinguish between these two conduits of change by saying that whilst the first operated in a 'top-down' manner, the second acted in reverse, that is, in a 'bottom up' mode gradually aggregating up the sum of institutional initiatives which eventually emerge as a *de facto* 'spontaneous' revision generated within and by, the higher education system itself. Amongst the more remarkable examples of the latter is the transformation of the role of institutional leadership.

9.3 Leadership: a shift in perspective

Strengthening the powers of institutional leadership almost by definition accompanies the drive to managerialism. In Britain, it involved the transformation of the vice-chancellor from the traditional figure of *primus inter pares* of the academic collegium to that of chief executive officer, a status largely modelled on the powers and responsibilities of the American university president. This change in role went far beyond mere symbolism. It stressed the executive status of the institutional head as deriving less from academia than from his managerial position at the head of an administrative hierarchy. It stressed the professional and essentially managerial nature of that post rather than its historic representational function. No less important, the initiative behind these changes came from institutional leadership itself, in a report issued in 1985 under the auspices of the Committee of Vice Chancellors and Principals and from the pen of the vice-chancellor of Birmingham University, Alex Jarratt (Jarratt Report, 1985).

The issues of managing an institution at a time when its mission is being redefined and oriented from the public sector to the far more volatile private sector of the nation's economy are, of course, not confined to Britain, though it remains a fact that the British higher education system was the first in Europe to be faced with so stark a programme of adjustment. By common admission, leadership remains a matter of key significance. Historically and in many countries still today, institutional leaders – rectors, presidents etc.. – are chosen from amongst academic staff (Neave, 1991). Their administrative and managerial abilities are variable, but tend mainly to be acquired 'on the job'. There is much to be said for creating both rectorial induction programmes and for redefining the rules that govern the holding of rectorial office and particularly, the length of its mandate. In most European universities, continuity of institutional heads is becoming a matter of concern. For if the period in office is relatively short, the range of skills required is becoming progressively longer – above all when devolution of responsibility from national centre to individual university is the order of the day. Austria employs an ingenious system to ensure continuity whilst maintaining a short period in office. The office of rector is preceded by a period as pre-rector and followed by a period as pro-rector. Thus, individuals destined for the highest responsibility pass successively through all three. Such a triumvirate makes for continuity, reinforces positional and organisational memory.

Continuity and thus stability at the highest level of management may be jeopardised by rapid rotation just as they may lead to stagnation and routine if prolonged unduly. Though few European universities subscribed to the traditional British practice of nominating vice-chancellors *aut culpam, aut vitam*, even those who subscribed to this practice have had second thoughts. The Jarratt Report recommended a period in office of no more than ten years.

9.4 Higher education administration: mainland Europe

Over the past fifteen years, the pace of change in higher education management has accelerated. New Higher Education Acts were passed which bore down upon such systems as the Austrian, the Danish, Finnish, French, Dutch, as well as those in central Europe. Amendments to existing legislation were made in Italy and in the Dutch speaking community of Belgium. The purposes of such law-making were many, but interlinked around the central theme of strengthening the role of 'the market' in higher education, to adjust both to changes in the labour market as well as changes in the major labour market with which higher education was now indissolubly tied, to wit, the private sector. Moves to *a posteriori* methods of verification and assessment, evident in procedures of quality assessment, accreditation, accountability and effectiveness, accompanied the reinterpretation of central government's role in higher education as a 'supervisory' one. Within the universities, internal governance was also overhauled and reinforced. The lines of responsibility between the 'academic managers' – the president, rector, vice-chancellor and the less exalted deans – between the executive boards, senates and university councils were clarified. In the Netherlands, management rationalisation introduced the post of university president in parallel to the rector, the former having responsibility for the university's funding and the latter the oversight for matters academic, including teaching and research.

As Europe's universities moved away from the collegial model of internal governance, so they acquired such rights as the internal distribution across the university of public funds, to determine how additional funds might be raised.

As government funding patterns increasingly endorsed the bloc grant principle, so institutions found themselves endowed with a corresponding latitude to determine their own investment policy, to acquire real estate, to engage in contracts with outside parties and to set out the terms of employment for their staff and personnel.

9.5 Professionalisation of higher education administration

Irrespective of the particular form of internal governance towards which an institution is moving, professionalisation of the administrative services and of management personnel is essential. However, professionalisation itself is a term not without its ambiguities. It is generally employed as synonymous with an activity acquiring and requiring certification of special knowledge which sets those possessing it off from those who do not and gives them thereby an identifiable status. That said, the expanding range of responsibilities an institution takes on and the more crucial the decisions to be made, the greater the need for administrative skills of both a specialist nature and of a high level. Nor are these skills wholly in technical domains such as financial planning and budgeting, fund raising or strategic planning, whether in operationalisation, implementation or assessment. The maintenance of strategic vision, the cohesion necessary if the myriad different interests of teachers, researchers, managers, students and employees are to be kept in a state of creative but balanced tension, call for a very high order of political skills, that is, the ability to reconcile conflict of interest around a common cause or objective. The mastery of such skills is no less relevant when one also bears in mind that they have to be applied not only to the inner dialogue between management and academia, but that they are no less indispensable to the external dialogue between higher education and the various external communities and interests which feel they have a stake in the university.

As the range of decisional competence accruing to a university expands, so the rules relating to the conditions under which they operate and apply should be set forth with the greatest of clarity in the university statutes. But one cannot legislate for cohesion any more than one can pass laws calling for that deftness and sensitivity which ensures and maintains agreement and consensus. That has to come from the rise of a professional ethic and the development of corporate and institutional identity.

There are, as with any reform, dangers and tensions to the institution that come from the devolution of decision-making from national government to the individual establishment. In some countries, legislation has actually contributed to amplifying the natural centrifugal tendencies always present at faculty level and below. Such fragmentation may be attenuated by management initiatives to strengthen cross-faculty cooperation. But fragmentation, even if accentuated by infelicitous legislation, is not wholly amenable to remedy by management alone, for fragmentation into different sub fields and specialisms is part of the natural dynamic of knowledge generation (Clark, 1995). And the introduction of order based only on the grounds of administrative tidiness and convenience may well risk compromising that dynamic. Yet, university leadership has an incontrovertible role to promote quality throughout the institution. It may do this by a policy of positive discrimination in favour of the weaker departments in order to bring them up to strength. But in all this, the role of administration remains a sensitive one which is perhaps best seen as servicing the university rather than steering it.

As we have noted in connection with university leadership, so with management in general: continuity is an important element and most particularly so when one bears in mind the often short periods in office of rectors, vice-rectors, chairmen of boards, senates and the less exalted dean. The continuity of professionalism is an important complement to the democracy of academia. Certainly teachers and researchers can develop into qualified administrators, though one may be forgiven for wondering how long this will remain so as the drive to professionalise management gets under way, and more especially so when those recruited to administration often remain there for the rest of their lives (Andersson, 1995, pp.18-22). However, the force of academic custom still makes it imperative that the rector be both a good manager as well as a respected and leading figure in his academic speciality.

9.6 Leadership vs self-government

Within the collegial model of university governance a complex skein of administrative bodies, committees and organs has accumulated. For some, these bodies are sharply and functionally separate. For others, their remits, powers and responsibilities overlap. In Europe's universities a bicameral system of administration has emerged based on an executive board on the one hand and, on the other, a self-governing body in the form of the senate, though nomenclature will, naturally vary from system to system, if not from sector to sector. Amongst other terms used for this entity are council or *Konvent*. The executive board brings together the rector or the president, as the case may be, and the rector's staff. Chaired by the rector, its responsibility covers the main fields related to the funding of the university and its operational working. The senate, (or councils) by contrast, are entrusted with internal, legal and electoral issues. They also have an advisory status *vis à vis* the executive board (rectorate).

There are naturally variations on this basic pattern. One splits the executive body into two, the first being the rector's college (rector and rectorate staff) the second, the senate which is chaired by the rector or by an independent elected chairman, the university council (*Konvent*), deans' committee, research committee etc.. The senate has the power to set up functionally defined executive sub-committees for budgeting, teaching, research, professional ethics, etc..

Some managerial models are based on the principle of participant democracy (see supra Ch.1) and insert executive and advisory committees within what is basically a bicameral system. Such an arrangement gives each member of academic staff the right to participate in the taking of decisions or to be part of the advisory committees. These advisory committees may be coopted into the legally constituted organs of internal governance. The exact ratios between different sub-constituencies – between say, full professors, mid level or junior academic staff, administrators, technicians and employees and the part reserved for management, president, vice-chancellor, rector and rectorate staff – is subject to wide variation across different countries irrespective of whether their internal governance is collegial or managerial in the way it conducts its affairs.

9.7 The 'double innocence' of bicameral structures

University governance involves structures that are both hierarchical and complex. Complex too is the composition of the collective interests represented by them. Given the multiple constituencies in its boards and senates – staff, students administrators and outside personalities, they are very often places where tension dwells. The bicameral arrangement of board and senate suffers from a further disadvantage. It is often by no means easy to move rapidly or to reach decisions expeditiously. Commenting on this obstacle, Claude Bissell, one-time president of the University of Toronto, called it a 'system of double innocence': "The lay members (outside personalities) of the Board are innocent of academic problems and are proud of their innocence... For their part, the academics gracefully retreat whenever an issue reaches a point where it requires expression in financial terms." (Bissell, 1974).

His solution lay in replacing the board and senate by a unicameral system constructed around a unified governing council, chaired by the rector (president) with the participation ex officio of vice-rectors and deans. It has proven an attractive scheme. Variations on it have been introduced by legal instrument into the internal governance of higher education in Austria, Germany, Hungary and the Baltic States. Others, amongst which Denmark, the Netherlands, Spain and the majority of the central European states, have standardised around the bicameral model. Yet, the bicameral pattern is very far from preserved in aspic. Some countries have injected a new vitality into it by setting up new bodies, creating new committees and reshuffling mandate, responsibilities and legal status.

To take a closer look at the variation in the internal structures of governance, their remits, operational ambit and workings, let us home in on management in the Dutch and German universities.

9.8 Two case studies from western Europe

9.8.1 Governance structures in Dutch universities

Under the Higher Education Act of 1992 (Act No. 59/1992 of the Kingdom of the Netherlands) management in Dutch public universities is divided between an executive board and a university council. A third body, the committee of deans, has an advisory relationship to the executive board, to the university council, to the faculty boards and councils in the area of teaching and research. The remit of the executive board encompasses the regulation and administration of the university as a whole. It is a triumvirate consisting of the rector and two others who are selected from amongst its members by the university council and appointed, suspended or dismissed by royal decree. The executive board is chaired by the university president, also appointed from the university council by royal decree. His remit embraces the areas of finance and personnel.

The rector represents the university in judicial and other matters. He is appointed by royal decree from a list of two or three nominees put forward by the committee of deans, approved by the executive board and by the university council. His responsibilities cover higher education and research.

The remit of the Executive Board includes:

- preparing, promulgating and implementing the proposals of the University Council,
- managing finances and university property,
- signing contracts and carrying out other legal transactions,
- having control over safety, health and other working conditions,
- protecting the confidentiality of personal data files in the university data base.

It is answerable to the university council and to the Minister of Education.

Membership of the university council does not exceed 25-30 persons drawn from academic staff, administrative staff and students, each group having an equal number of places. The council is elected from members of each academic department in proportion to the number of faculties (*Faculteiten*) in the university. The chairman is elected from amongst council members and has the right of participation in executive board meetings in an advisory capacity. The Minister of Education may, in addition, nominate five individuals from outside the university to seats on the university council.

The remit of the university council is to:

- lay down guidelines and appoint committees,
- draw up the biennial higher education and research plan for the university,
- determine the budget including an estimate of the institution's revenue and expenditure,
- start up or close down study programmes,
- draw up the code of conduct regarding teaching in foreign languages,
- set the numbers of students to be enrolled and the study programmes on offer,
- draw up internal regulations in conjunction with the government.

In this version of bicameral governance, power and responsibility in decision-making resides in the executive board. For its part, the university council sets down the formal conditions and procedures in decision-making and acts as an instance of control.

Finally, placed over the executive board is the board of trustees which may be created to further cooperation between the university, industry and the public sector.

9.8.2 Governance structures in German universities

As set out in the 1985 Higher Education Framework Law (*Hochschulrahmengesetz*) governance structures in German universities provide another variation on the bicameral model. Here, the function of executive board falls to the senate, chaired by the university rector or president, according to institutional circumstance. The composition of senate includes vice-rectors (or vice-presidents) the *Kanzler* (treasurer, registrar) and deans of faculty ex officio, in addition to which are full professors, students, members of research staff and administrative personnel. Different *Länder* may modify this pattern. In Lower Saxony, the 1991 Amendment to the Higher Education Act provided for senate membership to include the rector as chairman, seven professors, two members of research staff, two students and four members from other staff categories. The *Kanzler* and heads of departments may participate in an advisory capacity.

The university rector (or president) is elected by the university council (*Konvent*) from within the full professorate and nominated by the senate. He is appointed by the Minister of Education and Science. Head of the rectorate, itself made up of the rector, vice-rectors and *Kanzler*, the rector represents the university officially in its dealings with the world without the gates.

The *Konvent* or university council stands as the second administrative instance to which members are elected on a proportional basis by the subject group (*Fachbereiche*) senates.

The power of decision and the responsibility for it are split between rectorate, senate and *Konvent* with the former acting in a higher executive capacity and invested with prime responsibility especially in the area of finance. The senate, by contrast, is entrusted with:

- discussing issues fundamental to the university's development and curriculum reform,
- approving the allocation proposed by the rector of budgets within the university to faculties, departments, research units, libraries etc.,
- decisions involving the establishment of new fields of study and new degree or diploma courses,
- decisions related to general research and scholarship,
- proposals for changes or amendments to the university's bye-laws, statutes or legal instruments,
- decisions related to the nomination of full professors on proposition by faculties and departments (*Fachbereiche*).

The formal remit of the *Konvent* covers:

- the election of rector and vice-rectors,
- the approval of the university budget brought forward by the rectorate,

- endorsing all changes or amendments to the university's bye-laws, statutes or legal instruments as well as those touching upon the faculties, and departments (*Fachbereiche*).

One of the most significant responsibilities of the university is to draw up procedures that allow management and leadership to take due account of student expectations. Such bodies and procedures fall in with the conditions set out in national legislation for higher education. Keeping in touch with students is, it is felt, one way to keep abreast of social demand and society's expectations.

9.9 Further perspectives on structures of governance

So far, we have focused on the structure, formal remit, composition and inter-relationships between, governance bodies in western Europe. But does this summary portrayal apply elsewhere? What if it does not? And, if it does not apply, what are the outstanding differences?

In the higher education systems of central and eastern Europe, executive management consists of the rector, elected by senate from amongst academic staff with ranks of full professors or associate professors, and an administrative board of full-time professionals acting under the rector's authority. The academic senate, made up of academic staff, administration and students, exercises the democratic rights of advice and oversight which also extends to approving certain stipulated items (see below).

9.9.1 Governance structures and powers in Hungary

The internal governance of Hungarian higher education establishments is set out by the Higher Education Law, approved by the Hungarian parliament on 1st July, 1993 and which came into force on 1st September, 1993. Under the terms of this Law, a higher education institution is defined as a professionally independent legal entity, endowed with self-government and having the exclusive right to dispense higher education and to award degrees and diplomas that attest to their holder's being qualified. Higher education institutions include universities, colleges and vocationally-oriented higher education establishments. According to the terms of the law, universities and colleges are defined as follows:

A university is an establishment of higher education providing at a minimum first degree programmes of at least four years duration as well as specialised post-graduate education in at least two areas of learning in a minimum of two fields of study. It undertakes scholarly research, advanced doctoral level training and confers the PhD degree. It also awards the higher doctorate (Habilitation). The law requires the university to have appropriately qualified staff to carry out the tasks just mentioned and possesses the facilities – buildings, libraries, laboratories and equipment – necessary for teaching, learning and research.

By contrast, a college is defined as an establishment providing at minimum three year first degree courses, and putting on study programmes relevant to the local or regional community. It undertakes applied research provided that the appropriate conditions in terms of personnel and material support, permit.

In Hungary, an institution of higher education has the latitude to decide on all matters that concern it for which the law or other regulations make no legal provision or which do not fall under the area of responsibility of the state, local government or other authorities. In the interest of upholding the freedom of teaching, learning, artistic creativity and research, higher education establishments have the right, within the limits set down by the law, to determine their own internal organisation. The may select academic staff, research personnel and elect their leadership. They may also determine the internal allocation within the institution of the budget the state assigns them. They have the right to determine how financial resources, derived from third party sources are to be used. The institution also decides on curriculum design, introduction and development, on the educational and research programmes to be undertaken and the numbers of students to be accepted. Furthermore, the Law anticipates the right of higher education institutions and their staff to lodge appeal before the Constitutional Court against any action or decision which violates the internal regulations that bear on institutional self-government.

9.9.1.1 Internal self-government

The Law sets out the structure and operational workings of institutional management on the classic principle of unicameralism. A university is headed by a rector, a college by a director general, both of whom area assigned deputies and a head of administration who, as secretary general, is their subordinate.

The institution (faculty) council is the highest organ of self-government. For universities, the rector is its chairman and in the case of colleges, the director general. Heads of faculty (deans) or directors general are ex officio members of the university council. Student representatives shall account for at least one quarter and at most no more than one third of the institution council, with a further one third being made up of senior academic staff (professors and lecturers). In addition, the council includes permanent external and coopted members from other teaching or research institutes.

Members of the university council are elected for three years and their collective responsibility extends to all aspects that involve the management and operation of the establishment, and particularly budget submissions, the assignment of the voted budget, the drawing up of teaching and research courses, determining human resource strategy. Its other tasks include putting forward the names of candidates to academic posts in both colleges and universities, proposing the establishment of new faculties or the creation of other internal bodies. To other committees, councils or boards falls the charge of oversight for institutional and individual performance, the organisation of faculty administration as well as teaching and research organisation and such like activities. These latter bodies may be set up by senior academic staff, lecturers, students and other categories of employees.

9.9.2 Governance structures and powers in Slovakia

In the Slovak Republic, higher education is organised according to the amendment of the Higher Education Law No. 172/1990 of 20 November, 1996. In contrast to the Hungarian legislation, throughout the exposé of the Law, the term university embraces all establishments of a higher education level. Universities are defined as the highest institution of an educational, scientific and/or artistic purpose within the ensemble of scholarly and scientific establishments. They are self-governing and their internal organisation and management are determined in keeping with the law and within the powers laid upon the bodies of academic self-government.

Universities are subdivided into faculties and both university and faculty are legal entities. It is the bicameral principle which shapes the internal governance of higher education in Slovakia.

The university is governed by academic officers amongst whom the rector, vice-rectors, registrar and the president of the academic senate on the one hand and by academic boards on the other. The academic boards consist of the academic senate, the scientific council which is replicated at the faculty level in the form of the faculty senate, composed of the dean, vice-deans, secretary of faculty and the president of the faculty senate. The Higher Education Law requires that the academic officers – rector, vice-rectors, deans and vice-deans – are excluded from membership of the academic senate. Accordingly, the power of decision-making is split between the academic board and the academic senate.

The rector heads the academic board. He is the representative of the university, administers it and acts on its behalf. His is accountable in two directions – to the academic senate and to the Minister of Education. With the approval of the Ministry of Education and the academic senate, the rector sets up centres of research, teaching, information and other sub-units within the university. He nominates on the basis of the *lege artis* habilitation and associate professors. He proposes internal budgetary allocation to the individual faculties. Elected by the academic senate of the university and nominated into post by the president of the Slovak Republic, the rector heads the scientific council of the university.

9.9.2.1 Internal self-government

The academic senate of the university elects the rector from amongst the full professors and associate professors within the same university. In addition, it debates proposals for the setting up of new study areas, for the creation of new programmes of study, teaching and research as well as the development of operational research units, information centres and other facilities of special purpose. The academic senate approves the rector's proposal for the annual internal budgetary round, approves both university and faculty statutes, gives its assent to the rector's proposal for the nomination of vice-rectors and for membership to the scientific council of the university.

Amendments to the Higher Education Law define the legal competence of the Ministry of Education. According to paragraph 15, the Ministry sets down the basic conditions for the development of higher education generally, coordinates the activities of higher education institutions, apportions the annual budget to individual establishments. The Ministry monitors the use to which the budget is put in the light of the official policy of employment, the state's priorities for the development of higher education, national research priorities and science policy profile. A further source of oversight is exercised through the evaluation of the universities by the accreditation committee. The Ministry registers the statutes of universities and faculties, coordinates the activities of those academic bodies within universities that have responsibility for conferring academic degrees, diplomas and titles and approves the criteria set down for the conferment of such degrees.

Under the terms of the Higher Education Law, decisions taken by the representatives of academia, by academic boards, by academic and scientific councils may be contested by recourse to the appeal law which deals with administrative procedures. Following an appeal, the Ministry has the right to veto any decision taken by committees of higher education, boards or councils. The Ministry also has the right to introduce new procedures as a way of settling the issue under dispute.

In Slovakia, a separate student council was provided for under an amendment to the 1990 Higher Education Act. Since the student constituency is represented in academic senate, this latter arrangement appears to be redundant. In addition, and with an advisory capacity *vis à vis* the rector, the administrative board and senate stands the college of deans which brings together faculty heads into the domain of university management.

9.10 Structures of governance and administration at the faculty and departmental level

The predominant pattern of governance at the institution-wide level draws upon a bicameral arrangement. It is here that 'bureaucratic' and 'entrepreneurial' authority exert their influence and have their being. But, as we have insisted throughout this volume, there are other forms of authority which draw their weight and influence from other sources – principally, from within the basic functions of teaching and research. And, as we have also pointed out (see above Chapters 1, pp. 9-13 and 6, pp. 80-85) the roots of this 'academic authority' lie entwined deep in the organisation of the university, below the institutional level – within the faculties and most specially within the departments, *Vakgroepen* or *Fachbereiche*. They, just as their bureaucratic and entrepreneurial counterparts, are elemental in governance even if the current push towards managerialism may have dented their frontiers and, in the name of 'market-driven' rationalisation, have succeeded at the institutional level of decision-making in blunting their edge. The base units and their aggregate forms, the faculties – where they still exist – remain powerful players in academia's version of the Great Game and it is well not to leave them aside.

Not untypical of current governance structures below the level of institute-wide administration is the arrangement found in Dutch universities which splits into the faculty board and the faculty council.

The faculty board is chaired by the dean, elected by board members from amongst the full professors who, together with five further members predominantly from teaching staff, form the membership of this body. By law, the faculty board is empowered to act upon and to administer faculty business. Faculty business encompasses organising and coordinating research and teaching, enforcing the conditions that regulate teaching and examinations. It carries out the decisions of faculty council, and may advise the university executive board on issues arising from teaching and research undertaken within the faculty. It answers to the faculty council.

The faculty council brings together three constituencies of academic staff, administrative and support staff plus students, the places being distributed according to a ratio of 5:3:2 respectively. The dean of faculty chairs the faculty council and its duties include drawing up budget submissions, selecting academic staff, drawing up internal regulations governing the conduct of examinations and the conditions of teaching etc..

Faculty council determines the faculty's internal organisation, takes the initial steps to found or to close departments coming under the faculty. Departments, in their turn, are headed by a full professor who underwrites responsibility for teaching, research and the degree programmes provided by the department. To the head of department falls the development of research projects which are approved by faculty council.

9.11 Governing autonomous universities: the place of intermediary bodies

Lying beyond the myriad bodies – boards, senates, councils, *Konvents*, *Stirets* – which go to make up institutional self-management in higher education, is an untidy gaggle of organisms, agencies, commissions, committees, quasi autonomous non-governmental organisations, conferences, and authorities which, over the years, have swarmed over higher education. They cover a vast and largely uncharted territory which ranges from the most ephemeral to the most respectable, from the scarcely visible to the powerful Research Councils which dictate the fate of research projects and the standing of their proposers. Not all of these entities necessarily have bearing upon governance. Nor are they uniform in respect of their powers or, for that matter, the influence they may have upon 'steering', be it the national system or the institution (Neave, 1992; El Khawas, 1992; Frackmann, 1992).

Often termed 'intermediary bodies' because they stand between the university world and government, these institutions have, in certain systems, played an essential part in maintaining not merely a special type of relationship with government, but also at institutional level, of upholding a specific interpretation – some would argue, the original and the only authentic one – of governance itself (see Chapter 1).

9.11.1 The British model: once a model settlement

A classic example of the way an 'intermediary body' upheld a very precise interpretation of governance is, of course, to be seen in the workings of the now-defunct British University Grants Committee. The UGC served as the main channel for universities in the United Kingdom collectively and directly to negotiate their collective finances with the Treasury as opposed to having their individual budgets negotiated by the Ministry of Education with the Treasury and the former assigning them to the individual establishment. Distribution to each university followed on the bloc grant principle and was undertaken by the UGC itself. Created in 1919 and abolished in 1987 the arrangement built around this agency was widely regarded as quintessential of the British model of university/state relations (Berdahl, 1990) and was followed by India, Australia, New Zealand and Israel.

By acting as a 'buffer' between government and university the state was kept at a distance. Such a 'hands off' relationship was, in retrospect, largely instrumental in preserving intact a collegial model of internal governance which had long since been attenuated in Europe by the process of 'state incorporation', (see Chapter 1, pp. 21-22). In effect, the UGC was a structural instrument to preserve university autonomy against undue external influence – a function which in Europe was ensured by the state itself working through constitutional, administrative or public law.

9.11.2 Intermediary bodies: other arrangements

Other countries possess different forms of 'intermediary bodies'. Some, like the Irish Higher Education Authority, will have the powers of budgetary distribution. Others, like National Rectors' Conferences, will have the powers of persuasion and influence in high places. And others, for example the French National Evaluation Committee, possess a strategic purpose which is to pass on to individual universities that information about their strengths and weaknesses such that they may plan future institutional developments in its light.

It is certain that, as central government seeks to reduce its own profile and, at the same time, maintain a strategic hold and steering capacity – however remote – over national higher education policy, so the part of intermediary bodies as indirect agents of 'steering' is likely to increase. Clear signs of this happening are not difficult to find. But they take a slightly different form from what has usually been associated with intermediary bodies. To an increasing degree, these new agencies are 'bodies of public purpose' – that is, bodies which, whilst formally outside the ambit of the appropriate Ministry, nevertheless fulfil a monitory or evaluatory function in higher education, the results of which are then reported either directly to central authority or indirectly via their public diffusion.

9.11.3 The ambiguity of intermediary bodies

What one may say about intermediary bodies is that their simple presence guarantees neither one way nor the other the degree of institutional autonomy that exists in a particular higher education system, still less whether it will grow or, like the *peau de chagrin*, shrink out of sight. Much depends on who set them up, why they were set up in the first place, how the intentions of government have developed meanwhile and finally, whether government is prepared to respect or abide by, previous settlements. Intermediary bodies may certainly contribute to upholding established forms of governance, as we have seen in the British case – provided that is their avowed function. But those which have acquired the remit of 'agencies of public purpose' can also serve as direct instruments the demands of which without doubt amplify the move towards the 'managerialist' or towards the 'market' models of institutional governance. That said, the crucial element does not lie in 'intermediary bodies' *per se*. It lies in the intent of he who creates them which, in most cases, brings us back to national administration and to system wide authority, in short to government.

9.12 In place of a conclusion – three templates

In this Chapter we have examined the various assumptions, political, philosophic and technical which higher education has faced over the past decade or so, as part of the rise of complex management systems. These systems, techniques and practices have had a most substantial impact on governance. We have examined, too, some of the changes in the role of institutional leadership and in the governance structure of certain higher education systems that have had a referential role in this process. What lessons may we retain from this analysis?

Conclusions ought to be a synthesis of what has been said – hopefully elegant, thought-provoking and practical as well. Given the purpose of this series, it is obvious that if provocation is not wholly to be ruled out, the emphasis ought nevertheless to be on the latter feature in default of the former. Accordingly, rather than end in the expected fashion, we wish to conclude with a species of template that, drawing on this Chapter, serves as a synthesis of functions for three central actors in university governance – the rector, the executive board and the university council-cum-senate.

9.12.1 The Rector

- as chief executive officer holds executive power, is responsible for daily management of the university within the terms set down and provided by law, by university statute and by the decisions of the university council (*Senat, Konvent* etc.),
- is responsible for the preparation of all documents that need the approval of the university council, and for providing information adequate for the university council to take decisions,
- is responsible for the management of human resources (appointment and severance of employment),
- represents the university,
- has a deliberative vote in the university council,
- retains residual power over those matters not falling under the remit of the university council.

9.12.2 The Rectorate or Executive Board

- is made up of no more than 3-6 persons, with an unambiguous remit,
- under the guidance of rector and the university council serves as executive board,

- bearing in mind the responsibilities exercised by the deans of faculty within their respective faculties, acts under the rector's responsibility,
- submits proposals to the university council.

9.12.3 The University Council

- is elected through direct secret ballot by academic staff, non academic staff and students, academic staff being in the majority. Membership of the university council shall not exceed 35,
- elects its chairman from amongst the members of the executive board,
- has in all matters pertaining to the university a general right to give advice,
- enjoys the right to take decisions relating to the following items and may give its approval of:
- internal statutes,
- the institutional budget,
- strategic development planning undertaken by the University,
- new courses and study programmes, their merger or their abolition,
- the creation of new faculties, their merger or their abolition,
- the university's annual report to the Minister,
- the report of management to the Rector.

REFERENCES

Andersson, Johnny (1995) "Managing the Autonomous University", *Higher Education Policy*, vol.8, no.3, pp.18-22.

Berdahl, Robert, (1990) "Academic freedom autonomy and accountability in British Universities", *Studies in Higher Education*, vol.15, no.2.

Bissel, Claude (1974) *Halfway up Parnassus*, Toronto, University of Toronto Press.

Clark, Burton R. (1995) *Places of Inquiry: research and advanced education in modern universities.* Berkeley/Los Angeles/London: University of California Press.

El Khawas, Elaine (1992) "Are buffer organisations doomed to fail? Inevitable dilemmas and tensions", *Higher Education Policy,* vol. 5, no.3, pp.18-20.

Frackmann, Edgar (1992) "The Role of buffer institutions in higher education", *Higher Education Policy,* vol.5. no.2, pp.14-16.

Jarratt Report (1985) *Report of the Steering Committee for Efficiency Studies in Universities.* London: Committee of Vice Chancellors and Principals.

Kogan, Maurice & Kogan, Philip (1983) *The Attack on Higher Education.* London: Kogan Page.

Lane, Jan-Erik (1982) "Das Hochschulwesen in Skandinavien in einer vergleichenden Ubersicht", in L. Hüber (ed) *Europäischen Encyclopädie Erziehungswißenschaft.* Hamburg: Klett-Kotta Verlag.

Neave, Guy (1991) "On the procedures of Elevation: or, how the mantle of Elijah falls upon the shoulders of Elisha", in special issue "Organisation und Management von Universitäten Verhaltnis von Staat und Universität", *Plenum* 1/1991 [Vienna] pp.44-49.

Neave, Guy (1992) "On bodies vile and bodies beautiful: the role of 'buffer' institutions between university and state", *Higher Education Policy,* vol.5, no.3, pp.10-14.

Neave, Guy (1988) "On the cultivation of quality, efficiency and enterprise: an overview of recent trends in higher education in Western Europe 1986-1988", *European Journal of Education,* vol.23. Nos.2-3, 1988, pp.7-23.

Shils, Edward & Daalder, Hans (1981) *Universities, Politicians, Bureaucrats.* Cambridge: Cambridge University Press.

Templeman, Geoffrey (1982) "Britain: a model at risk", *CRE Information, No. 58* 2nd quarter, pp.22-30.

Trow, Martin (1994) "Managerialism and the Academic Profession: the case of England", *Higher Education Policy,* vol.7, no.2, pp.11-18.

Williams, Gareth (1995) "The 'Marketisation' of higher education: reforms and potential reforms in higher education finance", in David Dill & Barbara Sporn (eds) *Emerging Patterns of Social Demand, op. cit.,* pp.170-193.

CONCLUSION

How the university should be governed, by whom and to what ends have been recurring issues across the history of that institution. Each country has reached a different settlement, though sometimes drawing on the inspiration, success or symbolic importance of practices developed elsewhere. It has put in place bodies with variable and varying responsibilities, brought into them the various constituent interests present in the world of higher learning – and sometimes extended participation to interests that lie beyond the groves of academe. Such interests, whether internal to the university or external, have been assigned different degrees of presence and representivity. Such a task is highly delicate, involving as it does nice calculations as to the balance between the general interests of the nation as against the need to uphold those basic conditions under which the academic community can perform the responsibilities society has laid upon it. These responsibilities today, just as they were in the past, revolve around the transmission of knowledge, the certification of ability, the generation of new knowledge, the pursuit of excellence and the continual sustaining of quality in all of them.

In examining the evolution in the systems of governance across different countries and across different times involves, not surprisingly, considerable variety in the models scrutinised. More detailed information on the current status of individual systems of higher education is contained in the case studies which follow this overview. There is, however, a leitmotif within these variations. It has two parts, the first involves the injection into institutional behaviour of those features which are held to go with market forces, competition, efficiency, cost effectiveness, the assumption of responsibility on the one hand and accountability on the other to those who avail themselves of 'the services' – in this case, higher learning – thus provided. The second part turns around a fundamental shift in the way higher education itself is perceived by those responsible for its development.

Higher education is moving – and is doing so with great rapidity – beyond its historic status as a 'public service'. Instead, it is seen to an increasing degree as a "service to the public". This redefinition of mission brings in its train a quite massive series of consequences the end results of which are not easily foreseen. First of these is the ending of the monopoly of state sector higher education in providing both higher learning and research to the nation. Whether the developing 'non-state sector' of higher education stands as complementary to – or as an alternative competitive form of – higher education in parallel to the 'state sector', is a matter that time and the particular circumstances pertaining in a given system, will determine. The second of these key developments involves a similar redefinition in the relationship between central government and higher education. In essence, it involves placing emphasis less upon hierarchical and formal subordination and more weight upon partnership between government, society and higher education. This partnership is itself shaped and informed in part by the market which is an economist's way of operationalising certain dimensions that lawyers and political scientists would conceive in terms of 'the general interest'.

The exact nature of such a partnership turns around a functional separation between the strategic responsibilities of central government and an increasing latitude at institutional level to determine how, given the resources, capacities and potential the individual institution or university has at its disposal, it shall act to meet in detail the general objectives laid upon it. The increasing range of responsibility thrust upon the individual university, upon its leadership, management, academic staff – and the pressure of having to take decisions which carry with them very real consequence for the future well-being of the individual academic community – have, in turn, direct effects on the way such decisions are reached and expedited amongst the various interests and constituencies, internal and external, which go to make up institutional governance. In short, the ability of the individual university to meet, and to show it has met, the expectations of society – and they are far from being either constant or homogeneous – places governance, like Uriah the Hittite, 'at the forefront of the battle'. Put succinctly, whether the 'marketisation' of higher education is to be successful is in large degree dependent on changes in the way the individual university conducts both its 'public' and its 'private' lives, in short, on the adaptation of its internal system of governance. To parody the epigram of the 18th century American philosopher and statesman, Benjamin Franklin, "If governance, democracy and reform do not hang together, they will most assuredly hang separately."

10

COUNTRY REPORTS

10.1

ALBANIA

Ylli Gjançi

1 Introduction

There are eight universities, an Institute of Physical Education and an Academy of Fine Arts in Albania. The most important principles and definitions relating to these institutions' governance derive from the Higher Education Law no. 7810 of 1994. The Law generally provides for academic freedom and institutional autonomy, democratisation and the suppression of ideological influences, and stipulates adoption of the principles of the market economy. This latter aspect is reflected in the right of higher education institutions to earn income from research and other potentially profitable activities. General objectives, as set forth in the Law, are the creation of an accreditation and information system, and of proper academic and administrative structures. The Law envisions a reconstruction of teaching plans and programmes, including post-graduate qualifications of teaching staff. It also introduces admission procedures on the basis of competitive examination. Last but not least, it favours increased university cooperation and representation in international projects. According to Art. 7 of the Higher Education Law, higher education institutions are free to establish and maintain relations with foreign institutions, to exchange experience in science and teaching, to train staff, and to establish and participate in international associations of higher education.

2 Governance

The management of higher education institutions is subject not only to the Law of Higher Education, but also the Law of Science and Technology and to the statutes of the universities. The statutes of Tirana University and Tirana Polytechnic University may be regarded as model statutes. According to the statutes, higher education institutions are governed by the following bodies:

- a rectorate,
- a university senate,
- a deanery,
- a faculty council,
- a departmental council.

These bodies are headed respectively by:

- a rector for universities,
- a director for non-university higher education institutions,
- a dean for faculties,
- a head of department.

The rector represents the higher education institution. The rector is appointed by the Council of Ministers on the basis of nominations by the senate and also serves as a government delegate to the higher education institution. The rector has a three year mandate and is not eligible for re-election after two consecutive terms.

As provided in Art. 18 of Law no. 7810, the rector or director serves as head of the senate. As such, the rector appoints the chancellor from candidates nominated by the senate. The senate also nominates a candidate for deputy-rector, who is appointed by the Minister of Education.

The senate is a superior, collegiate organ which takes decisions on essential issues regarding teaching, scientific research, administration and finance.

Art. 16 of the Higher Education Law provides that the composition, tasks and competencies of the senate, and of the councils, shall be defined in the statutes of the higher education institutions. Accordingly, the senate of the Polytechnic University of Tirana comprises the rector, the vice-rector, the administrative staff of the rectorate, the faculties, the departments, as well as the students. Other entities which may be represented in the senate are the chancellor of the university, the Ministry of Education, the State Committee of Science, and representatives of trade institutions with which the university has established relations.

The faculty is the teaching and scientific unit of the higher education institution covering related academic disciplines. The faculty council is an elected decision-making body which steers faculty interests in the areas of education and scientific research. The faculty council of the Polytechnic University of Tirana is composed of representatives of the faculty staff and the student body. The ratio of staff-student participation in the faculty council is 1 to 5.

The chair of the faculty council is the faculty dean, whose term is 3 years, and who may not be elected for more than 2 consecutive terms. The basic units of faculties are departments, which themselves consist of sections. The members of departments elect department councils. The head of the department, who chairs the department council, is appointed by the dean from a list of candidates proposed by the department council.

All higher education institutions are represented in the National Council of Higher Education, and in the Conference of Rectors. The National Council of Higher Education advises the Ministry of Education on important issues of strategy and policy in higher education. Its competencies are defined by the Council of Ministers. It is composed of prominent personalities from higher education institutions and others in the fields of science, economy, law and the arts. Internal members are the rectors (directors) as well as the representatives elected by the senate. The external members are nominated by the Council of Ministers on the basis of suggestions made by the Ministry of Education.

According to Art. 15 of the Higher Education Law "the regulation of the National Council of Higher Schools is designed and approved by the Council itself, through open voting with no less than 2/3 of the votes". The Minister of Education is the chair of the Council of Higher Education. The Ministry controls the scientific, teaching and financial activities in accordance with the Higher Education Law, the Law of Compiling and Implementing the Budget, and the Work Code.

3 Legal protection

Individuals may lodge complaints with the deanery, the rectorate, the Ministry against decisions taken by higher education institutions. Collective complaints to these bodies are also possible. Students may challenge decisions or actions which are not in harmony with the rights defined by the Law, university statutes or Work Code. These complaints are presented by student unions and trade unions. A chairman presides over these unions.

Not every decision rendered by internal review bodies is subject to further appeal or review before a regular court of law, because many of these actions are discretionary. Other complaints may be submitted to the Council of Ministers or be lodged with a court of law.

10.2

ARMENIA

Avetik Kalantaryan

The constitution of the Republic of Armenia provides that every citizen shall have the right to an education. Elementary and secondary school and vocational education at state educational institutions shall be free. Every citizen shall have the right to obtain free higher education at state educational institutions on the basis of competition.

1 The legal framework: principles and structures

The absence of an educational law has had repercussions on the entire educational system and on higher education in particular. The educational system is currently regulated by the legislative framework laid down by the educational law of the former Soviet Union provided that it is not in contradiction with the new Constitution of the Republic of Armenia as adopted in 1995, or with the educational policy of the government.

Higher education policy, as stipulated in the Educational Policy Report 1994, describes a transition from the former two-level system comprising colleges and higher education institutions to a unified four-level higher education system. The first level of the new system includes junior colleges providing 1-2 years of specialisation leading to a professional diploma. The second level involves two-stage or regional colleges, providing 4-years of basic level higher education leading to a bachelor's degree. The third level covers universities and the master's programmes of higher education institutions and involves 1-2 years of specialisation leading to a master's degree. The fourth level, *aspirantura*, involves 2-3 years of research leading to a doctorate.

Currently, the Armenian higher education system comprises 16 state-run universities and university level institutions with a total enrolment of 35,903 students, as well as 41 private universities and institutes with almost 15,000 students.

The higher education system, as one of Armenia's most valuable human resource bases, has made vigorous efforts to respond and adapt to the emerging market relations, socio-political and economic changes of recent years. This sector is still in the process of systemic reform entailing structural adjustment, the introduction of cost efficiency mechanisms, a move towards western models of higher education, and a consolidation of its base and resources. Reforms continue to optimise the activities, management and structure of the system, revise the curricula, introduce independence for higher education institutions, as well as promote experimental and innovative teaching methodologies and the publication of new textbooks and teaching aids.

The specific tasks and responsibilities of the Ministry of Education and Science are carried out by its affiliated agencies: the Research Institute for Education, the Research Centre for Higher Education Issues, the Institute of Pedagogy (formerly the Teachers' Retraining Institute) which has an education resource library. They are mandated to elaborate the principles of state educational policy and standards, to develop curricula, new syllabi, textbooks, teaching aids and guides, and to set up licensing and accreditation criteria and procedures.

The higher education system is controlled by the Ministry of Education and Science, which operates according to the relevant laws and decisions of executive bodies. The Ministry has mainly organisational, financial, licensing, certification and verification functions. The mandate of the Ministry in executing its numerous functions is very general. Among its basic tasks and objectives are the implementation and control of the unified state educational policy and reform of the structure and content of education. As a result of these two priority principles, the Ministry has the status of a government agency assigned with the executive power needed for the governance of the education institutions irrespective of their type, level, affiliation and form of ownership. The Ministry is also responsible for the elaboration of state policy-related legislative acts, regulations and quality control, and for the provision of appropriate conditions for the successful functioning of education institutions. It must also ensure the intellectual development of students, guaranteeing qualifications at graduation in compliance with international standards.

In order to link higher education to the market economy and to protect it from the negative effects of socio-economic changes during the current transition period, the main task of the administrative organs of education is to secure the proper utilisation of financial, material, and human resources, to improve mechanisms for stimulating work, to provide training in how to introduce innovation and how to manage the new relationship between educational institutions and other sectors of the economy, which will result in additional finances for the educational system from non-governmental extra-budgetary sources.

Since 1985 a great deal of independence has been given to universities and higher educational institutions. They are guaranteed with complete independence in all spheres of intra-university life: choice of internal structures, organisation of the educational process, development of curricula and projects, application of educational technologies and methods, research, financial and other issues. State run universities organise their teaching activities according to model curricula elaborated by the Ministry, however they are free to change up to 15 per cent of the curricula, adapting it to their specific needs. The administrative rules and activities of each higher education institution are defined in their bye-laws, which require approval from the Ministry of Education and Science. At present, it is within the power of higher education institutions to elect their scientific council (academic senate), the supreme collegiate body of the institution. They also act independently in their decision to open/close faculties and chairs, and to introduce education-related fees and to set the amount of tuition fees.

2 Democracy

The principles of governance of higher education institutions are constituted in bye-laws. The higher education institution governing bodies are: university administration, scientific council (academic senate), faculty (department) council, dean's office and chairs.

Institutions/universities are governed by a rector, who acts under the authority of the university administration. The rector is responsible for overall management of the institution and is accountable to the Ministry of Education and Science.

The scientific council (academic senate) is the supreme collective body of the institution. It is a representative and decision-making body of all those enrolled and employed by the university.

Faculty (department) council and the dean's office are responsible for the operational/educational activities within faculties.

Chairs represent the first operational level functioning within faculties. They have methodological and discipline-oriented responsibilities and are accountable to the faculty council and the dean's office.

The academic and non-academic staff and students take part in the internal governance of institutions through their representatives on the scientific council (academic senate) and the faculty council. In addition, there are trade union committees and students' councils, which co-ordinate their activities with the university administration.

The rector is appointed by the Ministry of Education and Science with prior co-ordination with the government. He presents the candidatures of vice-rectors to the Ministry board, whose positive decision is decreed by the rector. Deans and heads of chairs are elected by scientific councils (academic senate), whereas professors and instructors are elected by faculty councils on the results of a preceding competition for vacant posts. They sign employment contracts with rectors.

3 External influence

The government, Ministry of Education and Science, university boards of trustees (if any), agencies and organisations interested in training specialists for their specific needs, are external stakeholders which formally take part in the decision making, advising and control of the higher education institutions.

The government can supervise universities through the Ministry, provided that the Ministry undertakes its exercises of quality control, licensing and accreditation.

Boards of trustees and other concerned organisations are advisory bodies able to influence universities through their proposals.

4 Hidden or indirect governance

No cases of hidden influence have so far been detected in the country.

5 Legal protection

In the absence of a comprehensive educational law, legal issues within the sector are regulated by government decrees, regulations and decisions issued by the Ministry, and the bye-laws of the higher education institutions. All universities/higher education institutions have the right to appeal decisions and actions by the Ministry or government in a court of law.

University bye-laws constitute definite regulations for the resolution of internal problems for students and professors/instructors, however the higher education institutions have no internal avenues of appeal. All complaints are subject to appeal in a court of law.

6 Conclusion

After the collapse of the Soviet Union significant and positive socio-political transformations have been introduced into the education sector. The role of the Ministry, as the most powerful central governing body of the sector, has changed too. Universities have acquired self-governance and independence from the Ministry of Education and Science.

These processes need and will be supported by a comprehensive national educational law. However, economic and financial difficulties peculiar to the period of transition to a pluralistic society are delaying the law-making process in this sector. The problem of higher education institutional governance is extremely important for Armenia, and the government, in its dialogue with the World Bank, OECD, Council of Europe, UNESCO and other international partners and has addressed this issue as a priority measure for the overall improvement of the quality and trustworthiness of the country's higher education system. The development of higher education is likely to be a lengthy process requiring collaborative efforts at national and international levels, extensive fiscal investments and highly qualified human resources.

10.3

AUSTRIA

Gerald Bast

1 Introduction

According to Article 2 of the University Organisation Act (UOG) of 1993, universities are federal institutions. They are set up and dissolved by federal law. Within the legal framework the governing bodies, the universities have the right to carry out their duties free from external orders. Article 8 of the UOG 1993 specifies that the universities are subject to legal supervision by the Federal Minister of Science, Research and the Arts.

Constitutional principles include the freedom of science and teaching, as well as the competency of the national parliament for legislation in the field. The principle of autonomy of the universities is considered part of the freedom of science and teaching.

2 Governance

As the numbers of students and teaching staff at Austrian universities have more than tripled since 1970, planning and decision-making processes have become very complex. The centralised system of university administration is no longer suitably equipped to accommodate these processes.

The UOG of 1993 incorporates the concept of deregulation and decentralisation in the Austrian university system:

- the legal framework does not provide details any more,

- detailed regulations about the internal structure of the university and the working procedures of the various governing bodies at the university are part of the statutes of the university senate,
- decisions formerly made by the Ministry have now been given to the university, e.g. internal allocation of budget and personnel, recruitment of personnel including professors,etc..

The main governing bodies at the university are the:

- senate: determines the budget estimate, all strategic decisions, and supervises the rector,
- rector: head of the university, allocates the budget and personnel between the faculties, and coordinates the deans and deans of studies,
- dean of studies: determines most decisions regarding the organisation of teaching, exams and teaching assessment,
- council of studies: determines the contents of the study programmes as laid down in the legal framework,
- dean: allocates money and personnel within a faculty,
- faculty council: determines the budget estimate of a faculty, supervises the dean,
- head of institute: makes all the important decisions regarding the institute under the supervision of the institute conference.

3 Democracy

The law makes a distinction between "monocratic" and "collegial" governing bodies for each of the organisational levels, e.g. the university, the faculty, or the institute. The monocratic governing bodies, e.g. the rector, dean, dean of studies, or head of an institute, are individuals elected by a collegial governing body. The collegial governing bodies, e.g. the senate, the faculty council, the council of studies, and the institute conference, are composed of representatives of tenured professors, assistant teaching staff, students and of non-academic staff.

The rector is elected by the university assembly from one of three candidates proposed by the senate. The rector's foremost tasks consist of negotiating the budget with the Federal Ministry of Science, Research and the Arts. The rector's other duties include allocating financial and other resources to the faculties, submitting proposals to the university assembly regarding the election of vice-rectors and deans, selecting candidates for tenured positions, and appointing the heads of administrative departments.

The rector is formally responsible to the university senate which determines the policy guidelines. Accordingly, the university senate may cancel the rector's decisions if they are not in consonance with the guidelines.

The dean of a faculty is elected by the faculty council from one of three candidates proposed by the rector. The dean prepares the annual faculty budget and sets up faculty commissions which confirm university lectureships. Together with the rector, the dean conducts negotiations regarding tenured positions. The dean is formally responsible to the faculty council, just as the rector is responsible to the senate.

Participation of all members of the university is intended to assure democratic transparency. Professors, junior teaching staff, students and non-academic staff co-operate in the different committees and take decisions by carrying motions with a majority. The proportion between professors, junior teaching staff and students in the committees usually is 2:3:3; without respect to this proportion one or two representatives of the non-academic staff have membership in the commissions. In the council of studies and in the institute conference the membership proportion between professors, junior teaching staff and students is 1:1:1. The community is represented on an advisory board. Each university has its own advisory board which gives its expert opinions on matters such as long-term budget requirements, evaluation and internal distribution of resources. The advisory board includes representatives from central or local government, as well as from industry. These external members give advice to the university on various issues. The advisory board meets at least twice a year. The members of this board also evaluate applications for the post of rector and act as a link between the university, the business sector and society at large.

The representatives of the collegial organs are elected by their respective groups with the exception of the students. They do not carry out elections for representation on the different committees, the student representatives are appointed by the students union.

4 External influence and hidden governance

In principle, the governing bodies of the universities, and the university as such, have the right to take all decisions free from external influences, ministerial or otherwise. Decisions in some key areas, however, e.g. university statute, the creation and dissolution of university institutes, the designation of scientific subjects for professors' posts have to be approved by the Federal Ministry of Science, Research and the Arts. Approval of a rector's decision can be refused and even cancelled by the Ministry but only on certain grounds, these are:

- illegality of the decision,
- lack of financial resources or,
- the decision hinders the university from performing its functions, e.g. a rector's decision to withdraw all resources from a faculty or institute which are necessary for it to carry out the study programmes it has to provide by law.

The Ministry refuses the approval of a decision or cancels a decision of the university by formal administrative act as a decree. Administrative law determines the procedure and in which form the decree has to be issued. The university has the right to appeal against the Ministry's act to the Supreme Administrative Court.

Financial control of the universities is maintained by the Austrian "Rechnungshof", an institution established under constitutional law; of which there is no comparable institution in other countries. Financial regulation, especially over the allocation of funds and posts, may be identified as an instrument of hidden governance. The large majority of university expenditures have to be accepted by the Ministry, and they are usually, at least in the short term, of a non-variable type, e.g. concerning personnel and maintenance. Each university has to elaborate plans about the development of teaching and research at its institution and provide a calculation about the resources the university requires to carry out these plans. These are known as long term calculation requirements.

5 Legal protection

In general, there are several internal avenues of appeal against administrative acts and decisions. They end at the levels of the academic senate, the faculty council and the council of studies. The Federal Minister of Science, Research and the Arts exercises legal supervision. All autonomous organs of the university, as well as the students' board have the right to appeal to the Supreme Administrative Court concerning decisions affecting them. Personnel issues are resolved internally by the rector, with advice from the Ministry if necessary.

6 Conclusion

The Austrian university system has undertaken a significant move towards deregulation and decentralisation after the new UOG 1993 was passed in parliament. Austrian universities are state institutions with about 97% of the universities' revenues coming from the state budget and all professors are civil servants. Despite close legal and financial connections to the state, it is the decision-making bodies at the university which allocate and decide on the internal allocation of the budget and personnel and the recruitment of personnel. The Minister can cancel decisions of the university or refuse its approval only on the grounds of illegality, lack of financial resources or serious organisational deficits. The governing bodies of the university can appeal to the Supreme Administrative Court against the Minister's decision to cancel or refuse approval.

10.4

BELARUS

Boris Kopyssky & Nikolai Listopad

1 Governance

Article 26 in the Education in the Republic of Belarus Act addresses state and public governance of the education system. The provision reads as follows:

Leadership of the education system in the Republic of Belarus has state and public characteristics. The Council of Ministers of the Republic of Belarus carries out the following functions in the domain of education:

- establishes state requirements for education, and ways of ensuring their fulfilment,
- acknowledges approximate provisions for educational establishments and organisations, establishes the order of their formation, reorganisation and abolishment, and the order of charter registration in educational bodies,
- gives approval for samples of educational documents and for their publication,
- establishes the financing, material and technical security and accounts of educational establishments and educational organisations; the payment of their personnel, standards and social security of pupils, students, others under training and for the educational system officials.

1.1 The Ministry of Education:

- carries out state policy and establishes state control in the domain of education,
- gives its approval for standard academic plans and requirements for general educational and professional training.

Article 27 of the Act provides the following regulation concerning, *inter alia*, the management of higher education institutions.

Management of educational institutions is carried out according to their statutes on the basis of participation by teachers, pupils, students, employees, parents and public representatives. The institutions take independent decisions concerning educational process organisation, financial and economic questions and other types of activity while preserving state interests and requirements for education and guaranteeing the rights of pupils, students, teachers and other employees according to the legislation.

State organs can interfere with the activity of educational institutions only when the activity contradicts the Constitution of the Republic of Belarus, the legislation in force, the principles of state policy in the sphere of education or the institution's statutes. Persons who carry out the management of educational bodies and institutions in an official capacity respect the relevant legal requirements and are not influenced by political parties and other organisations that have a political scope.

2 The organisational structure of higher education institutions

Ultimate responsibility for the activities of a higher education institution falls on the rector, who is appointed by the Ministry of Education and Science.

The higher education institution's council consists of members elected by the academic staff. The council is involved in decision-making regarding teaching, research, the selection of staff and financing. It performs its functions as a consultative body to the rector.

Faculties are teaching units training specialists in the various professions. A faculty is headed by a dean who is elected by the institution's council, and who is responsible for the faculty's activities. The dean is assisted by a faculty council which serves as a consultative body and is elected by the academic staff of each faculty.

The basic units of the faculty are chairs which conduct teaching and research in specific academic domains. The heads of chairs are elected by the faculty council for a term of 5 years. They are responsible for chair activities to the faculty dean.

3 Principles of governance

The foremost principle relating to the governance of the higher education institutions is the maintenance of a public funding and control system while assuring autonomous decision-making by public self-governing bodies. Accordingly, the state regulates the administrative activities, the curricula and teaching programmes, and defines the contents of education. The institutions adapt and implement these directives taking into account student enrolments, their interests and the availability of staff. The performance of higher education institutions' graduates is evaluated by state commissions.

The legal framework provides for discretionary decisions in education policy by the President and the Premier of the Republic of Belarus. These are used in solving strategic problems and developing the relevant tactics for the Ministry of Education and Science, in daily administration, the management of teaching and research, in dealing with the rector and the institution's council, as well as for heads of other structural units that come under their powers. Changes in the governance of higher education institutions resulted with changes in the home policy of the former Soviet Union from 1985, and in 1991 with the declaration of independence of the Republic of Belarus.

3.1 Changes during 1985 – 1990 involved:

- a relaxation of state controls over higher education institution activities and a corresponding broadening of the institution's autonomy,

- since 1991, an enhanced role for public self-governing bodies in the management of teaching and research within higher education institutions,
- a conferral of additional competencies relating to teaching contents and forms of teaching to the public self-governing bodies,
- the appearance and development of a non-state sector of education.

4 Participation

Decisions taken by higher education institutions' councils are subject to approval by rectors, and enter into force thereafter. The decisions of faculty councils are only valid after approval by deans. Chair decisions are taken by simple majority vote. Rectors and deans are chairmen of their corresponding councils.

All academic staff at higher education institutions participate by secret ballot in the nomination of candidates for election to faculty councils and the higher education institution. Representatives of the non-academic staff and the students may be nominated, depending on the representation quotas set by the institution. In addition, student groups select senior members of study groups who represent the students' interests in their relations with faculty authorities and the higher education institutions' governing bodies. Public self-governing committees have been established at student residences to assist students in their extra curricular life.

State higher education institutions are directly subordinate to the Ministry of Education or to another specialised ministry (Ministry of Agriculture, Ministry of Communications, Ministry of Culture, Ministry of Public Health, Ministry of Sport and Tourism). Non-state higher education institutions are consolidated into associations. They are served the Ministry's directive documents via their associations.

The state defines the main requirements concerning the enrolment of young people in higher education institutions. Higher education institutions are obliged to meet these requirements. The state also defines the numbers for enrolment.

State inspection attached to the Ministry of Education and Science monitors the comprehensiveness and precision of execution of normative documents. As the Ministry of Education and Science does not financially support the non-state education sector, it does not monitor this sector. However, the state taxation inspection's terms of reference cover the control of regular and proper payment of taxes by non-state higher education institutions.

Teaching staff and students may appeal against decisions of their administration to the Ministry of Education and Science. If the conflict cannot be settled by the Ministry then they may appeal to a court of justice.

5 Conclusion

The Ministry of Education and Science has completed the drafting of the "Vocational Education in the Republic of Belarus" Act. The keystone of its concept is to increase the autonomy of higher education institutions, and to implement standards derived from the European experience. The Act will pursue a policy of narrowing the sphere of state control over administrative and economic activities of higher education institutions, and, furthermore, it will introduce a system of assessment and accreditation for all higher education institutions, regardless of the form of property.

10.5

THE FLEMISH COMMUNITY OF BELGIUM

Marie-Anne Persoons

1 The legal framework: principles and structures

The legislative reform of higher education in the Flemish Community can only be explained in relation to the recent creation of a federal state in Belgium, with autonomous regions and communities.

Under this new arrangement all decision-making for cultural and social affairs, including education, now directly belongs with the Communities' competence.

The legislative reform of higher education in the Flemish Community was initiated in 1989 and was aimed at establishing new legislation. In 1991 the decree for the university sector was voted. Three years later, in 1994, the decree for non-university higher education institutions followed, based on the same principles as the university decree, while consecrating the historically grown dual structure of Flemish higher education and maintaining the difference between universities and non-university higher education institutions, the socalled "hogescholen".

1.1 The new regulations incorporate a number of basic principles:

- greater administrative autonomy for the former national state or Flemish Community institutions,

- increased scope for individual policy-making on the part of the higher education institutions, – adequate specification of the task and identity of university and non-university higher education,
- renewed educational organisation and improved ordering of education supply,
- the safeguarding of the basic rights of students,
- a draft framework for a flexible policy towards personnel and employment conditions at universities and non-university higher education institutions,
- promotion of the internationalisation of higher education and scientific research,
- development of an adequate quality assurance system. The Research Council was confirmed as a quality assurance instrument for scientific research,
- development of an adequate funding model for higher education.

In fact, both decrees balance between two major poles: autonomy and delegation of the decisive power to the institutions themselves on the one hand, and rationalisation and reinforcement of the competitive position of the Flemish higher education on the other. The principle of autonomy is stated in several measures in the new legislation in order to reduce governmental regulation concerning financial and personnel matters.

The universities already had a tradition of broad autonomy before the legislative reforms, particularly concerning their academic programmes. They still enjoy relative freedom, but now find they are held to their mission and their mandate as laid down in the decree.

For the non-university higher education institutions the introduction of autonomy and deregulation entailed more dramatic changes in comparison with the former situation. The whole sector experienced scaling down, the number of "hogescholen" in the Flemish Community was reduced from 163 to 29 in 1995. Also the non-university higher education institutions were made liable to a system of financing where by each institution has its own budget with which to develop adapted policies on personnel, equipment, infrastructure, etc..

The principle of rationalisation, especially by means of cooperation between institutions, within their own sector or between the university and non-university sector, plays the same dominant part for universities as well as for non-university higher education institutions. This prevents uncontrolled programme supply and its undesired financial effects.

Instruments to achieve these goals of rationalisation and programme supply are provided by law. In addition to this legal framework there is a system of scrutiny with a special commissioner appointed by the Flemish government for each higher education institution. The task of the commissioners consists of approving the hogescholen and universities' annual accounts and reports, and to ascertain whether policy is being pursued in accordance with the law. They are not required to form an opinion on whether or not this policy is appropriate. The legitimacy of financial transactions at the universities is monitored by an inspector of finances, who also assists the Flemish commissioners.

2 Democracy

Generally, the new legislation on institutional governance focuses attention on the concepts of representativeness of the governing bodies, including the participation of the students, in decision-making process, and on the openness of the administration as a whole.

Furthermore, the system of institutional governance in the Flemish institutions reflects the pluriformity of the teaching field as a whole, which is closely linked to historically grown interpretations in Flanders of the concept of "freedom of education".

It is a tradition in Belgium that a distinction is made between socalled "neutral" schools, pertaining to public law, and "free" schools (not to be confused with private schools), pertaining to private law. Federalisation and the new legislation on higher education did not alter this dual structure. Although both networks are liable to the same regulations in many aspects and enjoy the same system of financing by the government, there can be slight differences in the institution's governing structure.

The following description concentrates on universities formerly organised by the Flemish Community itself. The special decree of 31 May, 1991 on the University of Ghent (Universiteit Gent) and the University Centre of Antwerp (Universitair Centrum Antwerpen) is used as a model.

The description of the governance of the Flemish Autonomous "Hogescholen", the descendants of the former ARGO (Autonomous Council of Flemish Community Education) higher education institutions, refers to the rules laid down in the decree of 13 July, 1994 on the non-university higher education institutions of the Flemish Community, called "Hogeschool" decree hereafter.

2.1 Universities: the special decree

The crucial element in the concept of this decree is the idea of autonomy. Like in the stipulations of the (general) "decree of 12 June, 1991 concerning the universities of the Flemish Community" a university is considered as an autonomous legal person. The authority of organising academic programmes is transferred from the Flemish Community to the university itself.

The governing bodies of the university are the rector, the vice-rector, the governing board (*bestuurscollege*) and the university executive board (*raad van bestuur*), the faculty boards and the boards of faculty equivalent bodies.

Out of these, the university governing board is the highest governing body, nevertheless it must still report to the university executive board.

The governance of the university is mainly executed by members of the academic staff as a task in addition to their teaching and research activities.

Apart from the academic staff, there are non-academic staff, students and some representatives from groups outside the university which participate in the university's governance. All groups are appointed by election, apart from the last mentioned category. There are no professional managers that fully participate in the decision-making process of the university's governing bodies. The university administrators who are not academic staff merely attend the meetings of the university executive board, and have an advisory function only.

The rector has the general direction of the university. He is the chairman of both the governing board and of the university executive board. The vice-rector assists the rector in the fullfilment of his tasks and can replace the rector in case of absence. He acts as the vice-chairman of the governing board, which can assign him additional tasks, if necessary.

The university executive board consists of 33 members, of which the academic staff is the most important group the non-academic staff, the students and members from lobbies outside the university are also represented. Except for the last category, all members are appointed by election. The boards competencies remain open to further extension by decree. The 1991 legislative reforms have given the board clearer legitimising, controlling and representative functions. Specifically these include:

- legitimation: determining the general administrative regulations, examination and teaching rules, the main outlines of the organisation and co-ordination of teaching and research; drafting of a policy plan, a budget and the main outlines of personnel policy,

- control: approbation of the budget, the annual accounts and annual report of the university, determining the personnel policy, the nomination of members of independent academic staff and first rank non-academic staff, the formulation of the discipline regulations of the executive board itself,

- representativeness: involvement of representatives from all levels of the university or hogeschool community and from social organisations.

The competence of the university governing board consists in the approval of decisions of the executive board, the disposition of the finances and the goods of the university within the limits of the budget, the budget policy and financing plan established by the executive board; executing contracts and other legal transactions; the maintenance of the academic discipline and where necessary taking measures according to disciplinary regulations; the determination and declaration of vacancies; the nomination of the auxiliary academic staff and the lower non-academic staff; and the formulation of the discipline regulations of the governing board itself.

Each faculty has a faculty board of which the dean of the faculty is the chairman. The decisions of the faculty board are reported to the university governing board.

Other universities, to which the special decree does not apply, may have a somewhat different organisation, but the basic principles of participation in the university's governance by the different groups within the university community and of representatives of lobbies outside the institution, remain the same.

2.2 The "Vlaamse Autonome Hogescholen" (autonomous non-university higher education institutions)

There is much similarity between the governance structure of the autonomous non-university institutions of higher education and the universities under the special decree. The governing bodies of an autonomous hogeschool are the general director, the governing board, the executive board and the departmental boards.

There is a clear analogy between the competence of the autonomous hogeschool governing board and executive board with that of the universities under the special decree. The general administration is the task of the general director.

All Flemish non-university higher education institutions are divided into departments similar to university faculties.

Each department has a departmental board chaired by the department dean (*departementshoofd*). In contrast to the faculty boards the departmental boards also have representatives from groups external to the hogeschool.

3 Indirect actors on the institutional governance

Three official organisations have to be mentioned as important actors on policy making concerning higher education, and influencing as a consequence the regulations on institutional governance.

VLIR (the Flemish interuniversity council) is an umbrella organisation for the Flemish universities and functions as a debating and policy-making forum. It gathers information on all aspects of university operation enabling it to provide policy advice on university matters to the Flemish parliament and lobby policymakers on behalf of the universities. A similar organisation has recently been set up for the hogescholen, the VLHORA (the Flemish higher education council).

VLOR (the Flemish education council) was set up in 1990. Policymakers must consult VLOR before taking decisions on issues other than budgetary matters. It is also empowered to take the initiative in advising policymakers. It can sponsor documentation and surveys to support its advice and it provides a forum in which representatives of organising authorities, teachers' unions, parents' associations, socioeconomic associations and the Ministry of the Flemish Community and can deliberate on teaching matters with specialists in the field. Problems of a general educational nature are the preserve of the general council which has autonomous status. There are councils on four levels beside the general council, for higher, adult, primary and secondary education. VLOR has a staff of experts who prepare the work of the general council and its committees. This independent body facilitates democratic discussion between all the participants in the teaching process.

DVO (the education development service) is intended to provide the inspectorate with the tools it needs to carry out its work. The service also has to formulate proposals concerning the "final goals" of the teaching programmes for all educational levels apart from the universities. DVO has other tasks in addition to defining these goals, including the development of the professional profiles the study programmes are supposed to aim for. The service also provides specialists for screening onecycle basic courses at non-university higher education institutions.

Due to the fact that in the governing bodies of the institutions themselves, as well as in VLIR, VLHORA, VLOR and DVO, experts and other representatives from socioeconomic cultural, political and philosophical associations may participate, it can be stated that indirectly these lobbies do have some effect on the institutions' governance. However, this influence is bound by the limits of the basic principles of general policymaking on higher education in Flanders which aims at the guarantee of academic freedom in teaching and research.

This restriction also applies to the possibilities offered to the institutions to set up spinoff activities and engaging in joint ventures with industrial companies.

It is obvious that the relative degree of influential power from certain lobbies may differ slightly from institution to institution.

4 Legal protection

Although the decision-making of the institution's governing bodies is ruled by democratic principles, there may be situations in which conflicts arise with students, personnel or third persons outside the institutions. Usually, these will go as far as a court trial, only after the attempts at reconciliation by an appointed ombudsperson, union or professional organisation have failed.

In cases of conflicts with institutions pertaining to private law, the usual civil law procedures are followed. If the institution pertains to public law the judgment is at the competence of the Council of State. There have been cases in which staff of private law institutions establish legal proceedings directly to the Council of State, instead of waiting for the decision of the civil court first.

In the case of conflicts between the national (federal) constitution (in particular those articles on nondiscrimination and freedom of education) and Community legislation or between the legislations of different Communities, the competence for judging is at the Arbitration Court, who can even advise to abolish or change a particular law or legislation in order to solve the contradiction.

Due to the recent date of the legislative reform of higher education in Flanders, it is too early to determinate what impact the judgment of the Arbitration Court will have on eventual changes in the legislation. It is noticeable that there is growing tendency of appeal to the Council of State and the Arbitration Court by students as well as by personnel of higher education institutions.

5 Conclusion

Legislative reform of higher education in the Flemish Community is still an ongoing process. It can be expected that in the near future new refining regulations will appear due to the interaction and communication between government administration and the teaching field, i.e. the institutions of higher education themselves.

The basic principles of institutional autonomy and the guarantee of a competitive position for Flemish higher education in a fast changing international context, will remain the key for further legislation.

Keeping to these basic principles without abandoning the historically grown valuable tradition of multiform and pluralistic education policy will become the main challenge for any future regulation.

The ultimate goal can be no less than the affirmation of the cultural identity of the Flemish Community through its scientific and professional contribution to today's world educational forum which is characterised by ever growing international cooperation.

10.6

BULGARIA

Ivan Atanassov and Ervant Stepanyan

A new Higher Education Act has been in force in Bulgaria since the end of 1995. It replaced the 1958 Law on Higher Education, as well as the Academic Autonomy Act adopted in 1990. The new Higher Education Act set the legislative framework for an overall transformation of the governance of higher schools. Instead of a centralised system, the new management model being developed is in line with the recent democratic changes, and is based on academic autonomy and self-management of the higher schools. The state policy on education is carried out by uniform state requirements. These stipulate minimum standards for quality work in the higher schools, their funding, through the activities of the National Agency for Evaluation and Accreditation which regularly assesses and accredits the work of the higher schools at their request. Academic autonomy combined with the new institution for accreditation are probably the two major changes to the system of management of higher education institutions in the last 10-15 years.

The two most crucial legal provisions on the governance of the higher education system and the higher schools are specified in Articles 4 and 19 of the Higher Education Act:

Article 4 specifies:

No privileges or restrictions shall be allowed in higher education in connection with age, race, nationality, ethnic origin, gender, social background, political convictions or religious denomination, except for the cases expressly stated in the Regulations on the Activities of Higher Schools in accordance with the peculiarities of the training process and the future profession.

Article 19 specifies:

(1) Higher schools shall have academic autonomy. It shall express the intellectual freedom of the academic community and the creative nature of research and education as the highest values.
(2) Academic autonomy shall include academic freedoms, academic self-government and the inviolability of the territory of the higher schools.
(3) Higher schools shall perform their overall activities on the basis of the academic autonomy principle, while observing the laws in this country.

The role of the state in developing higher education and guaranteeing academic autonomy is achieved by the following:

- elaborating the state policy in higher education in partnership with the academic community,
- providing annual subsidies for higher education institutions, as well as tax exemptions and other benefits,
- guaranteeing the quality of the results through state requirements and the activities of the National Agency for Evaluation and Accreditation.

There are public and private higher schools, and depending on the specificity of their activities they divide into universities, specialised higher schools and colleges. Higher school autonomy is expressed in the principle of election of all bodies for a specified mandated term. The main principles of management and distribution of competencies are defined by the Act. Proceeding from this, the higher schools organise themselves independently on the basis of internal regulations, through independently set structures and with independently defined rights and obligations, with their own personnel, and scientific research and education policy carried out on the basis of their own budget.

Under the Higher Education Act the management bodies of the higher schools are the general assembly, the academic council and the rector. There are similar structures with the same major functions at faculty level, the faculty general assembly, the faculty council and the dean. All management bodies of the higher schools have a four-year term of office.

The general assembly is the supreme management body. It is elected from among the academically ranked teaching staff, the managerial personnel, students and *doctorands*, as well as from among the unranked teachers. The general assembly adopts the regulations on the workings of the respective higher school, and elects the academic council and the rector. It convenes several times a year.

The academic council is elected from among the academically ranked and unranked teaching staff, managerial officers and representatives of the students and doctorands, with academically ranked representatives having the largest share of the seats. The academic council determines the education, research and personnel policy of the higher school, sets up the departments, sets up special programmes and approves the plans of study to be used for training. It also adopts the budget, as well as the annual report of the higher school.

The rector elected by the general assembly, who is by right a member of the academic council and its chairman, carries out the operative management of the higher school. His responsibilities are determined by the Higher Education Act, or arise from the decisions of the general assembly and the academic council. In recent years the rector reports on the state and work results of the higher school.

The students council is a body protecting the general interests of the students. It consists of representatives of the students and doctorands who are on the general assembly. The students council is funded out of the higher school budget; the money is used for providing student entertainment, and for cultural, sporting, research, creative, and international activities.

The private higher schools have the above mentioned management bodies as well, but are also able to constitute others provided, as stated in the Higher Education Act, that their establishment does not violate the acknowledged and legally stipulated academic freedoms.

The academic community has the largest representation in the higher school management bodies, e.g. no less than 70% of the membership of the general assembly. The remaining places are distributed between the managerial staff and the students. Membership of the general assembly and the procedure of members election are set out in the Regulations for Work of the Higher Schools. The principle of election for a set term applies to all management bodies and is the major element of academic self-management. The same person cannot be elected to the same executive managerial post for more than two consecutive terms.

The state exercises its functions with respect to the management of higher education through the National Assembly, the Council of Ministers and the Ministry of Education, Science and Technology, these carry out the national policy in higher education. The National Agency for Evaluation and Accreditation is a specialised state body that assesses the quality of training, upgrades the qualification of specialists, and aims to develop science and culture in the higher schools. Accreditation of the different higher schools is carried out in compliance with its evaluations.

The National Assembly makes decisions on the opening, transformation and closing down of higher schools and determines the annual subsidies for the public higher schools.

The Council of Ministers establishes the general guidelines in the national policy on higher education, opens up faculties, branch establishments, colleges and institutes within the higher schools, approves a register of the education and qualification degrees for specialities, sets up uniform state requirements for obtaining professional or specialised degrees, approves the quotas of students for state funded education, as well as the maximum number of students and doctorands who can be trained in any higher school, and specifies the amount of semestrial fees.

The Ministry of Education, Science and Technology co-ordinates the interrelations between the autonomous higher schools and the state administrative bodies, prepares and maintains a state register of specialities, etc.

From 1992 there has been a rectors council, established as a non-commercial partnership. The rectors of all higher schools take part in its sessions. It represents the higher school community in the public arena, and takes part in the planning and development of higher education policy. It has an advisory capacity, yet its decisions exercise a considerable impact on the management of the higher schools.

Application of normative acts in Bulgaria does not presume any covert effects in state administration. The normative act-adopting bodies and the bodies exercising control over the implementation of the normative acts are democratically elected. Indirect influence on the management of the higher schools can be traced to the application of some provisions, for instance, when determining capacity and hence the funding, and indirectly the level of quality. However, such influences do not leave a notable imprint on autonomous management.

The interrelations between the founders and the academic management of some private higher schools, which under existing legislation are regulated by the constituent act, create preconditions for certain indirect influences on management. These interrelations are formed and regulated independently between the interested parties.

Considering the acknowledged autonomy of the higher schools, the Higher Education Act does not permit control on the part of executive authorities such as the Council of Ministers or the Ministry of Education, Science and Technology over the workings of the higher school management bodies; the Act only provides for judiciary control over their action and workings. The procedure of appeal before court is specified in the Administrative Procedure Act.

10.7

CYPRUS

Cristodoulos Cleopas

1 Institutional governance

Post-secondary education in Cyprus of both the university and non-university sector may be divided into two categories:

- state post-secondary education: where according to the provisions of Law No. 144/1989 the government is prohibited from intervening in matters of admissions, curriculum or examination, staff recruitment, staff promotion and general conditions of employment at the university level;
- private post-secondary education.

1.1 The administrative authorities of the University of Cyprus

The administrative matters are legally entrusted to a council whose president and three of its other members are appointed by the President of the Republic. The majority of the council members represent other interest groups (i.e. the permanent academic staff, the senate, the university students) and are elected by the bodies they represent. As decisions are taken by majority vote of the council members, the government cannot exert any decisive direct pressure on the university in matters of academic freedom except indirectly through the budget.

The University of Cyprus is fully state supported. Its budget is prepared by its council but it is submitted to the Council of Ministers for approval. After its approval by the Council of Ministers it is also approved by the

House of Representatives. The Law also states that the university may have other sources of income, such as donations and grants made to it, but these will be accepted only if they are made on such conditions as shall safeguard the independence of the university.

It should also be noted that the president and the members of the university's council cannot be removed from the office except in the same manner as a judge of the Supreme Court.

In academic matters the university enjoys an even greater degree of freedom. Article 22 of the University of Cyprus Law No. 144/1989, provides that the selection and promotion of members of the academic staff are exclusively in the hands of the senate, the council only ratifying the decisions of the senate, or refer back to its decisions concerning the selection and promotion of academic staff where there are strong reasons to believe that the relevant rules and regulations have not been observed.

1.2 University of Cyprus: academic authorities

The supreme academic authority of the university is the senate, which consists of the rector and the vice-rector, the deans of the schools, and three representatives of the teaching staff of each school who are elected by the board of the school.

The chairman of the senate is the rector of the university. The director of administration and finance and the director of the university library take part in senate meetings but without the right to vote.

The rector is elected from amongst the professors of the university at a meeting specially called for that purpose. His/her period of office is four years with the possibility of one re-election.

The vice-rector is also elected at the meeting at which the rector is elected and by the same people who elect the rector. The vice-rector acts as a replacement for the rector when he cannot fulfil his duties.

For each of the university schools a dean and a deputy dean is elected by the members of the departmental boards from among the professors and associate professors. They are elected for a term of three years with the possibility of one re-election.

The board of each school consists of the school's dean and deputy dean, a chairman and two members from each of the school's departments, and two student representatives.

Each department has a board which consists of the professors and associate professors of the department, representatives of the assistant professors and lecturers, their number being specified by law and two student representatives.

This organisational structure safeguards the university's independence and academic freedom. The decisions of both the administrative and the academic authorities of the University of Cyprus are subject to judicial and parliamentary control before the Supreme Court and the House of Representatives respectively.

2 State post-secondary education in the non-university sector

There are currently operating in Cyprus a number of public post-secondary institutions which offer courses of sub-degree level in various fields of study. The exception is one institution which offers only post-graduate qualifications for those people already employed in the civil service who want to gain higher qualifications as a part of in service training and for promotional purposes. These institutions are state supported, state controlled and serve the needs of the public sector in providing skilled man-power.

These institutions are annexed to several Ministries (Labour and Social Insurance, Agriculture, Health) and they are governed by means of internal regulations drawn up by the relevant Ministry and approved by the Council of Ministers of the Republic.

Their study programmes, the selection and promotion of their staff and other aspects of their operation are state-controlled, although they do have governing boards which advise the relevant Ministries in matters related to their administration and development.

3 Private post-secondary education in the non-university sector

A number of private post-secondary education institutions operate in Cyprus offering 1-4 year courses in various fields of study, e.g. secretarial studies, business administration, hotel and catering, banking, accountancy and computer studies.

The degrees awarded by the institutions in this sector are not recognised as yet. The process of accreditation of these institutions is in progress at present and it is hoped that by the end of 1997 some of them will have been successfully accredited.

These institutions are privately owned profit-making organisations. Their owner may be an individual or a company in which case the share holders of the company are usually members of the same family. Their establishment, operation and control is governed by the provisions of Law No. 67(I)/96 according to which no private school may be established and operate in the Republic unless in accordance with its provisions.

The decisions of the administration of these institutions is not subject to judicial or parliamentary control. The procedures followed for the selection and promotion of their academic and administrative staff are set by each institution with no uniform pattern being followed by the institutions in this sector.

10.8

DENMARK

Ulrik Jørgensen & Jane Planck

1 The legal framework: principles and structures

One of the most important principles in the University Act 1993 concerning governance is the combination of democracy and leadership. At all levels there are elected collegiate bodies and elected leaders. The leader, at all levels, is also the chairman of the relevant collegiate body. The collegiate bodies have their specific area of competency and responsibility described in the University Act. The rector is, according to the Act, the supreme head of the institution, with the heads at lower levels being the deans, heads of departments and directors of study. Their specific areas of competency are defined by a letter of delegation from the rector. Elected leaders' competencies are only limited in areas where the collegiate bodies approve of certain basic decisions, such as the budget and the field of activities.

The management and collegiate body structure is normally a column 4 levels deep. If an institution wants to be divided into several main study areas then a faculty council is elected for each area. All collegiate body levels provide the framework for the head's daily management of the institution concerning academic and economic activities.

As a consequence of the principle of university autonomy, the legal framework also provides for discretionary decisions in the daily administration of academic activities and strategic policy. The most important areas where the universities' autonomy is limited by the Ministry of Education are:

- in the area of study programmes,
- over the levels of education,
- the admission to study programmes,
- the budget.

The University Act and certain ministerial orders leave it up to the institutions to make professional discretionary decisions, for instance, in the choice of research themes and methods, on the appointment of academic staff, on awarding PhD and doctoral degrees and on admitting the best students amongst the qualified applicants, if there are more applicants than study places. The individual teacher/researcher has a certain freedom in choosing methods both in teaching and researching, but both of these areas are subordinated to the frame of activity decided upon by the elected leaders and the collegiate bodies.

One of the most important changes in the governance of the universities is the introduction of the decisive power of elected leaders, which in most matters has turned the collegiate bodies into advisory bodies with a few overall powers. This change was introduced to create a more efficient decision-making structure and to legitimate a wider autonomy for the universities than had been the case previously.

2 Democracy

Collegiate bodies comprise of 4 management levels, i.e. a senate, faculty councils, departmental committees and study committees. Their competencies are as follows:

The senate approves the university budget and lays down the overall guidelines and long-term strategy for the institution. Similarly, the faculty council approves, within the framework laid down by the senate, its budget and lays down the overall guidelines for its activities. Finally, the departmental committee approves, within the framework laid down by the faculty council, the budget of the department and lays down the guidelines for its activities. The study committee approves of teaching plans, including the assignment of teaching resources and draws up proposals for curricula development.

The collegiate bodies are concerned with more overall issues in relation to education and research policies, but they and the committees have a few specific competencies of their own. A superior/inferior relationship, e.g. by these competent to supervise the work of lower authorities, has not been established between the collegiate bodies. Thus, neither delegation of authority by superior bodies nor recourse to these bodies is available.

All employees and students at the university can exert their influence on the governance of the university through their elected delegates in the collegiate bodies. Students are not formally represented at the departmental level, but may have observer status, while the technical-administrative staff are not represented on study committees. The composition of the senate is 2:2:3 for academics/teachers, technical-administrative staff and students besides the 2 nominated external representatives and the 5 leaders. The composition of the faculty council is 2:1:1 for academics, technical-administrative staff and students and includes 2 nominated external representatives. Study committees have a 1:1 composition of teachers and students, while the departmental committees have a composition close to 2:1 of academics and other staff.

Leaders at all levels of the university including the rector are elected by the academic staff, the technical-administrative staff and the students. The rector and the other leaders come from the permanent academic staff (professors or associated professors). Members of the collegiate bodies are also elected.

The senate consists of a chairman (rector), 2 external members appointed by the Danish Council for Research Policy and by the chairmen of the National Advisory Boards on Higher Education, 5 members representing the management, 2 members representing the academic staff, 2 members representing the technical-administrative staff and 3 members representing the students. The faculty council consists of a chairman (the dean) and up to 14 members, including 2 external members appointed by the relevant National Research Council and by the relevant National Advisory Board on Higher Education, and representatives of the academic staff, technical-administrative staff and students in the proportion of 2:1:1. The departmental committee consists of a chairman (head of department), 2 members of the permanent academic staff and 1 member of the technical-administrative staff.

The study committee consists of an equal number of teachers and students with a maximum of 10 members. The chairman of the study committee is also the study director.

Elections for the collegiate bodies are held within 4 electoral groups, comprising the following categories: academic staff, part-time teachers, technical-administrative staff and students. Within each group everyone is eligible and entitled to vote and can stand for election to the collegiate bodies. Each category elects its own representatives, and the voting is carried out by secret ballot either as letter ballot, or a traditional ballot at a polling station.

3 External influence

No other stakeholders other than those governing the institution (including the external members of the senate and the faculty council) directly take part in the decision-making at the universities. In practise other external bodies influence the activities and decisions of the universities. The Ministry of Education has formed an independent Centre for Quality Assurance and Evaluation of Higher Education. The ensuing evaluations can be used by the Minister of Education to limit an institution's offer of study programmes and to regulate the intake to study programmes if the quality and academic level do not meet the requirements in the ministerial orders. Furthermore, the National Board of External Examiners controls the quality of education.

With regard to the universities' research activities these are financed by the Ministry of Education by a basic grant. The teaching activities are financed by a student/exam-related measuring system. In addition, the universities have the possibility of getting financial means from other sources, primarily for research (external financing). Such grants may come from other ministries, the business enterprise sector, private foundations, and the research councils. The following comments on research council stipulations exemplifies the conditions universities must accept when obtaining external financing.

The research councils act on the basis of strategic plans which identify priority fields of research. These plans have been worked out in a process involving all interested parties in Danish society, and so, are built on consensus. Significant contributions to the plans come from the universities themselves.

When the research councils finance activities of a significant size and duration, a contract between them and the university in question is drawn up, specifying the obligations for each party. Normally, the university guarantees a financial contribution via their basic grant. When relevant, the participating scientists undertake an obligation to cooperate with users in the business enterprise sector and elsewhere with a view to disseminating the research results.

Universities are free to choose whether they want external financing, but in fact external grants often supply up to 50% of research costs in specific fields which means that in practice external financing plays a major role in university research.

To control the legitimacy of the institutions' use of appropriated means parliament has established a National Audit Office.

4 Hidden, or indirect, governance

Even though the institutions are given a lump sum of money for which they theoretically have free disposal of, there are often certain premises set for spending the state grants that influence the decision-making process and deprive the universities of their autonomy.

It is currently under discussion whether there is a hidden influence built into educational and research evaluations and in the availability of research grants derived from strategic planning. There have been criticisms of the way in which the quality criteria for education and research have been decided upon. There is also some reluctance over the use of external referees or evaluators and in the way in which they are appointed, which has often resulted in limiting the influence of the institutions' academic staff.

In practical terms also, industrial interests play an important part in the definition of new areas of research.

5 Legal protection

At the great majority of higher education institutions in Denmark, the students have a formal right to complain about examinations according to the following rules:

The complaint, which may concern the assessment, the basis of the examination or the examination as such, must be submitted to the original examiners who may then either make a new assessment, offer a re-examination or reject the complaint. The examiners' ruling may be brought before a board of appeal which consists of 2 external examiners, one teacher and one student. The board of appeal may raise the mark, decide that a new assessment must be made with new examiners, offer a re-examination with new examiners or reject the complaint. If the board of appeal decides to discuss raising the mark, the student member of the board withdraws from the board during the further treatment of the complaint. If the complainant finds that the ruling made by the examiners or the board of appeal has legal shortcomings, he or she may submit a complaint to the institution. The institution's ruling may be brought before the Ministry of Education.

The rector, as head of the institution, is responsible for all decisions made by heads at lower levels. Thus he has the possibility to alter their decisions, but in cases of complaints he is not obliged to do so as the decisions have been made on his authority. The rector cannot interfere or alter decisions made by the collegiate bodies, but he is responsible for the legitimacy of their decisions.

Complaints about the legitimacy of decisions made by the institution pursuant to the University Act or other rules laid down in pursuance of the Act can be brought before the Minister of Education.

6 Conclusion

The new University Act of 1993 will, in the coming years, form a test site for the possibility of combining democratic principles in university governance involving all employees and students at the university, with a hierarchical structure of leadership. It will also form the basis for the ongoing negotiations about the role of universities and the principles and practices of university governance. As yet it is too early to make any statements on the outcome of these processes.

10.9

ESTONIA

Ain Heinaru

1 Higher education in Estonia is divided into

i applied higher education,
ii diploma programmes (3-4 year study period = 120-160 credit points).

Academic higher education consists of:

i Bachelors degree (4 year study period = 160 credit points),
ii Masters degree (2 year study period = 80 credit points),
iii Doctoral degree (4 year study period = 160 credit points).

There are four types of higher education institutions in Estonia, namely: public universities, e.g. Tallinn Technical University, private universities, e.g. the Estonian Business School, state higher education institutions, e.g. Tartu Teacher Training College, and private higher education institutions, e.g. the International University of Social Science "LEX" or Estonian American Business College amongst others.

2 The legal framework: principles and structures

The basic principles of current higher education policy are as follows:

- institutions of higher education are autonomous,
- that the effectiveness of higher education institutions is increased,

- that higher education institutions become self-regulating and self-developing; accreditation is seen as the most important mechanism for improving the quality of higher education,
- that international co-operation is encouraged,
- that applied higher education is developed,
- that the financing of higher education institutions and the number of students are increased,
- that higher education, research and development financing maintains a certain percentage of the GDP,
- that one of the bases for financing higher education institutions should be financing according to speciality,
- that a clear direction is given for integrating research and higher education,
- that a credit point system and mutual recognition for higher education institutions is introduced,
- that an electronic database network for higher education is developed,
- that clear ties are created between higher education institutions and industry,
- that the concept of the state commissioning certain fields of study is introduced.

The establishment of universities is regulated by the Law on Universities where Article 6, Para. 1 states that the establishment of universities is initiated by the government on proposal by the Minister of Education, and Paragraph 4 states that the establishment of a university is decided by the Riigikogu (parliament) on proposal by the government. Private universities require a teaching license from the Ministry of Education in order to carry out instruction at a higher education level. Statistics on admission, instruction and graduation are kept by the Ministry of Education's Information and Statistics Section. All issues related to universities are resolved by the Research and Universities Department in the Ministry of Education, while for institutions of applied higher education, issues are resolved by the Ministry's Vocational Education Department. All course curricula are required to be registered in the Ministry of Education and these are entered into the curricula register.

Currently, all research in Estonia is administratively regulated by the Ministry of Education, and the research budget, as a part of the state budget, is channelled through this Ministry. The Estonian Research and Development Council, chaired, according to law by the Prime Minister, is the main advisory body to the government concerning research and development issues. The Estonian Science Foundation's main responsibility is to allocate competitive research grants, based on peer review. The Science Foundation operates under the jurisdiction of the Ministry of Education but is virtually independent in its main function. The Estonian Innovation Foundation operates under the jurisdiction of the Ministry of Economic Affairs and its responsibilities lie in issuing competitive grants and loans, mostly for development work and market oriented applied research, as well as to small and medium enterprises and industry in general. The Estonian Informatics Foundation operates under the umbrella of the State Secretary's office and is responsible for distributing state budget resources to finance mainly the development and maintenance of a variety of state registers.

Estonia is currently undertaking reforms in its system of education and research. Higher education institutions are regulated by the Law on Universities, the Law on Private Schools, the Law on the Organisation of Research and the Law on the University of Tartu. Institutions of applied higher education are currently unregulated; a draft Law on Applied Higher Education Institutions is currently being prepared. Amendments have been scheduled for both the Law on the Organisation of Research and the Law on Universities in order to bring them into concordance with other recently adopted laws as well as with the legal acts of the European Union. A Law on the Academy of Sciences is also being drafted. Intellectual property rights are regulated by the Law on Copyright and the Law on Patents.

Centres of excellence is a new concept for Estonia. The first two, the Centre for Strategic Competence in Material Sciences and the Centre for Strategic Competence in Gene Technologies, are currently in their planning phase. They are being organised within the framework of a 3-year national PHARE-sponsored project: Reforming Research and Higher Education in Estonia, and as such are included as pilot projects for the programme. Both these centres are, at present, network structures bringing together the intellectual and hardware capacity of the most competent research labs in these fields at the University of Tartu, Tallinn Technical University and several state research institutions. Their activities are linked to graduate study schemes and intensive international cooperation.

The next two centres of competence currently recommended by the Ministry of Education, and in principle approved by the Research and Development Council, are the Centre for Strategic Competence in Infotechnologies and the Centre for Strategic Competence in Environmental Technologies. Their organisation is still in the initial stages. It should be noted that there has been a recommendation to include these centres in the allocation of 10% of the national PHARE funds for research, technology and development (RTD), the proposal adopted by the Commission in 1996.

These four centres of competence in innovative technology research and development will primarily serve as strategically important links between basic research and education, and industry, health and other sectors of the economic and social infrastructure. Centres of Strategic Competence will also focus their attention on human resource supply according to the demands at state and regional levels.

Estonia has short, medium and long term priorities in RTD.

Long term priorities for RTD are:

- to narrow the gap between Estonian RTD financing and that of an "average" EU member state, both in terms of the amount of money spent on RTD in general, as well as in terms of the structure of the expenditure (ratio of public vs private funding, ratio of expenditure on basic research vs applied research, ratio of expenditure on research vs developmental work),

- to orient RTD, and specifically its research component, more towards the RTD priorities of the European Union, as manifested in its framework programmes. Also to actively participate in the formulation of these priorities and ensure the awareness of them by the Estonian RTD community,

- to encourage Estonian industrial and service sectors to increase spending on RTD; to facilitate this by legislation, and specifically through taxation and other direct economic means,

- to promote entrepreneurship in establishing small and medium-sized enterprises (SMEs), specifically in the high added-value areas of industry and services; to build up the informational, legal and financial infrastructures necessary for this.

Medium term priorities for RTD are:

- to establish an advanced, easily accessible informational infrastructure as a service for RTD, and be pro-active in guiding the use of this resource,

- to pay specific attention to the needs of SMEs regarding RTD which they cannot afford themselves, and to find mechanisms (including financial) allowing them to overcome these obstacles, specifically in the case of export-oriented production,

- to achieve a consensus in understanding that the basic precondition for a high standard of RTD as a vehicle for innovation, must be created primarily through national measures,

- to offer, on a much larger scale than is presently available, shorter university courses in areas where the demand for a skilled professional workforce in the private sector emerges (e.g. in informatics services and technologies, molecular diagnostics etc.).

Short term priorities for RTD are:

- to harmonise Estonian legislation covering RTD, higher education and intellectual property rights with those in use in the European Union,

- to use innovative new concepts like centres of excellence to promote RTD in areas considered vital for the further economic and social development of Estonia. As recommended by the Estonian Research and Development Council, these areas are: biotechnology, information technology, material science and environmental technology,

- to ensure that the state budget allocations for research are kept at the level of 2% of expenditure,

- to increase substantially state budget expenditure on technological innovation, predominantly via the Innovation Foundation under the Ministry of Economic Affairs.

2.1 Evaluations

There have been two evaluations carried out on research. In 1991 the Royal Swedish Academy of Sciences and the Swedish Research Council evaluated Estonian research covering the years 1988-1991, in 1995 the Estonian Research and Development Council carried out an evaluation. The basic recommendation of both evaluations was the integration of research and higher education, in order to better utilise the existing personnel and material resources. The implementation of this recommendation has already begun.

3 Democracy

The Ministry of Education's Research and Universities Department and the Information and Statistics Section are responsible for the collection of information and the monitoring of university operations.

According to the Law on Universities, universities are autonomous to the extent determined by the Law. This autonomy means that the universities have the right to independently determine their academic and organisational structure, the content of the teaching and research work, the organisation of teaching, the course curricula, the employment conditions of teaching staff and researchers, and the selection of candidates. Institutions are defined by their constitutions which outline their mission, governance and politics. A constitution of a university is first ratified by the council of the university and then by the Ministry of Education. Institutions are run under the direction of a rector (president) who acts under the authority of the institution's council or board of trustees.

The role of academic staff, non-academic staff and students is defined by the university constitution. The community is also active in discussing the problems of higher education and applies appropriate pressure to the internal governance of the universities.

At the election of rectors, all professors, a certain ratio of academic and non-academic staff, and students, are present. The university council includes elected student representatives. The same system regulates the formation of faculty councils. Students have various types of student unions.

4 External influence

Public universities and institutions of higher education obtain finances mainly from the state budget. The state may also finance certain curricula according to national needs. These cases are determined by the Ministry of Education and will be regulated in more detail in the future. The budget for a higher education institution is ratified and amended by the council of the institution.

5 Hidden or indirect governance

The evaluation and accreditation of higher education institutions is carried out by the Higher Education Evaluation Council, which was formed by government decree. Its task is to accredit the curricula of all universities, within four years of the entering into force of the Law on Universities. In future, accreditation must be carried out no later than every seven years. Foreign experts are an obligatory presence in the Council.

Through accreditation the state recognises diplomas, as well as commissions fields of study by setting priority areas for accreditation.

6 Legal protection

To date, only problems of a financial and management nature have occurred in universities and higher education institutions.

7 Conclusion

The Estonian university system is basically well-developed and balanced. The formation of institutions of applied higher education has began. Reforms are taking into account Estonia's aim of integrating into European Union structures.

10.10

FRANCE

Sophie Decker

1 Introduction

The principles of governance of higher education are laid down in the Higher Education Act of 26 January 1984, and the two most important legal provisions on governance are found in Sections 22 and 26. Section 22 states that "institutions shall, by means of constitutional decisions taken by a majority of two-thirds of the sitting members of the governing board, determine their internal regulations and organisation in conformity with the provisions of this act and its implementing regulations, while always ensuring fair representation on governing boards for each major branch of learning. The regulations shall be transmitted to the Minister for Education."

Section 26 is concerned with the administration of higher education institutions and states that "Universities shall be administered on the basis of decisions taken by their vice-chancellors, decisions taken by their governing boards and the proposals, opinions and wishes expressed by their scientific boards and their boards for studies and university life."

2 The legal framework: principles and structures

The basis of the legal framework of higher education is the Higher Education Act of 26 January 1984. One of the most important features of governance as stated in it, allows for all members of academic society to be represented and for their involvement in the main decision-making process. As stated in Section 20, "scientific, cultural and vocational institutions, including universities, are managed democratically with the co-operation of all staff and students and of prominent outside persons". Furthermore, these institutions are "multidisciplinary" and "independent". Independence is to be understood as the right of an institution to make its own decisions concerning the content of studies and research, and internal regulations which must comply with higher provisions (such as government orders, Acts and the constitution).

The National Board for Higher Education and Research (CNESER) represents scientific, cultural and vocational institutions of "major national importance", especially in the educational, cultural, scientific, economic and social fields. It is made up of appointed individuals representing "major interests" and elected staff and student representatives. Universities are represented by the Conference of University Vice-Chancellors (CPU).

Over the past ten years more rights have been delegated to institutions of higher education aimed at providing better facilities and working conditions for the staff and students. The Framework Education Act of 10 July, 1989 provides that the state may make public higher education institutions the contracting authority for the construction of university buildings. The Act also increases the powers of higher education institutions over real estate allocated to them by the state. In respect of such property, institutions exercise all the rights and obligations of ownership with the exception of the right to sell and the right to change their use. An Act of 4 July, 1990 extended the same possibility to local authorities.

From 1991, a number of universities have been set up which are exempt from the normal rules of operation. The changes that have been introduced are as follows:

- the establishment of two university boards instead of three; one of the boards comprises representatives of local and regional authorities and the business world and acts in an advisory capacity, while the other carries out the tasks normally performed by the three standard university boards,
- the head of the institution is appointed by the Minister rather than being elected.

This is the first time that Section 21 of the 1984 Act, which allows for such experimentation, has been applied. The aim is to achieve greater flexibility in university "government" and to give local and regional authorities and the business sector a greater role in determining the goals and direction of each institution. A further objective is to establish a more appropriate legal framework for the development of university buildings.

3 Democracy

The governing bodies of higher education institutions consist of two parts: elected vice-chancellors who manage the universities, and governing boards which determine policy and approve budgets etc (see Sections 27, 28, 30 and 31 of the Act of 26 January, 1984). The tasks of scientific, cultural and vocational institutions are those listed in part II of the Act.

Universities are made up of various constituent bodies, which are teaching and research units, internal institutes and schools, laboratories, departments and others, depending on the profile of studies. They have their own management bodies (directors and boards) and exercise certain responsibilities. For instance, scientific boards propose scientific policy options and objectives to the governing boards; boards for studies and university life propose policy options and objectives concerning teaching and student life to the governing boards. These boards play a purely advisory role, any decisions can only be made by the governing board. The statutory division of responsibilities is broadly between policy and executive functions. The powers of the governing board may be delegated to the vice-chancellor.

The Act contains no provision designed to maintain a balance between the controlling bodies. The outcome depends to some extent on the state of relations between individual vice-chancellors and their governing boards. When it comes to a question of democratic governance of higher education institutions, staff and students participate in the exercise of power through their representatives on the boards, especially the governing board. Staff and student representatives are elected under a proportional representation list system. While 'prominent outside persons', whose number and origin are laid down in each institution's regulations, are appointed by the bodies they represent, i.e. local and regional authorities, trade unions, chambers of commerce and industry and so on.

4 External influence

As mentioned above, 'prominent outside persons' (representatives of local and regional authorities, research bodies, the business world and trade unions) are able to participate in the decision-making process, as they are included on the three boards in varying proportions, according to maximum and minimum levels set by law.

The Ministry of Education in each of the educational districts (whose boundaries roughly correspond to regional boundaries) is represented by chancellors who attend meetings of the governing boards and have the rights of supervision. All decisions and resolutions concerning regulations are addressed to the chancellor, who may request a court to set them aside where they are in breach of the law. Chancellors play a similar role in respect of institutions' budgets, in consultation with Regional Audit Offices.

Chancellors, as part of their administration, may have to manage expenditure and property common to several institutions. In the event of serious operational problems in an institution's management bodies, they may take the necessary emergency measures.

Accountants are appointed by the Ministry responsible for the budget and attend meetings of the governing boards in an advisory capacity. They ensure that any expenditure ordered is in accordance with the approved budget and with public accounting regulations.

The National Evaluation Committee, a body which is independent of the state, evaluates the educational dimension of institutions' operations. Institutions are also subject to management supervision by the General Inspectorate of Education Administration and to auditing by the Auditor-General's Department (for the largest institutions) or the relevant Regional Audit Office.

5 Indirect governance

In general, the institutions' independence is restricted by the state's powers in the following areas: authorising institutions to award national diplomas, determining the geographical location of higher education courses (distributing training options throughout the country), allocating funding, setting staffing levels, etc.. Since 1989, part of that funding (less than a half) is subject to a four-year contract setting out the institution's obligations, rather than being automatically allocated according to exclusively quantitative criteria.

6 Legal protection

Any person claiming to have been wronged by a decision taken by an institution's controlling bodies (in practice, such person is usually a student) can apply to the body in question for reconsideration of the decision. Such an application preserves, for a certain period of time, the applicant's right, in respect of time limits, subsequently to take the matter to court. Cases may also be brought before a court (usually the Administrative Court, the Administrative Court of Appeal for appeals or the *Conseil d'Etat* for cassation) on the same conditions as under general law. Chancellors may also refer such cases to these courts in order to have set aside decisions deemed to be in breach of the law. It should be noted that neither chancellors nor the Ministry can set decisions aside directly.

10.11

GEORGIA

Georgi Machabeli & Irakli Machabeli

The two most crucial legal provisions on governance are:

On the Status of the State Higher Education Institutions, No. 17, January 17, 1992, and the Plan of Urgent Measures to be Carried out in the Field of Education, No. 965, December 31, 1993.

There are two types of higher education institutions:

i state higher education institutions which are financed partly by the state budget at the federal or local levels, and partly by tuition fees charged by certain departments of the institution,

ii non-state secular higher education institutions which are financed by tuition fees only. In accordance with the ordinance No. 6 from January 12, 1992, issued by the cabinet of ministers, all higher education institutions are autonomous although there are no normative documents determining the scope of the autonomy.

The most important changes since 1985 are:

i the declaration in 1992 of autonomy for higher education institutions, which came as the result of establishing democratic institutional governance after the Soviet period of central government control,

ii the opening of non-state secular higher education institutions in response to an overwhelming demand for higher education.

The main governing body within higher education institutions is the scientific council, consisting of deans (presidents of faculties), heads of departments, leading professors, representatives of student communities, and trade union organisations. The members of the scientific council elect a rector, determine educational and scientific policy of the institution, confirm ordinances and decisions of the rector, confirm nominations of deans, heads of departments, professors and other personnel. Daily administration of higher education institutions is carried out by the rector and his staff (vice-rectors, departments of study, science, finance, economics, international relations, administration and other services).

The rector, with his staff, has executive functions. Vice-rectors are in charge of different fields of activities, for example one directs the development of educational problems, the second manages science, the third administration and economics, the fourth international relations, etc..

Vice-rectors have their own staff united into proper departments. Financial problems of the higher education institutions are solved at the level of the rector or vice-rector. Deans and heads of departments produce an application on their financial needs and the rector considers the applications and decides whether to accept the request.

The main governing body of a faculty is the faculty council which consists of the dean, vice-deans, heads of departments, leading professors, representatives of students and trade unions. The faculty council elects a faculty dean, produce nominations of heads of departments to the university scientific council, approves decisions taken by the dean, etc.. The executive managers of faculties are deans. They have two or three vice-deans, which have their own fields of activity (study, science, etc.). Deans, with the help of the vice-deans, guide all the educational and scientific problems of the faculty, monitor progress in students' studies, work out lesson time-tables, and approve the decisions of heads of departments which then need confirmation by the rector or scientific council of the university.

Heads of departments are responsible for educational and scientific programmes in one branch of science. They distribute teaching loads to members of the department, manage the scientific research of the staff, and invite in new teachers. There are other scientific divisions such as research institutes and laboratories; the institutes are divisions of higher education institutions and the laboratories are subdivisions of a faculty. Their guidance is realised by directors and vice-directors. The main goals of scientific divisions are to carry out any scientific problems ordered by state or private institutions.

One of the most important governing bodies of the higher education institutions since attaining autonomy has become the rectors council, which also includes the rectors of the state higher education institutions from Tbilisi.

The beginning of the council's activities coincided with deep political and social changes due to the disintegration of the Soviet Union and formation of an independent state of Georgia. As a result the most revolutionary changes in functioning of the higher education institutions were connected with the activities of this council. For example, in accordance with the decisions of the council, two-level study in the institutions was introduced. Formerly students in Soviet universities studied for five years and received a diploma which allowed them to obtain a variety of skilled labour employment opportunities. Now the first level involves four years of study and students gain a bachelors degree with a limited list of employment opportunities. The second level involves two or three years of study and students receive a masters degree and have obtained a full higher education. Furthermore, the rectors council decided to introduce fee paying departments in state higher education institutions.

The Ministry of Education and in particular its Department of Higher and Special-Higher Education and Science is one of the most important governing bodies for the higher education sector. It is responsible for determining the quota of students enroling at the institutions; it confirms dates and rules of admissible examinations, curricula, and lists of professions at the institutions; it approves the nomination of a rector elected by the institution's scientific council, and controls their activities. Newer functions have appeared more recently, for example, licensing the new fee paying higher education institutions, and organising attestation and accreditation of the higher education institutions.

External influences on the activities of higher education institutions comes from the Ministry of Trade, the Ministry of Health Protection which helps finance the medical university and approve its curricula and lists of subjects, etc., and also from the Ministry of Agriculture for the agricultural university, and the Ministry of Culture for fine art institutions.

There are no mechanisms of hidden or indirect governance for state higher education institutions. The same cannot be said for the non-state higher education institutions as their educational activities have not been studied, and their governance by the Ministry of Education only amounts to the registration of these institutions.

Though, it is important to note that on 27 June, 1997, the Parliament of Georgia has adopted the Law on Education of Georgia and some important changes in management of higher education institutions have been made there. The most important among them are as follows:

1 the candidature of the rector of a state higher education institution needs the approval of the President of Georgia,
2 all higher education institutions have to surpass attestation and accreditation to continue their activities,
3 special accreditation council managing the accreditation of higher education institutions and members of the council are to be appointed by the President of Georgia,
4 the Ministry of Education is responsible for activities of the attestation committee and committee of licensing.

10.12

GERMANY

Kornelia Haugg, Werner von Trützschler
& Michael Daxner

1 The legal framework: principles and structures

All institutions of higher education in Germany are, apart from certain exceptions, such as the administration colleges, public law entities (*Körperschaften des öffentlichen Rechts*) and, at the same time, state institutions of the individual Länder. They enjoy autonomous rights within the legislative framework. The limits to this autonomy are set by the supervisory rights of the Land Ministry concerned. The fundamental order and other important statutes resolved by the individual higher education institution require official approval. The same applies to the examination regulations at higher education institutions.

The basic principles for the structure of the internal organisation, the governing bodies and their functions and the rules for election are laid down in the Federal Framework Act for Higher Education. Within these principles the Higher Education Acts of the Länder lay down the directly applicable rules for the higher education institutions.

Following fierce arguments about the democratisation of higher education institutions in the shape of group universities with strong rights of codetermination by assistants and students in the 1960s, the Framework Act for Higher Education laid down the principle of graduated participation in line with function taking into account previous rulings by the Federal Constitutional Court. Consequently, all members of a higher education institution are entitled and obliged to participate in self-administration in line with their qualifications, function, responsibility and degree to which they are directly affected.

There have been no changes in the basic structures and rules for the governance of higher education institutions since 1985. But governance is one of the main topics in the current discussion about the reform of the Federal Framework Act.

2 Democracy

The Federal Framework legislation gives the Länder a certain amount of latitude for specific provisions to be covered by Länder laws. This is illustrated, for example, by the variety of governing structures and university bodies in these laws. Nonetheless, the Federal Framework permits a broad characterisation of the internal organisation and governing structures throughout Germany and for all types of institutions:

The members of a higher education institution are divided into four groups:
- professors (chaired and non-chaired),
- students,
- sub-professorial and artistic staff,
- non-academic staff.

All of these groups must be represented in the departmental council as well as in the two central bodies of the institutions. The professors have the absolute majority on all bodies, not just with regard to certain issues.

The basic organisational units of the institutions are departments (*Fachbereiche*; also sometimes called faculties). They are headed by departmental councils and always chaired by a professor. Departments either consist of the member of one large academic field or of several smaller, related fields.

The institution is governed by a full-time head (rector or president) with a term of office of at least two or four years respectively, elected by the council/convent. The function of the head may also be carried out by an elected presidential committee, presided by the rector or president serving as full-time member and including the chief administrator (chancellor) ex officia. State participation exists in as much as the responsible Ministry of the Land may veto a presidential candidate or selection.

Central tasks are dealt with by two central composite bodies. One of these is the parliament of the given institution called, variously, the council, the convent, the consistory, the large senate, or the assembly, according to the different Länder laws. Its most important functions are to elect the head of the institution and take decisions pertaining to its constitution. The second body, the senate, is responsible for current operations in as much as they concern matters of principal importance of the individual institution. Senate functions relate to decisions on development and budgetary planning, the number of students to be admitted, the establishment of departments and scientific units, basic issues concerning research and the promotion of young scientists and artists, examination regulations, and decisions about nominations for professorships made by the departments.

The chancellor, the chief administrator reporting to the rector or president, takes care of the administrative matters of the institution as a whole. In particular, s/he is responsible for the budget and participates in this capacity in the administration of departmental matters and facilities.

3 External influence

Beside the governing bodies and the Land Ministry concerned, there are no other stakeholders involved in the process of decision-making or controlling of higher education institutions.

As mentioned above, the Land Ministry has the right of supervision, for example the head of the institution has to be officially appointed by the responsible Land Ministry. Also decisions about nominations for professorships made by the departments have to be confirmed by the Land Ministry. As the higher education institutions are funded primarily through the Länder budget, there is a big financial influence on the decision-making process. For their annual budget the individual institutions submit detailed budgetary requests to the responsible Land Ministry and these have to be passed by the parliaments of the Länder. These may be subject to modification at various levels.

As there is an increasing need for external funding, organisations promoting research and industry may also have a hidden influence.

4 Legal protection

Liabilities are fostered with the strengthening of responsibilities, the decentralisation of decision-making, greater accountability for resources and a broad base of bottom-up action. However, it is difficult to effectively establish competitive structures because of many regulation which require homogeneity.

Study programme incentives are becoming popular despite a lack of sufficient funds. In many Länder there are innovative procedures to establish shortcuts towards these new study-programmes and curricula. The best results for study-related innovation come out of the evaluation processes. When these operate independently from any state influence, they are even more effective and create a climate of sustainable reform.

The idea off buffer-institutions has promoteded a discussion about the internal and external share of responsibilities. The influence of external evaluators, associations of sponsors, regional or local advisory boards etc., is growing. Quite frequently, the activities of these bodies create a spin-off for the reform debate inside the institutions. The pressure for efficiency has pushed a counter-activity in the universities aimed at more effectiveness.

A new debate on participation in the decision-making process is likely to replace the outdated structures of a very inflexible and frustrating model of corporate group interests. This has a notable influence on the rights and the self-awareness of the professorate, which reflect their role as the top of the scholarly hierarchy. More autonomy and competence in governance is going to renew the quest for double qualification of senior staff, e.g. if serving as chairpersons over a longer period. All these are examples of what is being discussed or implemented in existing Länder legislation and in the drafts for a new Federal Act on Higher Education.

5 Conclusion

The Federal government and the Länder are aware that more contemporary management structures are needed to bridge the gap in the field between institutional autonomy and state supervision. In the current discussions about the reform of the Federal Framework Act one of the main issues is whether state deregulation and greater responsibilities for the head of the higher education institution would achieve a more efficient use of resources. And also whether a new stage of professionalisation with longer periods in office and more rights for rectors and deans, with a reduction in the regulation of the state bureaucracy, would achieve better management and controlling functions for higher education institutions.

10.13

GREECE

Frida Meropouli

1 Higher education system

The identity of universities is formulated in Article 1 of L. 1268/1982 which assigns the university the tasks of producing and transmitting knowledge through research and teaching. According to Article 16, para. 5, "higher education is rendered exclusively by institutions, that are legal entities under public law with full self-government". These institutions act under the supervision of the state, they have the right to be financially supported by the state and operate according to the laws that concern such institutions.

University immunity is recognised under para. 4 of Article 2 of L. 1268/1982, and aims at "safeguarding academic liberty, free scientific research and free movement of ideas".

According to paragraph 5 of this Law, university immunity consists of "hindering any interference by the public force on these grounds without the invitation or the permission of the competent official of the HEI (higher education institutions)".

According to Article 6 of the Law, higher education institutions are composed of schools and departments or independent departments. Each of these organisational units has a different subject and carries different authorities and responsibilities.

Schools cover a group of related sciences, so as to secure the necessary interaction and teaching coordination for their research and for scientific progress.

The department is established as the basic functional academic unit and covers the cognitive subject of a science. A sector coordinates the instruction of part of the cognitive subject of the department.

Higher education institution bodies are determined by Article 2 of L. 2083/1992, which replaced Article 11 of L. 1268/1982, and include the senate, the principal's council and the principal.

The senate constitutes the basic personification of every university action and exercises directive management, aiming at supervising and controlling the university procedures. The authorities of the senate are provided for in paragraph 2b of Article 2 of 2083/1992 and can have a general and a more specific character.

The principal's council is a body with a smaller representative composition so as to be able to function with greater flexibility. According to paragraph 3a of Article 2 of L. 2083/1992 it is composed of the principal, the vice-principals, the representative of the students that participates in the senate as well as the superintendent of the registrar's office who acts as a spokesman and who also has a voting right in administrative, financial, technical and managerial personnel issues.

The principal is the highest one-member body of the higher education institution. He represents the institution and exercises managerial duties. His executive authority has recently been reinforced with Article 3 para. 1f of L. 2083/1992, so that certain functional obstacles, arising from the reluctance of HEI's officials to make decisions, can be overcome with his mediation.

The principal is assisted, in his exercise of duties, by the vice-principal of financial planning and progress and the vice-principal of academic issues and personnel (Art. 3, para. 1f, VIII, L. 2083/1992). The vice-principals do not exercise authority directly from the law.

2 School bodies

Schools have three bodies, the general assembly, the deanery and the dean (Art. 10, para. 1n 1268/1982). These bodies have limited authority over co-ordinating activities.

The general assembly of the school is the largest of these representational bodies, being composed of the general assemblies of all the departments that constitute the school.

The deanery comprises the dean, the presidents of the departments and a representative of the students of each department. It is a body with limited authority of a suggestive character.

3 Departmental bodies

At departmental level the representational bodies are the general assembly, the administrative council and the president (Art. 8, para. 1n, L. 1268/1982).

The general assembly is composed of the members of the department, that is the educational and research personnel, students and post-graduate students. Representation of the latter two categories is fixed at 50% and 15%, respectively, of their total number in the department.

The administrative council is composed of the president and the substitute president of the department, the directors of the sectors, two pre-graduate students and a representative of the post-graduate students and EMY. A representative of the assistant supervisors or scientific collaborators may also participate in administrative council meetings when subjects that concern them are discussed.

4 Bodies of the sector

The sector bodies are the general assembly and the director (Art. 9, para. 1n L. 1268/1982). The general assembly is composed of the faculty members, two to five student representatives and one representative of the post-graduate students. Its authorities are of a coordinating, suggestive as well as decision-making character.

5 Suggestive bodies of the HEI

The Council of Higher Education is a collective body assigned to make proposals to government on issues concerning higher education such as the establishment, abolition, merges, organisation and function of higher education institutions.

6 Educational and Research personnel

Higher education personnel are divided into four levels: professors, substitute professors, assistant professors and lecturers. There is no hierarchical dependence between these groups.

These positions are filled through election or progress. Election defines the manner in which the intellectual property of the prospective staff member is obtained. Progress allows for the possibility of promotion of the staff member in service.

7 Proclamation of positions

Filling higher education and research positions is done through an open process that begins with their proclamation (Art.6, para.2, L. 2083/1992). Professors and substitute professors are elected as permanent personnel while lecturers and assistant professors are elected for a three-year service which can be renewed for another four years. After the renewal and before the end of their service the lecturers have the right to request to be promoted to the level of assistant professor while assistant professors may request to become permanent.

The proclamation of higher education and research positions is announced by the general assembly of the department following the suggestion of the general assembly of the related sector.

8 Other higher education staff

The law also provides other categories of personnel as well. These categories are temporarily occupied with the educational task, and provide special technical administrative services or special educational services.

9 Post-graduate studies

Post-graduate studies constitute an instrumental part of the educational and research activities of higher education institutions. Post-graduate programmes are organised individually by each academic unit or through the cooperation of more than one department.

10.14

THE HOLY SEE

Mgr. Walter Edyvean

1 Introduction

The Supreme Pontiff, John Paul II, in his foreword to the promulgation of the "Sapientia Christiana", took note *inter alia* that:

> "(...) a new attitude has arisen about the structure of universities and Faculties, both civil and ecclesiastical. This is a result of the justified desire for a university life open to greater participation, a desire felt by all those in any way involved in university life.
>
> Nor can one ignore the great evolution that has taken place in pedagogical and didactic methods, which call for new ways of organising studies. Then too there is the closer connection that is being felt more and more between various sciences and disciplines, as well as the desire for greater cooperation in the whole university environment."

It is with these objectives in mind, that the structure and governance of institutions of higher education which are subject in whole or part to canonic law must be approached.

The Holy See is the supreme organ of government of the Roman Catholic Church and the juridic personification of the Church in its contacts with other members of the international community. The juridic personality of the Holy See is international, as is the nature of its activities. Questions concerning university education which fall within the competence of the Holy See, are treated by the Congregation for Catholic Education.

Academic centres at university level for which the Holy See bears responsibility are:

a) the ecclesiastical universities and faculties,
b) the Catholic universities,
c) the other Catholic institutions at tertiary level.

The classification follows from the objective and contents of studies, as well as from the authority on the basis of which degrees are awarded. As regards the first category, ecclesiastical universities and ecclesiastic faculties are severally and separately subject to the same rules. Where faculties form part of an ecclesiastical university, their governance must be coordinated through the statutes with the governance of the entire university in such a way that the good of the single faculties is assured, while at the same time the whole university is promoted and the operation of all the faculties with each other is favoured. Art. 20.1 states that the canonical exigences of ecclesiastical faculties must be safeguarded even when such faculties are inserted into non-ecclesiastical universities.

Ecclesiastical universities and faculties are engaged in teaching and research in the sciences proper to the Church. These institutions are governed by universally valid academic legislation, e.g. the aforementioned Apostolic Constitution "Sapientia Christiana" of 15 April 1979 and the annexed Norms of the Congregation for Catholic Education of 29 April 1979. These texts confer authority in academic matters to the Holy See. At present, about 150 institutions, as listed in the *INDEX GENERALIS Universitatum et Facultatum Ecclesiasticarum*, are governed by the "Sapientia Christiana".

The Norms of Application relevant to the Apostolic Constitution "Sapientia Christiana" specify, inter alia, that university or faculty is understood to include those Athenaea, institutes, or academic centres which have been canonically erected or approved by the Holy See with the right to confer academic degrees by the authority of the same See. The canonical value of an academic degree means that such a degree enables one to assume an office in the Church for which a degree is required. (Norms of Application Art. 1, 7.1).

Apart form these institutions, other Catholic universities and university colleges exist, which follow the academic legislation and structure of the respective nations. They teach and conduct research, in the light of the Christian faith, in the disciplines common to all universities. These universities award degrees on the basis of civil authority. They number about 900 in the world, and are subject to ecclesiastical legislation as set forth in the Apostolic Constitution *Ex corde Ecclesiae* of 15 August 1990.

Some countries have Concordats with either the local ecclesiastical authority or the Holy See relative to questions concerning the university-level institutions for which the Holy See is competent. The Holy See is furthermore signatory to several international treaties on university matters.

2 Governance

2.1 Relations between the institutions and the Holy See

2.1.1 The chancellor

The Apostolic Constitutions provides that higher education institutions subject to canonic law are represented to the Holy See by a chancellor who is also the representative of the former to the institutions. The chancellor is usually, although not always, the Roman Catholic Bishop *pro tempore* of the place where the institution is located. If the university or faculty depends upon a collegial entity (for instance, on an Episcopal Conference), one designated member of the group is to exercise the office of chancellor.

Where the Roman Catholic Bishop is not the chancellor, he may serve the function of patron of the institution. The assent of the patron is required, for instance, before any appointment is made that requires a *nihil obstat* from the Holy See. Whenever something in the university or faculty is known to be contrary to doctrine, morals, or ecclesiastical discipline, the patron may take the matter to the chancellor so that the latter may take action. The Bishop may have recourse to the Holy See, without prejudice to his own obligation to provide personally for action in those cases which are more serious or urgent and which carry danger for his diocese.

The duties of the chancellor are:

- to promote continually the progress of the university or faculty, to advance scientific progress, to ensure that Catholic doctrine is integrally followed, and to enforce the faithful implementation of the statutes and the prescriptions of the Holy See,
- to help ensure close relationships between all the different ranks and members of the community,
- to propose to the Sacred Congregation for Catholic Education the names of those who are to be nominated or confirmed as rector and president, as well as the names of the teachers for whom a *nihil obstat* is to be requested,
- to receive the profession of faith of the rector and president,
- to give or take away from the teachers the canonical mission or permission to teach, according to the norms of the Constitution,
- to inform the Sacred Congregation for Catholic Education about important matters, and to send to that Congregation every three years a detailed report on the academic, moral, and economic condition of the university or faculty.

The Norms of Application Art. 5 confer responsibilities in educational matters to the Bishops' Conference joined to the Apostolic See. The Bishops' Conference along with the chancellors, monitors the universities and faculties to foster their progress and are solicitous for their scientific and ecclesial conditions; while, of course, respecting the autonomy of science according to the mind of the second Vatican Ecumenical Council.

2.2 Governance of institutions

Generally, statutes specify the application of the general legislation set forth in the Apostolic Constitution to a particular institution. Often the statutes reflect and incorporate elements of the practice of other universities in their country or region. Of course, statutes are of subsidiary nature, and cannot confer competencies which encroach upon authority conferred by the Apostolic Constitution. Accordingly, where a board of trustees, for instance, has the power to maintain doctrinal orthodoxy and to ensure a just freedom in teaching, such power is without prejudice to the personal duty of the chancellor, independently of the trustees, 'to ensure the Catholic doctrine is integrally followed'.

The statutes of each institution are subject to approval by the Congregation for Catholic Education. The statutes are approved experimentally for three years and may be revised and approved definitively thereafter. Faculties which are legally connected to civil authorities may be granted extended periods of revision. In these matters, and to assure appropriate planning of universities and faculties and a suitable distribution of institutions in different parts of the world, the Sacred Congregation for Catholic Education may seek the advice from the Bishops' Conferences and from a commission of experts. Prior to approving a new university or faculty, the local Ordinaries, the Bishops' Conference, and experts, especially from neighbouring faculties, must be heard.

The personal and collegial authorities to be instated by institutional statutes are defined in the Apostolic Constitution. Personal authorities are, in the first place, the rector or president and the dean. The collegial authorities are the various directive organisms or councils of the university or faculty. The statutes of the university or faculty must set out the names and offices of the academic authorities, determining the way they are designated and their term of office, taking into account both the canonical nature of the individual university or faculty and the university practice in the local area. Those designated as academic authorities are to be people who are truly knowledgeable about university life, usually they come from among teachers of some faculty.

Statutes must also determine how the personal and the collegial authorities collaborate with each other, and have to give credence to the principle of collegiality. The statutes should define how the students, either individually or collectively, take part in the university community life in those aspects which contribute to the common good of the faculty or university.

Statutes must establish a university council (general council, academic senate) and a faculty council, the denomination of these bodies may vary. Other special councils or commissions for scientific learning, teaching, discipline, finances, may also be established.

Statutes must provide for the positions of a rector or a president, as well as for that of a dean. According to the terminology of the Apostolic Constitution, a rector presides over a university; a president over an institute or a faculty which exists separately; and a dean presides over a faculty which forms part of a university.

The rector or president is the principal bearer of personal academic authority in an institution. The rector or president is usually appointed by the university council (general council, academic senate) with the approval of the chancellor, the vice-chancellor, if any, and of the Holy See after the assent of the patron has been obtained. The president is normally selected from among the professors and permanent lecturers of the institute. The office of the rector or president is:

- to direct, promote and coordinate all the activity of the academic community,
- to represent the university or the institute or faculty existing separately to society at large,
- to convoke the council of the university or of the institute or faculty existing separately and preside over the same according to the statutes,
- to watch over the administration of temporalities,
- to refer more important matters to the chancellor,
- to send, every year, a statistical summary to the Sacred Congregation for Catholic Education, according to the outline provided by that same Congregation.

It is the duty of the dean of a faculty:

- to promote and coordinate all the activities of the faculty, especially matters regarding studies, and to see to providing with due speed for their needs,
- to convoke and preside over the faculty council,
- to admit or exclude students in the name of the rector according to the norms of the statutes,
- to refer to the rector what is done or proposed by the faculty,
- to see that the instructions of higher authorities are carried out.

2.2.1 The board of trustees

As mentioned above, the statutes may establish other governing bodies than those defined in the Apostolic Constitution. Often boards of trustees are instated which are legally responsible for the institution.

Where instated, boards of trustees are usually the highest authority as regards constitutional, juridical and financial matters. The composition of boards differs; they may comprise ordinary and honorary members. Ordinary board members may be the Provincial Superiors *pro tempore* with jurisdiction over the institution, and other such ordinary members as may be appointed. Honorary board members usually have the right to be present and to participate at board meetings. They may also have the right to vote before the board on other than financial matters. Honorary board members are free from all financial obligations which arise from the trustees out of board decisions.

2.2.2 The university council

Where a board of trustees exists, the university council (general council, academic senate) is a body whose authority is subject to the board of trustees but superior to that of the faculty councils. It advises the trustees, determines policy and directs its implementation. Furthermore the university council may:

- establish regulations concerning the affairs of the whole institution,
- review, and where necessary cancel, regulations issued by faculty councils,
- provide disciplinary procedures for cases not otherwise provided for in the statutes,
- administer the financial affairs of the institute,
- make academic appointments of more than one year's duration, and terminate any academic appointments in accordance with the statutes.

In the execution of its responsibilities the university council (general council, academic senate) may work through both regular and ad hoc committees. Such committees may be an admissions committee, an appointments committee, or a finance committee to assist the board of trustees, where such exists, in the board's financial responsibilities.

2.2.3 The faculty council

A faculty is governed by its own council whose chairperson is the dean. The faculty council shall comprise the dean, all the faculty's professors, senior lecturers, lecturers and assistants. Student representatives may participate, subject to faculty regulations. Frequently, student members shall not constitute more than a portion of the faculty council and may be excluded when delicate matters, particularly concerning staff, are being discussed. Other persons may also be excluded, for example visiting staff, as the council may from time co-opt for important reasons and for a determined period.

The duties and powers of a faculty council may be as follows, according to the statutes of the institution:

- to provide an internal policy for the faculty and to ensure its execution by the dean; within each faculty the council may have the ultimate responsibility for all matters that pertain to the internal administration of the faculty, such as faculty regulations, syllabus, teaching methods, examinations, awards, appointment of assistants,
- it may advise the general council on admissions, on financial policy, on academic matters proper to the general council, and on the appointment of its deans, professors, senior lecturers and lecturers,
- to establish particular departments and staff/student committees and to ensure that such bodies are governed by appropriate regulations and terms of reference,
- to meet regularly or whenever summoned, usually by the president or the dean, or whenever a certain quorum of its members so requests.

2.2.4 Deans

A dean is the chief executive officer of a faculty, an ex-officio member of the general council and chairperson of the faculty council. A dean is appointed by the general council, having heard the advice of the faculty council. The dean is normally selected from among the professors or permanent lecturers. It is usually the responsibility of the dean:

- to represent the faculty in accordance with the statutes,
- to convene and preside over the faculty council and over other official meetings within the faculty, unless the president or vice-president presides,
- to administer the ordinary internal affairs of the faculty,
- to sign certificates for degrees and other awards.

3 Conclusion

When the Sacred Congregation for Catholic Education, by command of Pope Paul VI, commenced renewing the now abrogated Apostolic Constitution *Deus Scientiarum Dominus* in 1967, it consulted the ecclesiastical universities and faculties throughout the world. As a consequence, the Apostolic Constitution "Sapienta Christiana" now affords a wide framework regulation under which individual institutions may respond appropriately to local exigencies as well as to an ever changing social environment, while preserving their proper mission.

10.15

ICELAND

Thordur Kristinsson & Arnor Gudmundsson

1 Introduction

There is no legislation covering higher education as a whole, but each institution has special laws defining its operational structure, its role in education and research, the degrees awarded and the length of the various programmes offered. All higher education institutions are directly responsible to the Ministry of Culture and Education.

There are 13 institutions of higher education in Iceland, one traditional university with 9 faculties, 2 other more specialised university institutions with research tasks, and 10 non-university institutions. The universities are governed by university councils, which are composed of representatives of the faculty members, students and staff. State non-university higher education institutions have school boards, the members of which are appointed by the Minister of Culture and Education, based on the suggestions of parties associated with the school. Private colleges are privately administered, but have one representative appointed by the Ministry of Culture and Education on their board.

The basic principle of governance for universities in Iceland is collegiality. Universities are governed by the members of the academic community and are independent in all academic and research matters. The governance of non-university higher education institutions, which are situated in a grey area between the upper-secondary and tertiary levels of education, is characterised by administrative structures similar to those of the upper-secondary level. These institutions are ultimately governed by external school boards and are subject to closer control by the Ministry of Culture and Education.

2 Governance of higher education institutions: the example of the University of Iceland

The University of Iceland is the oldest institution of higher education and is the principal university in the country. It is a state university founded in 1911 as the result of merging three professional schools, namely, the School of Theology (establ. 1847), the School of Medicine (establ. 1876), and the School of Law (establ. 1908).

The governance and administration of higher education institutions is shared between the university council, the rector, the deans of faculties and the administrative directors. The main tasks of the university council are the development of policy for the university as a whole and the allocation of funds from the university budget. The rector and administrative directors implement the decisions of the council and are charged with the daily administration and management of the university.

Regulations for university institutions outline in more detail the role and function of each administrative instance, the university council, administrative directors, deans, faculties, departments and the study regulations for students and the degrees offered. Changes in the university regulation are in general made by the initiation and approval of the university council. The regulation for the University of Iceland is particular in that changes in it have to be confirmed both by the Minister of Culture and Education and the President of the Republic of Iceland. Regulations for universities, other than the University of Iceland are, confirmed by the Minister of Culture and Education.

The laws for the University of Iceland state that the university council has the final decision in matters of the university and its institutions unless otherwise stated in its laws and regulations.

The Law on the University of Iceland places 2 limitations on the powers of the Minister of Culture and Education to regulate the matters of the university. First, the university council has to be consulted regarding changes in the regulation for the university. Secondly, the Minister of Culture and Education has to seek a confirmation from the President of the Republic for changes in the regulation.

The legal framework provides for discretionary decisions in strategic policy, general management, daily administration and the management of teaching and research. The criteria being that decisions must be within the framework of the law and regulations and in accordance with university policy laid down by the council. Its collegial government, with no external members on its governing board, and the independence of the university council, gives the institution considerable discretionary powers in its decisions. A complaint against decisions made by authoritative bodies within the institution has to be brought to all administrative levels within the university and finally to the university council, before a plea can be brought to the Minister of Culture and Education, and then only in matters specifically mentioned in the Law.

The faculties of the University of Iceland have considerable discretionary powers with regard to the allocation of funds, the curriculum and other academic matters.

The codes of the Law of the University of Iceland concerning the governance of the university were changed by the Althing (parliament) in 1990. In December 1986 the university council appointed a special committee of 4 professors and 1 student to examine the governance of the university as a whole. The committee's main objective was to propose changes in the function, responsibility and authority of the university administration because many additional tasks had emerged within the administration during the preceding decade which were not properly defined in the Law, and as a consequence had led to conflicting competencies. The committee's final report was published in March 1989 and many of the proposals contained therein were accepted by the university council. The university council, in turn, proposed to the Ministry of Culture and Education several changes to the University Law which the Althing passed in December 1990.

The results are clearer lines of function, responsibility and authority of individual administrative instances and increased financial autonomy and responsibility of the individual faculties and their deans. Obligatory regular evaluation of the performance and activities of faculties was also introduced, as were permanent study committees comprising equal numbers of staff and students for each department, the establishment of 6 central administrative directors (instead of 2 as before for finance and academic affairs) to be directly responsible to the rector and the university council, and the introduction of standing committees to assist and advise the university council (some of these had already been established but without due support in law and regulation).

3 Democracy

The highest authority of the university is the university council, chaired by the rector, who also presides over the university. The rector acts both as the academic and the executive head. Professors only are eligible to be elected rector or dean. The rector is elected for a term of 3 years in general elections open to all full time academic staff members, full time non-academic staff members holding a university degree, and registered students who carry a 1/3 of the votes.

In addition to the rector, the university council is composed of the 9 faculty deans, 2 representatives from the union of academic staff members elected by the union members for a term of 2 years from amongst those members not eligible to be elected deans of faculties, 4 students, the director of finance, 1 member elected from members of the administrative staff and the director of the National and University Library. The deans of the faculties are elected by the permanent academic staff members of the faculty for a term of 2 years. The students are elected for a term of 2 years by a general election amongst all registered students. The director of finance, the member elected from members of the administrative staff and the director of the National and University Library are without voting rights.

Administrative directors of the central administration are appointed by the university council for a term of 5 years. The central administrative offices are: finance, academic affairs, research, public relations and international affairs, personnel, building and construction.

The university council appoints several standing committees for 3 year terms. Their task is to advice the council and assist it in policy making as well as to work on particular projects or topics designated by the council. They consist usually of 1 member from the council, 5 representatives elected by the council from faculty nominees, 1 student and the director of the relevant central administrative office. These committees are: the administration and governance committee, the development and planning committee, the finance committee, the academic affairs committee, the research committee, the international affairs committee, the buildings and construction committee, the personnel committee, the public relations committee, the legal affairs and regulation committee and the appeal and conciliation committee.

The faculty general meeting is the highest ranking authority within each faculty and is chaired by a dean. All permanent members of academic staff, as well as student representatives are obliged to attend. In large faculties the faculty general meeting has certain administrative competencies with regard to the faculty and the faculty council. In all faculties there exists permanent study committees comprising equal numbers of staff and students. These study committees discuss curriculum development and other matters related to individual courses and study programmes. They advise the faculty general meeting.

Faculties have considerable financial, and unrestricted academic autonomy with regard to design and development of the curricula and teaching and research. Changes in the regulations concerning each faculty must be discussed and approved by the faculty general meeting and then by the university council before being passed to the Ministry for confirmation.

All permanent academic staff members are appointed to their respective posts following an assessment of competency. The assessment is conducted by a committee consisting of 1 member of the university council and a representative from the Ministry of Culture and Education; the committee's chairman is appointed by the respective faculty. The proposal of the committee must be adopted by a faculty general meeting; students do not have a vote in these cases.

The activities of the academic staff members in the internal governance of the University are mostly concerned with administrating study programmes, curriculum development, research, and the administration of departments, faculties etc. Full time academic staff members are obliged to attend department meetings and faculty general meetings. Their duties are, approximately, administration (12%), teaching (48%), and research (40%). Non-academic staff members not holding administrative posts have no role in internal government.

Students are represented in almost all committees and working groups appointed by departments, faculties or the council. The university council, faculties and departments may ask for representatives from the outside community to sit on committees appointed within the university.

4 External influence and hidden governance

There are no external members to the board of the universities. Stakeholders influence is indirect, through legislation and regulations and overall budget decisions. For instance, while the universities allocate their funds autonomously, they are constitutionally answerable to the Minister of Culture and Education – and current expenditures are financed through governmental appropriations in the national budget. In this respect the Althing (parliament), the Ministry of Culture and Education and the Ministry of Finance influence decision making regarding the use of funds by the universities. This may affect course offerings as well as the management and feasibility of research projects.

Indirect state governance occurs mainly through the appropriations of funds from the national budget. As already mentioned, the Althing (parliament) appropriates funds to the universities, but the Ministry of Culture and Education and the Ministry of Finance prepare proposals for university financing within the framework of the national budget. Budgetary decisions also take into account other sources of financing.

Parliament has also passed laws on student enrolment at universities. As a general rule, the University of Iceland is required to admit all students who have successfully passed a matriculation examination at the upper-secondary school. An exception applies to students of medicine, dentistry, nursing and physical therapy who are required to pass a competitive examination during the first year of study. However, in principle all students who have passed the matriculation examination are eligible for admission to the University of Iceland, while other higher education institutions may impose their own selection criteria.

The general admission rule for the University of Iceland has some hidden side effects, in particular, large student enrolment numbers and a high drop-out rate during the first year, which compel faculties to structure their study programmes accordingly. Hidden or indirect governance by other sources is limited, but can be detected in the influence of the Union of University Teachers in the negotiation of salaries and work conditions.

5 Legal protection

The University of Iceland enjoys complete internal autonomy in financial and academic matters. The legal framework and regulations provide for successive stages of appeal, from department to faculty to the university council, which is the highest authority in all matters not otherwise prescribed for in the Law or regulations. The external appeals procedure is to the Ministry of Culture and Education.

According to a law on state administration decisions made by the university council can also be set before the parliamentary ombudsman, who can give a legal opinion on the decision; the ombudsman does not have formal powers to rule in university matters.

10.16

ITALY

Wladimiro Gasparri

1 The legal framework: principles and structures

The Italian constitution states in Article 33:

> "The arts and sciences are free and their teaching is free (...). The institutions of higher learning, the universities and the academies, have the right to adopt an autonomous regulatory system within the limits laid down by the laws of the state".

Law no. 168 of 9 May, 1989 provides furthermore:

> "1. The universities are endowed with a legal personality, and by virtue of Article 33 of the constitution possess didactic, scientific, organisational, financial and accounting autonomy. They are self-regulatory bodies which draw up their own articles of association and internal regulations.
>
> 2. In conformity with the principles of autonomy laid down by Article 33 of the constitution and specified by statute law, the universities are regulated in addition to their own respective articles of association and by-laws, only by the statutory laws that make express reference to them. Provisions promulgated by circulars are not applicable to them.
>
> 3. The universities undertake didactic work and organise their respective academic bodies with every respect for the freedom to teach of the university teachers and of the general principles laid down by the university teaching regulatory systems. In observance of these principles the articles of association establish the didactic programmes leading to the award of diplomas (also if carried out in schools with special objectives), degrees

and post-graduate degrees. They define and regulate the criteria for holding specialised courses, PhD programmes and complementary didactic services.

4. The universities are the primary seats of scientific research and work to achieve their own institutional missions, while respecting the freedom of research of university teachers, and also that of the academic bodies."

The fundamental principle on which the Italian university system is organised is that of autonomy. Article 33 of the constitution allows the individual universities to draw up regulations which by themselves constitute a systematic regulatory framework which, in spite of a lack of an internal source of reference, makes reference to sources of general regulatory provisions. The realisation and the development of university autonomy represents an effective organisational formula against interference particularly from government policy positions. The tasks assigned to the universities – the maintenance and development of academic and didactic liberty in order to promote and sustain civil progress – does not tolerate any exceptions for reasons of political choice or convenience. Therefore, the principle of autonomy enshrined in the constitution represents a barrier against pressures to conform by political majorities, prevents the state from using statutory regulation and limits legal intervention to setting out limits.

Constitutional law recognises a reserved regulatory domain which is unalterable by ordinary statute law; Article 33, first clause of the constitution refers to the freedom of teaching and enquiry in the universities. In using the expression university autonomy two different concepts are usually confused. On the one hand the term refers to teaching and on the other to administrative organisation. University autonomy is, first and foremost, an organisational formula that refers not to the freedom of teaching and academic enquiry, but, instead, to the administrative aspects of the university regulatory system. However, by emphasising the organisational aspect of the meaning of the principle of university autonomy is not intended to deny that it is functionally unrelated to the freedom of academic enquiry and teaching.

The latter concept, far from constituting an institutional guarantee for academic work is, instead, an individual freedom whose institutional guarantee is provided for by university autonomy.

University autonomy, that is, the right of the university to adopt self-governing regulatory systems is set out in Article 6 of Law no. 168 of 9 May, 1989, and covers regulatory, organisational, didactic, academic, financial and accounting autonomy. The prescriptive powers of the articles of association, or charters, is, furthermore, enforced by such a distribution of autonomy, and it is the university charters, or articles of association, which constitute the most direct and fullest expression of autonomy. Their special character is due to the fact that they can derogate from what other laws establish and as part of their intrinsic characteristics, can replace the laws of the state.

The statement of the principle of academic autonomy is accompanied by a corollary definition of organisational structure for each of the individual charters which provides a guide, in terms of privileged regulatory powers, for describing university organisation, identifying responsibilities and allocating powers.

On the basis of the charters and the national legislation referring to them, the organisation of individual universities does not contain true management structures endowed with powers to make choices and autonomous strategic policy decisions. The individual charters have been drawn up to follow a common pattern with regard to the distribution of responsibilities and tasks between a university's bodies. Legislation and the various university charters have desisted from defining managerial structures for university bodies entrusted with strategic policy development decisions and more specifically the decisions of didactic-academic policy. Major strategic choices, either for the university or for the faculty, are, instead, entrusted to bodies which represent the academic world, in particular, the rector, the academic senate and the faculty board.

The rector represents the university and is attributed with full legal force for the initiation, implementation and overseeing of activities. He also provides a link between the central governing bodies of the university. The senate defines the executive action and lines of development of the university, plans the phases and oversees the co-ordination of the didactic and academic activities while at the same time taking due account of the autonomy of the individual didactic and academic structures. The senate may also appoint permanent or temporary committees with preparatory functions to help with senate tasks. These can include external experts if suitable experts from among the university staff cannot be found.

The position of administrative director is somewhat different from the above bodies. His/her responsibilities are to run the offices and the central administrative structures. In addition, he/she is responsible for management policy and co-ordination and control of the plans and objectives decided upon by the university's governing bodies and concerning the technical and administrative personnel.

The regulatory framework for the universities in the period between the 1948 Constitution and Law no. 168 of 1989 comprised a series of measures which did not always have a single common purpose. The only measure which followed the spirit of the 1948 constitution was presidential decree no. 382 of 11 July, 1980, concerning the re-organisation of university teaching staff, and the relative provisions for training as well as organisational and didactic experimentation. This decree, besides reorganising the relations between the various types of teacher in the university system, made it possible for the universities themselves to proceed to an initial form of differentiation of their own structures and procedures in order to carry out their functions in the best manner possible.

This reform proceeded in two directions. One concerned the re-organisation of the entire teaching staff with provisions made for the roles of the professors, ordinary and associate, and the creation of research positions. The other concerned organisational aspects and marked the start of an experimental phase. The 1980 decree did not define binding or definitive structural models but helped stimulate the autonomy and the primary initiative of individual universities in terms of organisational structure. First and foremost, the universities were given powers to set up departments (Articles 88 ss. of presidential decree no. 382 of 1980), i.e. establish one or more homogeneous research area in terms of objectives or methods and teaching work, even if more than one faculty and more than one degree course within a given faculty were involved.

Law no. 168 of 9 May, 1989 established the Ministry of the Universities and Scientific and Technological Research. This Law began a process of rapid transformation and development within the entire university system.

Besides re-organising the Ministry's functions, it defined and circumscribed its responsibilities, and set in motion a process of reform by attributing major areas of autonomous responsibility to individual universities concerning the regulation of their government and administrative organisation.

This Law and the others which followed in the course of the 1990s set out to satisfy the demand for autonomy made by the academic and research world. The objective was to break the organisational link with the state by delimiting the role of national law in order to provide scope for other alternative regulatory sources for defining policies and the exercise of university functions. Law no. 168 of 1989, in the absence of an outline law on university autonomy, has become a cornerstone for this process, offering a new guarantee for university teaching staff, and differentiating organisational structure, thereby enhancing flexibility.

On the basis of Law no. 168 of 1989 and an enactment of Article 9 of the constitution, the Ministry has the task of promoting scientific and technological research as well as developing the universities. In pursuance of this aim the Ministry "shall proceed to formulate and co-ordinate policy in matters of research with reference to the universities and the research bodies, taking due account of the principles of autonomy laid down in Article 33 of the constitution".

Article 2 of Law no. 168 specifies the Minister's previously adopted managerial and bureaucratic functions that the Minister no longer enjoys. This change recognises the autonomy of the universities and the research bodies, whose managerial and bureaucratic functions are now directed by a set of regulatory principles suitable for guiding the actions of both the government and the universities in the pursuit of their objectives. The charter process has been entrusted to the universities which are expected to adopt a charter or articles of association and internal regulations for teaching, administration, accounting and finance. They are exempt from the applicability of any legislative statute which does not make express reference to them.

The details of the Law are very complex and take into account the need to offset university autonomy against an organisational arrangement which is likely to impede innovative potential. Financing, which for the most part derives from state funding, the juridical status of staff, which is drawn up along the same lines as state administrative personnel, the rigidity of the teaching systems, and the legal value of academic titles are some of the main obstacles against the full realisation of the universities' didactic, academic, organisational, financial and accounting autonomy which Article 6 of Law no. 168 of May 1989, recognises.

Notwithstanding these major obstacles, Law no. 168 of 1989 opened the door to the process of autonomy. The successive stages of this transformation have been as follows:

1 New provisions for planning the development of the university system and for the establishment of new universities and faculties through Law no. 245 of 7 August, 1990: Regulations of the three-year plan of development for the universities and for the fulfilment of the four-year plan 1989-1990.

2 Re-definition of the teaching system and re-distribution of tasks between the Ministry and the universities, Law no.341 of 19 November, 1990: Reform of the university teaching systems. The teaching system, which is still substantially regulated by the Consolidation Act no.1592 of 31 August, 1931, and by royal decree no.1269 of 4 June, 1938, concerning regulations for students, has, in part, been reformed by the foregoing law which re-defines the arrangement of the courses and introduced diploma, degree and post-graduate courses. The Law also provided for the up-dating of the teaching arrangements through a regulation which also delimits the autonomy of the universities as such arrangements are based upon ministerial schedules. The measure was adopted after its approval by the National University Council.

3 The new Law on public measures to provide material support for those who are capable and meritorious of a university education Law no.390 of 2 December, 1992: Regulations on the right to university education.

4 The reform of the sources of funding for the universities and the manner of transferring state financing Article 5 of Law no.537 of 24 December, 1993: Measures to rationalise public financing.

2 Democracy

The government has espoused the principle of university autonomy within the consequent redistribution of tasks at the national level ie. the Ministry, and at the local level ie. the individual universities. The universities, through their charters, are responsible for their own organisational structure and for defining their own governing organs and those of their didactic and research bodies. The law provides that the Minister will be exclusively concerned with planning functions and with the promotion of scientific and technological research, together with the development of universities and the para-university 'higher institutes'.

The responsibilities of the Minister are as follows: preparation of a development plan for the universities to be presented to Parliament every three years; a report on the state of university education based upon evidence received from the universities and written in consultation with the National University Council and the permanent conference of university rectors; proposal and adoption in circumstances envisaged by law, of the acts of the annual and multi-year plans; the allocation of funds assigned to its budget and destined for the universities on the basis of objective criteria as defined by the Minister's own decree; presentation of an annual report to Parliament on the state of scientific and technological research, drawn up from reports received from individual universities and other research bodies.

The Law also provides for a series of consultative bodies for the Minister, in particular there is the National University Council (Law no. 31 of 7 February, 1979) which has consultative functions, such as making assessments of the co-ordination work conducted between the universities on development planning, and the national regulations on didactic arrangements. It has consultative functions of a binding character such as the preparation of regulations for the competitive examinations for university teachers and researchers for which the Minister is unable to formulate policies. It also has deliberative functions, such as the distribution of the funds destined to finance scientific research of national interest in accordance with Article 65 of the presidential decree no. 382 of 11 July, 1980. The Council's composition and electoral system allows for representation from those working in the universities i.e. ordinary and associate professors, etc., and also of those from the various disciplines, with a clear prevalence for the latter group, which makes the Council not only a consultative organ but also an organ of self-government not so much of the overall university system but as much for the categories and disciplines themselves. The composition of the Council is laid down in Article 10, fourth clause of Law no. 341 of 19 November, 1990, and the electoral procedures are established by presidential decree no.167 of 1 February, 1996.

Other important consultative bodies are the National Council for Science and Technology (*Consiglio nazionale della scienza e della tecnologia* – CNST), a high level consultative council for both the Minister and the Council of Ministers, in which the scientific community participates in drawing up the policies and main lines of scientific and technological research (Article 11 of Law no. 168 of 9 May, 1989), and the Permanent Conference of Italian University Rectors (*Conferenza permanente di rettori delle università italiane* – CRUI) which was formally recognised by Law no. 168 of 1989 and then by Law no. 341 of 19 November, 1990. The CRUI is an association of rectors from state and non-state universities, while the CNST is presided over by the Minister and made up of two elected members for each major area of academic study and by twelve members of considerable qualification and academic experience in the sphere of scientific research chosen by the Minister, as well as other members representing the various scientific and academic organs in Italy.

Law no. 390 of 2 December, 1991 on the right to a university education provides for the establishment of a National Council on the Right to University Education as part of the Ministry of the Universities and Scientific and Technological Research. This Council has consultative functions and gives advice and suggestions to the Minister as regards the right to university studies; it helps in the preparation of the report on the use made of the resources allocated for this purpose, which is subsequently attached to the report on the state of university education that the Minister presents to Parliament. As part of this work it promotes studies and surveys on student conditions and tutoring services. The Council is presided over by the Minister and is composed of five representatives from the universities, five regional representatives and five student representatives.

With the ministerial decree on the universities and scientific and technological research of 22 February, 1996 a permanent institute for monitoring and evaluating the national university system was set up. Its purpose is to evaluate the findings concerning the efficiency and productivity of scientific research and training, to verify programmes for the development and re-equilibrium of the university system, and to assign financial resources.

In conformity with the law, the range of university governing bodies permitted is left up to the university charters. This has led to a number of different forms varying in terms of composition, function and allocation of powers. In general, the governing function of the universities is divided between the following bodies:

1 The rector who has overall representative powers recognised by law, and who also has been assigned powers for initiating, implementing and overseeing of university activities along with the task of ensuring links between the central bodies of the university. The rector presides over the academic senate and the administrative council, exercises disciplinary functions, stipulates co-operation agreements with external bodies and plans the didactic and research work of the university. The manner in which the rector is appointed to his post varies according to charter. However, in all cases Law no.168 of 1989 states that he/she must be elected from among full time, permanent professors teaching at the university by an electorate made up of permanent and semi-permanent professors, confirmed researchers (or their representatives) and in some cases also by student representatives from the council of administration, the academic senate and the faculty councils, and also by a quota of the technical-administrative and managerial staff.

2 The academic senate which defines the polices of intervention and development of the university, plans the stages involved and oversees the co-ordination of the didactic and scientific work of the university. It also has powers to control the manner in which the university's autonomy is exercised. Law no.168 of 1989 established that the senate must be representative of the faculties making up the university. In general the various charters state that the academic senate comprises the rector, the faculty heads and other representatives of the academic and non-academic community. The latter group includes, for example, the students and the technical-administrative personnel, and very occasionally external members who may be representatives of the region, province or municipality.

These members are elected on the basis of procedures set out in the charter.

3 The administrative council establishes policy and maintains the university's finance and accounts and manages the technical-administrative personnel, but has no responsibilities for the teaching, research or service structures to which both the law and the charters attribute financial and spending autonomy. It also approves the annual statement of accounts of the university. Its composition varies according to the provisions found in the different charters. In general it is composed of the rector, the administrative director and other representatives of the academic and external economic world.

4 The board of auditors is entrusted with the control of the management of the university finances and accounts.

5 The evaluation nucleus is a body placed in an autonomous position with the task of measuring the efficiency of the structures and services for research, teaching and the technical-administrative management of the university.

The law which preceded the creation of the charters provided for another body, the academic assembly, which could be convoked by the rector in order to express its views on questions of general interest for the university. Over time it became so large and cumbersome as to make its convening impractical.

There are various provisions contained in individual charters for a variety of organisational structures which cut across the usual distribution of responsibilities. In particular, there is the university executive committee (*giunta d'ateneo*) which undertakes tasks delegated by the rector, the academic senate and the administrative council. This committee comprises the rector, the pro-rector and the administrative director, as well as members designated by the academic senate and the administrative council.

The council of students (consiglio degli studenti) which is formed by student representatives from the various university bodies and, in some cases, also includes representatives directly elected by the students. It has powers to suggest and advise on matters involving teaching regulations, the right to an education and university fees.

Finally, there may also be student-professor committees with competence for didactic matters, conferences or inter-departmental councils, area councils, and a permanent council of representatives for the technical and administrative personnel.

The organisation of the didactic and research structures and activities, in particular the faculties, and how the university organises itself in the various cultural sectors includes the following:

1 The faculty head who represents the faculty, convenes and presides over the faculty council, carries out its deliberations, and co-ordinates the general services which are faculty responsibility.

2 The faculty council which runs the faculty, particularly the planning, promotion and co-ordination of the scientific, cultural and training needs of the various faculty disciplines, and implements the overall development plans of the university which refer to the faculty.

In faculties where more than one degree course is taught, degree course councils have been set up which co-ordinate teaching activities and monitor the operation and attainment of the academic qualifications provided. Some faculty didactic rules provide for the setting up of a didactic commission as well as student-professor councils in which both parties are equally represented. These bodies monitor the level of implementation of the rules regulating teaching at the university and in the faculty.

The department which is also concerned with research using methods set by professors and researchers, from the same or different faculties, has the following bodies: the director, the departmental council and the committee.

The administrative director is the most important body for the university's administration and personnel organisation, and mirrors somewhat the position of the rector. He/she is head of the offices and central administrative structures and carries out the general tasks of policy making, co-ordination and control as regards the technical and administrative personnel according to the plans and objectives defined by the governing bodies of the university.

The system of checks and balances between the university's governing bodies centres upon an equal distribution of competencies among the various organs and the various didactic and academic structures (university, faculties, departments, institutions). A truly controlling body does not exist, apart from the board of auditors which has the responsibility for ascertaining the regularity of the financial and accounting management of the university, and forms the nucleus of evaluation to assess the university's management structures.

Law no. 537 of 24 December, 1993 provided for establishing in each university an internal evaluation committee with the tasks of verifying the correct management of public resources, the productivity of research and didactic activities on the basis of a comparative analysis of costs and performance as well as assessing the impartiality and correctness of administrative actions. This committee is also entrusted with determining control reference parameters on the basis of indicators provided by the general governing bodies to which it reports annually.

The reports of the evaluation committees are also sent to the Ministry for the Universities and Scientific and Technological Research, the National University Council and to the permanent conference of rectors who evaluate the results of the efficiency and productivity of research and teaching work, and who verify the development and re-distribution programmes of the university system with a view to the appropriate allocation of financial resources. This evaluation is the task of the permanent monitoring institute for the evaluation of the national university system.

It is through the balancing of powers between the rector, academic senate and administrative council that a clear understanding of the checks and balances of the university system can be gained. Despite a different approach to governance faculties and departments also maintain a system of checks and balances of the sort inherent in such collegiate bodies.

The rector oversees all the structures and services of the university, issuing directives necessary for running university affairs and for the correct application of the regulations of university governance. The academic senate coordinates didactic and academic activities by establishing criteria for the distribution of full time, permanent teaching and research appointments and deciding on their distribution between faculties. It also proposes criteria for the distribution of financial resources and allocation of technical-administrative personnel among the didactic and research structures to the administrative council. The administrative council exercises a control over the functions of the technical-administrative management of the university.

In some cases a special joint university-local authority council is created in order to examine common problems. This committee comprises the rector and representatives of the region, the province and the municipalities in which the university and its secondary institutes are situated.

The function and participation of the various groups ie. academic staff, non-academic staff, students, etc. in the governance of individual universities and their administrative bodies is regulated by the charters of the individual universities. As a consequence there are various differences in the university regulatory systems.

In general terms, Article 16, fourth clause of Law no.168 of 9 May, 1989 establishes that the university charters must state that the administrative council shall provide representation for all the various components identified by existing legislation, that is the technical-administration personnel and the students. There are other laws which ensure that students can participate in the governing organs of the university and the faculties, particularly the academic senate and the faculty councils.

An examination of some university charters shows that the line proposed by national legislation has been adopted, the membership of the academic senate includes full-time permanent professors and researchers and also students. Some charters, at the request of the rector, allow for a representative of the region, province or municipality to participate in academic senate meetings when the preparation, approval or verification of the development plans of the university are on the agenda.

On the university administrative council there are representatives of the students and teaching staff, it is also possible for representatives of the technical-administrative personnel to participate. Furthermore, some charters allow for local authority representatives i.e. from the regions, provinces and/ or municipalities, and for representatives of other public or private bodies which contribute towards the funding of the university.

Faculty governing bodies allow for the representation of researchers and students via the faculty councils, which also include the faculty head, and full and part-time professors, on degree and diploma course committees, and for representation of the technical-administrative staff via departmental committees.

The charters may also contain provisions for establishing centres for external relations solely related to the management or participation with organisations for commercial purposes. For instance the charter of the University of Bologna states that when one or more didactic or academic structure makes such a proposal, a joint-stock company may be set up with the task of promoting the results of the academic and especially the scientific activities of the university, in order to improve the information and technology available to industry.

Some charters permit the creation of special committees which allow for the involvement of external interests in the governance of the university. In some cases these are committees of organisations which help to maintain the university, while in others they are organisations or bodies from civil society providing advice and information.

The representatives of the teaching, non-teaching staff and students etc. are elected onto the various university governing bodies. The electoral procedures are set out in the charters of the individual universities and also in the statute law still applicable to the universities, for example, the election of a student representative or representatives to the faculty committees as laid down by Article 9 of decree no. 580 of 1 October, 1973 and enacted as Law no. 766 of 30 November, 1973.

The manner in which the academic senate is made up is of particular interest. The rector belongs to this body ex-officio, and also presides over it, the other ex officio members are the vicar pro-rector who acts as vice-president, the faculty heads and the administrative director. In addition to these ex-officio members, the academic senate comprises an elected membership of staff and students. Thus, for example, the charter of the University of Florence establishes that the senate be made up of a representative for each area of research elected from full-time professors and researchers belonging to the departments from those research areas, as well as by three student representatives. In other cases it is also possible for there to be elected representatives of the technical-administrative staff. The election of representatives is called by a decree of the rector who also determines the time and the procedure.

3 External influence

A major role in external influence is played by the national conference of the rectors of the universities. This is an association made up of the rectors from state and non-state universities and first received legal recognition with Law no. 168 of 9 May, 1989. This law set out to:

a) handle the problems of the universities in more detail by bringing their needs to the attention of government authorities and to parliament;

b) express opinions on the state of development of the universities and level of university teaching in conformity to Article 2 of Law no. 168 of 1968;

c) promote and sustain university initiatives in national and international assemblies through relations with analogous community and non-community associations.

External participation in university governance has been extended by some charters which provide for the involvement of bodies external to the university.

These charters allow for the setting up of a joint committee between the university and local government bodies in order to ensure the most appropriate forms of co-ordination with the various territorial authorities and to examine common problems. These committees are in addition to regional committees of co-ordination where more than one university is present. They comprise the rectors of each university and the faculty heads and have the task of co-ordinating the activities of the university seats on matters such as the right to a university education, and the utilisation and development of the university structures in the region (Article 3 of Law no. 590 of 14 August 1982).

The conference of students or the student committees provided for by some university charters can make requests and proposals to the university governing bodies i.e. the academic senate and the administrative council. They also express opinions as prescribed by the bye-laws and regulations of the university, in general, on the development plan, the university's end of year accounts, the didactic rules of the university, the determination of the contributions and fees payable by the students, and on the right to university education.

Some charters allow for a civic defending counsel which takes actions to safeguard the interests and rights of those who claim to have suffered damages, malfunctions, shortcomings or delays attributable to acts and omissions on the part of bodies, offices or single individuals belonging either to the teaching staff or to the technical-administrative personnel of the university.

Finally, the region acts to remove economic and social obstacles to the 'right to a university education' by providing scholarships. These funds may be transferred directly to the university so that it can allocate the scholarships.

4 Hidden or indirect governance

The principle form of indirect government or hidden influence on the autonomy of the university derives from the fact that the university is substantially financed by the state.

Recently, Law no.537 of 23 December, 1993 redefined the universities' financial funding procedures by augmenting their spending autonomy. According to the new procedures there are now no longer separate items of expenditure for personnel, management, research, major plant and equipment, etc. However, the Law has not eliminated the invisible power of the central administration over individual universities. There is now a single fund and transfer of money to each university. The universities receive funds related to their specific expenditure for their running costs and institutional activities which covers the spending on teaching and research, the non-teaching staff, and maintenance of university structures for research activities. With this single transfer the universities can make their own choices on how to use their monies and are thus able to rationalise their costs and enlarge their development prospects as they see necessary.

The university charters and latest regulations concerning income give the universities the capacity to determine and provide for their own needs and help reduce their dependency on the state.

The reduction in the size of state financing and its substitution by other sources of financing i.e. from private or public bodies, does not exclude, a priori, similar forms of external influence driven once again by funding. The reduction in the state's financial commitment to the universities, and the consequent weakening of its relations with them could find university autonomy being conditioned by local interests or merely economic interests to the detriment of academic and didactic freedom.

University access requirements up until 1969 depended upon prospective students having specific high school qualifications. Law no. 910 of 11 December, 1969 provided for the wholesale liberalisation of access, so that whoever wanted to enrol in a graduate course could do so, provided that he or she had a school leaver's diploma, which is obtained after five years of high school education. More recently access to the universities has been regulated. The Ministry for the Universities and Scientific Research has issued a number of decrees aimed at decongesting some faculties, and introduced a planned number of posts and the prior selection of candidates.

5 Legal protection

The protection of the different subjective positions in the university system is left to the normal instruments of protection provided for by the judiciary with regard to acts and measures adopted by the offices of the public administration. The instruments foreseen for safeguarding the legitimate interests and subjective rights of subjects are: appeal to a superior administrative authority or appeal to a court of law i.e. appearing before an ordinary judge or before an administrative judge.

Examples of administrative appeal procedure can be found in some administrative, financial and accounting regulations. They provide for the lodging of an appeal within a fixed term, with respect to measures taken by the various functional structures of the rector, in order to obtain a modification to that measure.

6 Conclusion

Law no. 168 of 9 May 1989 has set in motion a reform process which is still taking place and which is destined to make radical changes in the manner in which the university system is set up, thus bringing it into line with the framework set out in the constitution of 1948. It also means that the statutory law which until recently governed the universities and managed the university system according to a ministerial like centralising logic with tutorial functions, is now quite out of date.

The university charters represent the key to redefining responsibilities within academic institutes and in the Italian academic world, and refer above all to organisational structures, their competencies and to decision-making procedures.

For the future, the issue of autonomy must be resolved not only in terms of financial autonomy but also in terms of didactic autonomy. At present legislative measures are being prepared which are aimed at recognising and guaranteeing the capacity and right of the universities (and also the faculties) to be really autonomous in the field of teaching, and by extension to include the form and content of the curricula offered to students. These are measures which, if approved in the coming months, will make a major contribution towards the transition from a structure comprising of rigidly defined didactic paths, as set out in the ministerial schedules of law no. 341 of 1990 which annulled the autonomy conceded by law no. 910 of 1969, to a flexible structure which recognises proposals for curricula development advanced by individual universities.

10.17

LATVIA

Andrejs Rauhvargers & Janis Čakste

1 Introduction

Governance of higher education institutions in Latvia is premised by the principle of autonomy of higher education institutions, which is reflected in the rights of the institutions:

- to devise and adopt statutes, which are called Satversme,
- to hire its staff,
- to determine independently the content and the forms of studies,
- to define additional admissions criteria,
- to formulate the basic objectives of scientific work carried out at the institution,
- to regulate their organisational and administrative structures.

2 Governance

The representational, management and decision making bodies at higher education institutions are the Satversme meeting, the senate, the rector, the audit commission, and the court of arbitration. The competencies of the governing bodies are given in the 1995 Law on Education.

The Satversme meeting elects the senate and the rector, it approves the basic principles of financial management and is the highest collegial and decision-making body in the institution. Its members are elected by the staff of the higher education institution in accordance with quotas for different staff groups, i.e. professors, academic staff, non-academic staff, administrative personnel and students. In some institutions, e.g. the University of Latvia, all full professors are privileged by automatically being members of the Satversme meeting, while the rest of the academic staff (associate professors, *docents*, lecturers and assistants) elect their representatives.

The Satversme meeting adopts and amends the Satversme (statutes) of the higher education institution, elects and dismisses the rector, elects the senate, audit commission and the members of the court of arbitration. It also confirms measures taken by the senate, audit commission and the court of arbitration. In practice, however, the Satversme meeting convenes too rarely to function as the real ruling power in every day life. Its actual powers are, therefore, concerned with the election of the rector and the senate.

The senate is the decision-making body which determines the contents of bye-laws and regulations, and it issues decisions on virtually all matters. It is the collegiate governing body of the personnel, and as such it organises the election of the rector, approves the vice-rectors, deans, and directors of institutes, and it decides upon the establishment of new faculties, departments etc., as well as on the institution's budget. It also approves study programmes. In most higher education institutions the senate is the most powerful governing body. The rector implements administrative policy, determines the competencies of vice-rectors and other administrative staff, and represents the institution externally.

The senate and the rector are assisted by academic (research) councils, which, in their capacity as elected advisory bodies, prepare decisions in appropriate fields for approval by the rector or the senate. For example, the academic council prepares decisions on strategic changes in the study programmes.

The senate approves the regulations in all the fields of activity of a higher educational establishment, examines and approves study programmes, establishes and liquidates structural units, approves vice-rectors (on proposal of the rector) and deans (on proposal of faculties), and decides on the use of the budget.

The rector implements the general administration of a higher education establishment and represents the higher education institutions. The rector is personally liable to the government for the implementation of legislation, the financial activities and quality of education in the higher education establishment.

Other units involved in the governance of higher education institutions are:

- the director, who administrates the economic/financial sphere and carries out economic planning,
- the legal department, which provides legal assistance to individuals, groups or structural units, and to governing bodies at all levels,
- the faculty boards, which take decisions in academic, economic, and financial matters at the faculty level,
- the faculty deans, who implement the administrative policy of the faculty,
- heads of departments, who fulfil the same function at the departmental level.

The audit commission and court of arbitration examine applications from students and academic staff reporting infringements or violations of the academic freedoms and rights appointed by the Satversme. It also examines disputes between officials of the higher education establishment, as well as between institutions administrating structural units at a subordinate level.

3 The legal framework – principles and structures

Until 1985, Latvia was under Soviet rule and the Communist Party committees effectively controlled all governing bodies at higher education institutions. Thus, the first important change was the introduction of autonomy to higher education institutions by the Law on Education of 1991. Despite its positive intentions, the Law was too concerned with democracy and freedoms, and entirely omitted an accountability aspect. The borders of institutional autonomy were eventually defined by the 1995 Law on Higher Education which, *inter alia*, created a quality assessment and accountability system.

The 1995 Law sets forth in general terms the rights and duties, and general principles of election of governing bodies. The implementation of these provisions is left to the institution's Satversme. According to the Law, the Satversme meeting elects the senate and the rector as the main governing bodies. Their decisions are binding on all structural units and staff members of the institution. However, a hidden governance is exercised by the higher education quality assurance system.

Although not expressly stated in the Law, the legal framework in Latvia provides for discretionary powers at all the administrative levels. On many issues the appropriate governing body inside a higher education institution makes discretionary decisions, and is entitled to lay down internal regulations etc.. Their criteria are not formulated in written documents but are arrived at by due consideration of the possible outcome of their decisions on the quality of studies and research, the economic use of funding and the interests of staff and students.

The role of the academic staff in the institutional government is set forth in the Satversme of most higher education institutions. Academic staff, e.g. professors, are the most widely represented group in the Satversme meeting, the senate, and on the faculty boards.

Students are represented by a quota in the governing bodies, and most Satversme provide for a larger quota than the minimal 10% required by Law; for instance, the student participation quota is 29% at the Satversme meeting of the University of Latvia. Non-academic staff are represented with a quota of 14% in the Satversme meeting of the University of Latvia.

Representation of professors at the Satversme meeting is not stated in law, it is understood that the academic staff comprise no less than 60%, and students no less than 10%. In practice, as at the University of Latvia, all full professors automatically participate in the Satversme meeting and the percentage of students is estimated at 25%. These percentages depend on the number of professors; and the maximum number of student members of the Satversme meeting which is fixed at 100. Representation on the senate is set according to law with no less than 75% of academic staff of which 50% are professors and associate professors and students comprising no less than 36%.

The audit commission has no legally defined quotas of different personnel groups. In the University of Latvia members are professors and other senior teaching research staff. The audit commission has the right to examine how all the fields of activities of the higher educational establishment comply with the existing legislation including the Satversme of the institution. It, therefore, has the right to be familiarised with all the documentation relating to the financial and economic activities of the institution. The audit commission is elected by the Satversme meeting; representatives of the administration of the higher education establishment must not sit on the commission. Audit commission reports are sent to the senate no less than once a year and, if necessary, the follow-up decisions are taken by the senate.

The election procedures for staff and student representatives may differ in different higher education institutions. At most institutions the staff representatives to the Satversme meeting are elected at the departmental level at numbers proportional to their staff numbers. Student representatives are usually elected by the student body of a given faculty.

In principle, general stakeholders have no part in the decision making process at higher education institutions. An exemption applies to final examinations and to the defense of degree papers. One of the new aspects of the recently adopted Law is the existence of a convent of advisors at higher education institutions. This body includes representatives of the labour market, society in general, and in some cases representatives of the state as appointed by Minister of Education and Science. At most higher education institutions the convent of advisors has not yet been established. However, several Satversme have been amended accordingly, and in some cases the Minister may order their establishment.

External stakeholders consist of employers, professional associations, the Ministry of Education and Research, the Latvian Science Council, and research institutions of the appropriate field. They are involved in the examination commission for final examinations and defense of degree papers (Bakalaurs and Magistrs degrees). This commission is formed from both university staff and leading representatives from the appropriate branch of industry or science, or appropriate professional association. The chairperson of that commission is selected from outside the higher education institution.

4 Hidden governance

Possible non-accreditation of a study programme is the foremost powerful instrument employed to overcome possible institutional reluctance to implement changes, or undergo time-consuming modernisation procedures, and to discourage insular institutional autonomy. Furthermore, once fully implemented, the new Law will tie financing to quality assessment and accreditation results of study programmes.

A novel type of indirect governance has emerged as a result of continuing European integration. Policy measures on the part of national external bodies, e.g. the Ministry of Education are much more likely not to be rejected on institutional autonomy grounds if they are motivated or even explicitly supported by the Council of Europe or European Union. For instance, the introduction of a quality assessment system proposed by the Ministry of Education and Science was completely rejected by the higher education institutions since it was seen as a measure violating their autonomy. This situation rapidly changed when provision for quality assessment was strongly recommended by the Council of Europe as one of the crucial points in the forthcoming Council of Europe/UNESCO convention on the recognition of higher education credentials. Also third-party suggestions for making changes to the curricula have not been appreciated by the higher education institutions. However, such ideas are accepted when they are motivated by the harmonisation of education in certain professions with EU countries.

5 Legal protection

As part of the legacy of Soviet times, legal protection in Latvia must still be regarded as a weak concept. Latvians have grown accustomed to legal rights as merely formal promulgations which inevitably fail whenever called upon. As a result, even when higher education institutions were free to include in their Satversme democratic principles, procedures of legal protection were virtually always missing because nobody expected any action to be stated thereunder.

Current legislation stipulates a number of possibilities for the legal protection of staff. The 1995 Law provides that a court of arbitration shall be established at all higher education institutions. In principle, complaints or objections may also be submitted to the rector, because the rector is personally answerable to the Law and the Satversme.

However, neither the Law nor the Satversme provide clear mechanisms of appeal, other than a submission of the complaint or objection in person to the appropriate body. In practice, individuals in these cases can be represented by a trade union, a student association or by the head of department or the dean. In all cases, individuals may lodge their complaints with a court of law, which may hear the case irrespective of whether internal appeals have been made or not.

In many aspects the Satversmes of higher education institutions entitles the governing bodies to make discretional decisions, but the legislation does not spell out any concrete criteria for making these decisions. In practice the governing bodies consider the expected effect of a decision on the quality of studies and research, the use of finances, and on the interests of staff and students.

6 Conclusion

In principle, governance of higher education institutions in Latvia is democratic. It is based upon institutional autonomy. The main governing bodies of higher education institutions are elected by Satversme meetings. Legislation providing for the protection of the rights of individuals, groups or smaller structural units and even of the higher education institutions, against the state, appears to be weakly elaborated at all legal levels, although representatives who could (and should) insist on such provisions, were actually strongly represented during the elaboration of the relevant legislative acts. This seems evidence of a lack of democratic tradition in society at large. These conclusions have to be taken into account during the present period with the implementation of the 1995 Law. The shortcomings of the existing legislation must be overcome by elaborating the bye-laws of the Court of Arbitration, the Court of Appeal, and the Audit Commission.

10.18

LITHUANIA

Gediminas Dubauskas

1 Introduction

There are currently 15 higher education institutions in Lithuania: eight universities, six academies and one institute. Higher Education reform is a priority for the Lithuanian government and academic institutions, and is being pursued in a number of different contexts and through a variety of institutions and schemes.

Conditions for higher education and research are now changing more rapidly than at any other time. This is due to several reasons, the most important being independence which was gained on 11 March 1990. Internationalisation of economics, trade and information are crucial factors as well; Lithuania has not been immune to the entirely new opportunities they have created. In times when change is a key feature, centralised systems of education of the kind that Lithuania inherited from the Communist system, become impossible to preserve in higher education.

The aims of research and higher education reform are democratisation of the system of research and higher education, development of self-government as well as modernisation of higher education programmes. Lithuanian higher education aims to draw closer to west European models and to world achievements and promote international partnership relations.

2 Governance

The statutes of higher education institutions are the legal acts which regulate the activities of the institution. The statute laws regulate the activities of other research establishments. The statute (charter) of the institution to be established is drafted by the provisional (constituent) council appointed by the founder, and is approved by the founder. The statute of a functioning institution is adopted or amended either by the meeting (conference) of the institution's employees holding research degrees or academic research titles by a simple majority vote, or, on the instructions of the meeting (conference), by the council (senate) by two-thirds of the votes.

The university consists of a number of faculties, institutes, departments, laboratories, libraries, research centres, subdivisions, enterprises, etc., which are governed by the set regulations. The faculties, research centres, institutes and the libraries enjoy the rights of the faculty concerning their organisational structure. The heads of research centres are approved by the senate on the proposal by the rector. The divisions of the university can acquire legal personality on the proposal of the senate according to the procedure set by the government.

The university has the following permanent management bodies:

- decision-making councils, which are the senate, the faculty councils, institutes and other departments, and the student government,
- executive councils, which are the rector and the rectorate, the deans and heads of institutes, and other departments and directorates,
- the collegium for the supervision of the statutes and professional ethics (hereafter: the collegium).

According to Article 16 of the Law on Research and Higher Education 1991: "The highest decision-making body of institutions of higher education shall be the senate which shall be elected by the employees of the institution who have research degrees or academic (research) titles. The senate shall elect and appoint the head of the institution (i.e. rector, director) and shall approve deputies by means of a simple majority of votes. The same person may not be both the head of the senate and the head of the institution. The limits of the independence of other institutions, the structure of their management and the procedure for their formation shall be established by their statutes and the Laws of the Republic of the Lithuania."

In the event that statutes are adopted or changed upon proposal of the senate, the Conference of the University Teachers is convened. The conference is presided by an elected chair. The representation quota at the conference is determined by the senate, but it must be not less than 1/3 of all universities teachers having research degrees and pedagogical (science) titles. The decisions made by the conference are of a recommending nature as are those of the senate and the rectorate.

The bye-laws of the Lithuanian Agricultural University provide an example of another organisational structure. The university's legislative bodies are the university assembly and university council and the executive bodies are the rector and the rectorate. The board of statute supervision and ethics resolves conflicts and performs supervisory functions. Economic and financial activities are supervised by the revision commission of the university.

The university senate can be constituted only from the staff members with academic degrees or pedagogical titles. They are elected in faculties or subdivisions by secret ballot of majority votes for a three year period. Seven representatives from each faculty or subdivision equivalent to faculty are elected to the university senate. Elections are legitimate if 2/3 of voters from faculty or its subdivisions are present.

The university senate is led by the chairperson, assistant chairperson and secretary, who are elected for not more than two terms of office in turn. Senate managers/leaders are elected and recalled by secret ballot by an absolute majority of votes. Rector, vice-rectors, deans, deputy deans can not be elected as top managers of the university senate.

All sessions of the university senate are public. They are convoked at least once during a term. Special sessions are convoked by the request of the rector or the chairperson of an academy subdivision council no later than ten days after the request has been presented to the leaders of the university senate.

2.1 University Senate:

- confirms and changes regulations and other legal acts of the university,
- forms the board of statute supervision and ethics, revision commission and other regular commissions,
- elects and recalls the rector of the university,
- confirms or recalls vice-rectors appointed by the rector,
- listens and evaluates annual reports presented by the rector and the revision commission,
- confirms and changes the university's estimates of income and expenditures and also annual or long-term financial/economic programmes,
- establishes and closes faculties or other independent subdivisions of the university according to proposals of the rectorate,
- by the suggestion of the statute supervision and ethics commission revokes the rector's orders or decisions of independent subdivisions by 2/3 of the votes,
- solves questions of study and research organisation, confirms the main trends of research,
- approves the suggestions of faculty councils for conferring the titles of professor or associated professor,
- confirms committees for PhD studies and Habilitation committees; evaluates faculties or other subdivisions, establishes the certification order of academy personnel,
- solves other important questions of the university and establishes commissions to investigate them.

The decisions of the university senate are adopted by majority votes in open or secret voting. Decisions are adopted with 2/3 of university council member votes. Decisions are signed by the chairperson and secretary of the council. Decisions come into force after they have been publicly and officially announced.

The university assembly is convoked by the decision of the university senate or by the requisition of 1/3 of the members of the university assembly, to adopt or change the statutes. All the university's employees with scientific degrees or pedagogical titles constitute the university assembly.

Statutes of a higher education institution regulate the following main rights of those who are studying:

- to have their representatives with a deliberative vote on the senate, rectorate and departmental council,
- to help organise the study process, and solve questions concerning students and their private life, the allocation of scholarships, and the establishment and maintenance of regulations.

Other statutes delegate student's rights and duties to regulations approved by the senate of the institution. There are also government regulations pertaining to the rights of academic staff and those studying, in particular:

- the qualitative regulations of higher education and the regulations for the establishment and assessment of higher education institutions,
- the procedures for allocating scholarships to higher education students, and establishing scholarships bearing the name of a prominent person,
- rules for granting credits to day-time students,
- procedures concerning Lithuanian citizens' studies abroad and foreign persons' studies in Lithuania,
- governmental resolution on state scholarships for Lithuanian citizens' studies and research abroad and foreigners' studies and research in Lithuania,
- ministerial orders on rules of quality assessment for institutions of research and higher education,
- the orders for using public transport on favourable terms for students,
- the orders providing students with dormitories, students' sanatorium treatment and other issues.

3 External influence and hidden governance

The Ministry of Education and Science formulates general policy and implements targets for higher education development. There is some indirect governance detected in the financial regulations and educational quality assurance. All higher education institutions are financed from the state budget, and do not have sufficiently defined independence on the allocation of these financial means. Higher education institutions must follow the rules laid down by Seimas (the parliament) and the state government, the Law on Research and Higher Education 1991, the Qualitative Regulations of Higher Education 1993, the Regulations for the Establishment and Assessment of Institutions of Higher Education 1993, On the Approval of the General Regulations on the System of Awarding Research Degrees and Academic (Research) Titles in the Republic of Lithuania 1996, Regulations of the Lithuanian State Research and Higher Education Fund 1993, Governmental Resolution on State Scholarships for Lithuanian Nationals' Studies and Research Studies Abroad and Foreigners' Studies and Research Studies in Lithuania 1996, Ministerial Order on Rules of Quality Assessment for Institutions of Research and Higher Education 1996; as well as general labour laws, environmental laws, criminal codes, and other deeds.

The Centre for Quality Assessment in Higher Education was founded in 1995. This Centre is a state budgeted institution, organising the assessment of scientific and pedagogical activity of research and higher education institutions and giving information, consultation and recommendations about the recognition of higher education acquired abroad.

4 Legal protection

Transition from the former system of higher education began after the promulgation of the Law on Research and Higher Education 1991. The avenues for the internal and external appeal of decisions and actions taken by the institutions are still not well defined. Legal protection is organised according to the general labour laws, environmental laws, criminal codes, etc..

5 Conclusion

Democratisation, self-governance and the modernisation of higher education programmes have been the aims of higher education reform in Lithuania. Integrating studies and research is the next important objective of the reforms and will be implemented through joint graduate programmes within higher education and the research institutions. Efforts will also be taken to increase collaboration with foreign universities in order to update scientific developments.

Autonomy and sufficiently defined limits of independence for higher education institutions are stated in the Law on Research and Higher Education 1991. The functions of the government and/or Ministry over the detailed rights and duties of students, the procedure for financing higher education and for using property allotted to the institutions by the state, as well as some other issues require further determination.

After detailed survey of the regulations declared in the Law on Higher Education and Research 1991, it is obvious that some important regulations are not included, e.g. those concerning study fees, and the legal status of higher education institution statutes which are supposed to be realised in the Law on Higher Education Institutions. It is planned that a new version of this Law will be prepared in the near future.

10.19

MALTA

Paul Heywood

1 Introduction

Authority to govern the University in Malta is derived from the Education Act No. XXIV of 1988. The main principles, conceptions, notions and definitions relating to governance of the University of Malta issue from the provisions of Art. 28 which empowers the university:

- to provide for instruction in such branches of learning and to make such provisions for research and the advancement and dissemination of knowledge as it may from time to time determine,
- to determine the conditions for admission into the University and into any course of study provided by it,
- to provide appropriate procedures to determine the persons who have attained the necessary proficiency in the various branches of study,
- to constitute faculties, departments and other academic sections of the University,
- to institute academic and non-academic posts as required from time to time, and to make appointments thereto,
- to establish entities with their own statutes and to monitor the administration of such entities as well as of other entities already existing or which may be created by others in the field of higher education,
- to administer the funds voted by the House of Representatives for the implementation of its programmes and any other funds it may receive from other sources,
- to make statutes, regulations and bye-laws in accordance with the provisions of the Act,

- to act in any other way conducive to the attainment of its aims.

The last sub-section quoted above is noteworthy for the blanket coverage it extends to the University of Malta in so far as governance is concerned.

Prior to 1988, under the Education Act of 1974 as amended in 1976, 1978 and 1980, institutional governance was very narrowly circumscribed. The University was required to submit its recommendations concerning most aspects of governance to Government through a commission set up by the same Government for the development of higher education. How large the commission bulked in the mind of the Government of the day was reflected in the provision of the 1980 amendments to the Education Act 1974. The relevant Article 34 ran as follows:

1 "The Council of the University shall, not later than the end of June of each year, cause to be prepared and approve estimates of its financial requirements for the following financial year commencing on 1st January, and proposals for the allocation of its resources, and shall submit such estimates and proposals to the Commission.

2 The Commission shall, not later than the end of September of the same year, make a report to the Minister containing its recommendations on the estimates and proposals to the Commission.

3 The estimates and proposals of the University shall be submitted for consideration and decision by a Committee of the whole House by the Minister responsible for finance who shall, together with such comments or recommendations as he may deem appropriate to make, indicate to the Committee the sum the Government proposes to include in its next annual estimates to the House as a vote of expenditure in respect of the University or the sum already so voted by the House, as the case may require. The submission to the Committee shall be made by such motion as the said Minister may deem appropriate.

4 The Committee shall devote three sittings to the debate on a motion moved under this section and shall so regulate its procedure that representatives of the Council of the University and of the Commission may make their submissions and may give answers and explanations.

5 Any sum voted by the House for expenditure by the University shall be expended in accordance with the estimates and proposals approved by the Committee of the House under this section".

This direct state governance had a constricting effect on the development of tertiary education in Malta. In terms of the new law in 1988, the Government of the day at Art. 28 expressly stated that "The University of Studies of Malta is, by means of the present Act, being refounded under the name of University of Malta..."

In terms of Art. 30(1) "the following shall be the governing bodies of the University:

- the council,
- the senate,
- the faculty boards."

In terms of Art.30 (2) "the following shall be the Principal Officers of the University:

- the chancellor,
- the pro-chancellor,
- the rector,
- the pro-rector,
- the secretary,
- the deans of the faculties."

2 Governance

The chancellor is the highest officer of the University. He is appointed for a term of seven years by the President of Malta acting in accordance with the advice of the prime minister given after he has consulted the leader of the opposition.

His main responsibility is to ensure that the University of Malta conforms with the law. The chancellor promulgates the statutes, regulations and byelaws of the governing bodies of the University. Before doing so he may refer back once to the governing body concerned, any such statutes, regulations or bye-laws which in his opinion are not in accordance with the law. The chancellor, in special circumstances, shall also have the power to summon the council, senate and faculty boards.

The pro-chancellor is appointed by the chancellor for a term not exceeding five years. Whenever the office of chancellor is temporarily vacant, and until a new chancellor is appointed and whenever the holder of the office is absent from Malta or on vacation or is for any reason unable to perform the functions conferred upon him by this Act, these functions shall be performed by the pro-chancellor. The pro-chancellor also performs the functions of chancellor whenever required to do so in writing by the chancellor. Moreover, it is to be noted that the pro-chancellor is the ex-officio president of the council which is the supreme governing body of the University.

The rector is the principal academic and administrative officer of the University and is responsible for the day-to-day administration of the University. He is the ex-officio president of the senate and faculty boards and is vested with the legal representation of the University. The pro-rector is appointed by the rector for a term of one year and shall perform the functions of the rector for the same reasons and in the same circumstances that the pro-chancellor would perform the functions of chancellor. The secretary is the second highest administrative officer of the University and shall be appointed by the council for a term of five years. The dean of a faculty is elected for a term of two years by the academic staff of that faculty and from among the heads of departments of that faculty. He is president ex officio of the faculty board in the absence of the rector.

Together with the academic staff, both the non-academic staff and the students are represented on the council. The students are also represented on senate and faculty boards. As for the community in general, the membership of both council and senate has, down the years, been affected by major social issues as they arise.

The University has the power to make statutes, regulations and bye-laws in order to provide for its own administration and for the administration of its activities and of the entities created by it. Statutes, which are made by council, bind the whole University as well as the entities created by it.

Regulations, which are made by senate, provide for matters of an academic nature. These bind the whole University whereas bye-laws, which are made by the faculty boards, provide for matters of an academic nature and shall bind the faculty represented by the faculty board that made those bye-laws.

Art. 29 subsection 5 expressly states that "no statute providing for a matter of an academic nature may be made, or, when made, may be amended or revoked by the council, unless the council requests the advice of the senate on that statute or on that amendment or revocation but if such advice is not tendered within the term established by the council, which term shall in no case be less than twenty-one days from the date of the said request, then the council may make that statute or amend or revoke it without that notice."

All statutes, regulations and bye-laws made by the competent governing bodies of the University are without effect unless promulgated by the chancellor and published in the Government Gazette. When they are so promulgated and published, they have the force of law, provided that they are laid on the Table of the House of Representatives.

Membership of council, the main governing body of the University of Malta, reflects the importance given by the Government to vital sectors of the community. These include banks, industry, commerce, financial services, the Education Department and the Church.

The governance of the University is transparently defined in the Education Act. Members of council representing specific interests of stakeholders express their views and influence the council both directly and indirectly. As the membership of council virtually covers all interests of the various sectors of the community, including all the social partners within Maltese society, there is no hidden element which can be detected. There remains no scope for hidden attempts from other sources to influence the governance of tertiary education.

The structure of organisation mapped out by the Education Act ensures that grievances at all levels may be internally redressed effectively within a reasonable period. Internal decisions may be contested through appeals to council. The chancellor, furthermore, is required by law to ensure compliance with the provisions of the Education Act. The above remedies, moreover, do not preclude resort to the civil courts and other commissions and tribunals set-up by the Government for various purposes.

3 Conclusion

This healthy legal regime is borne out by the University's gradual and constant growth since 1987; results have been achieved over the past eight years which normally would have taken a far longer period to attain. Up to the 1950s the population of the University of Malta did not exceed 400. By 1987 the student population had grown to 1400. Between 1987 and 1996 it topped 7000 and is still growing.

It is obvious that the present governing methods have made it possible for the University to explore new approaches in management, both in the long and the short term. Decentralisation facilitated by the latest information technology is set to further promote this growth. At the moment seventeen per cent of the total local age cohort make it to University; the goal set by the present administration is twenty per cent. Of course the progress registered so far has been made possible by sustained financial investment in the human resources of the island. It is not by pure coincidence that the Ministry responsible for University matters is also responsible for Human Resources.

10.20

MOLDOVA

Stefan Tiron and Dimitrie Ungureanu

1 The legal framework: principles and structures

a) The Education Law established a modern system of organisation and monitoring based on principles such as:

- decentralisation of managerial and educational functions vertically and horizontally,
- the establishment of assessment, licensing and accrediting procedures in education,
- a higher education system based on university autonomy, and juridical, didactic, financial, scientific and editorial independence etc..

b) The existing legal framework assures a standard which is adequate for the responsibilities of decision-making both at the state level of educational and general management as well as at the institutional level of daily administration and teaching and research management. Decisions are commonly adopted by the collective governing bodies and the control of their implementation and assessment is performed by the qualified public authorities.

c) After 1985 one of the essential changes in the governance of higher education institutions was the introduction of the eligibility of rectors. Later this rule was withdrawn from those institutions where Communist Party committees were being set up and governing the universities.

Before these changes the rectors of higher education institutions were established by the staff of the institutions acting under external influence, i.e. government or Communist Party, and without consulting public opinion. This was undoubtedly antidemocratic. Often these candidates did not match the criteria of professionalism and high qualification needed, but represented figureheads faithful to the communist regime, and who also had influence in government circles.

2 Democracy

In the Republic of Moldova the governing bodies at higher education institutions are:

1) at university level:
- senate, senate office, administration council, under the direction of the rector,

2) at faculty level:
- faculty council, faculty council office, under the direction of the dean,

3) at department level:
- department office, under the direction of the head of department.

The departments are fundamental structural units which are responsible for formal educational activities and research. Administratively they belong to faculties. There are subordinate units and present their activity reports to the faculty council.

The faculties represent the basic functional units of the higher education institutions. Within this framework the study procedure for one or more sections of specialisation is organised in the same domain. The faculty performs the daily administration and control of the study courses, it provides evidence of the students' success and attendance at lectures, it promotes students to the graduation exams, accepts diploma theses, organises the teaching courses, chooses the dean and the heads of department, and the didactic staff, etc.. Faculties present their activity reports to the university senate.
The senate has the following roles:

- it adopts the university charter and the detailed regulations on the basis of the stipulations of the charter together with any necessary modifications,
- it approves the establishment and abolishment of sections, departments, research units based on the proposals made by the faculties or departments,
- it proposes the establishment of new faculties and university colleges,
- it approves educational study plans proposed by the faculties or the departments,
- it validates the constitution of the administrative council,
- it approves the activity report of the administrative council.

Academic staff, non-academic staff and students, trade union committees of the university staff and students, and the students' league participate, via their representatives who are chosen in a democratic manner, in the respective forums for the governance of department, faculty and university affairs. The way these representatives are chosen is governed by Order no. 24.4.3 approved by the Decision of the Council of the Ministry of Education on 19 March, 1996.

3 External influence

Higher education institutions decision-making concerning the level of didactic activity, the establishment or closure of specialised subject study and courses has to take into account the decisions also made by the Ministries and Departments concerned.

A convocation including representatives from outside the universities takes place as required in the form of a general meeting with the administrative council where problems are discussed.

Periodically the higher education institutions undertake quality assessment of the level of training of specialists and production specialists involved in this activity. On the basis of their opinion, conclusions are drawn and the necessary measures are taken to correct the situation.

Annual meetings are held with the directors of industry, firms, organisations and with university graduates having advisory capacity. Here again there are external influences which impact on the strategy and politics in higher education.

4 Hidden – or indirect – governance

The possibility of indirect governance of higher education institutions exists, and can be seen as a desire by the government to indirectly influence the governing staff of the institutions. Indirect intervention occurs through the financial dependence of the institutions on superior hierarchical government bodies. Such influence can be avoided by transparency such as the publicised exposure of the activities of the government and of the responsible Ministries. Undoubtedly such hidden governance can be detected. However, it is more difficult to produce the respective proofs which can be considered as subjective.

5 Legal protection

Decisions and actions taken by the administration of institutions can be disputed both by internal means, within the institution, as well as by external means, in a hierarchical chain from department office to faculty council, university senate and above to the Council of the Ministry of Education which is the central body of public administration in the domain of education.

Besides this there are general meetings of bodies which discuss problems of institutional governance. There is also the possibility of using the press as a means of resolving possible confrontations or conflicts.

6 Conclusion

The reform of higher education in Moldova is taking place in accordance with new principles and the Education Law which have created the pre-requisites necessary for a modern, institutional governance characterised by the decentralisation of governance (university autonomy), democratisation (eligibility of persons and forums of governance) and through the removal of responsibilities for decisions taken (assessment licensing and accrediting of institutes). The legislative framework for the creation of these conditions is still in the course of development.

10.21

THE NETHERLANDS

Ernst M.H. Hirsch-Ballin & Paul J.J. Zoontjens

1 Universities and hogescholen: institutional independence

Publicly and privately funded institutions have been enumerated in the Higher Education and Research Act 1992. Private universities and hogescholen originate from non-profit making associations with full legal competence or from stichtingen (non-profit making foundations). Three public hogescholen originate from public bodies having legal personality; in two cases this is a municipality, in the third it is a public body based on a public agreement between several decentralised public bodies in accordance to the Common Regulations Act. The public universities, four public hogescholen and the Open University have received corporate personality by Act of parliament: the Higher Education and Research Act. The status of legal personality is an important condition for the institutions if they are to act effectively and decisively in the new market-oriented situation in which they have been placed by the Act.

The institutions are funded by means of a block grant, which includes funding for initial education, and in the universities' case research, personnel and accommodation. This funding system corresponds to a global setting of the legal norms where the institutions have discretionary powers to determine their curricula and research programmes, their staff policy, personnel management and their accommodation management. The institutions are free to develop contract activities as long as the scope and content of these activities are in line with, and are not detrimental to the activities for which they obtain government funding.

2 Universities: principles of administrative organisation

The Higher Education and Research Act 1992 has made no change to the provisions governing university administration and organisation of the previous act. These provisions were introduced with the University Administration Reform Act 1970, and were altered, although not fundamentally, by the University Education Act 1986. The provisions contain detailed rules concerning a democratised system for the administration and organisation of the public universities. The same rules are observed by the publicly funded private universities, unless, in the opinion of the board, the special nature of the private university dictates otherwise. In practice, the board of only one private university has decided to depart from essential parts of the law. In April 1996 the government presented a bill to parliament in order to realise a fundamental change to the governance of universities. In that bill, the government proposed a system of participatory decision-making like that prevailing in hogescholen and companies. The following presents a general survey of the current system of university governance.

Within university administration a distinction is made between three levels: a central level (university), a middle level (faculty) and a basic level (department, working group, research institute or research school). This distinction corresponds to the legal elaboration of the federal principle of division of powers. On each level there are governing bodies with their own competencies and responsibilities. Between the levels a system of supervision provides for administrative and organisational unity, over which the executive board, at the central level, possesses special competencies.

The current administrative organisation is supposed to guarantee a full measure of freedoms down to the basic level where, in many cases, the actual organisation and operationalisation of education and research takes place. This is exemplified by the principal separation of powers concerning personnel and management and those concerning education and research. The legal responsibility for personnel and institutional management resides fully in the hands of the central level, especially the executive board. This responsibility cannot be delegated to the faculties or departments. In practice, the faculty board is able to exercise powers in personnel management if, which is often the case, those powers have been mandated by the executive board to the faculty's secretary. The cone of responsibility for education and research matters resides in the hands of the faculties at the middle level, and especially within the departments, at the basic level.

3 Democratised governing bodies: central level

At the central level there are two administrative bodies: the executive board and the university council. The executive board comprises the rector and two other members who are professional administrators. All duties are assigned to the executive board that have not been explicitly assigned to the university council. The executive board is accountable to the university council for the exercitation of all its powers. The main duties and powers of the executive board concern the appointment and discharge of personnel, the social policy over working conditions and accommodation, the legal and administrative representation of the university, the creation of research institutes and research schools, the day to day coordination of education and research activities at the institutional scale, and the suspension and rescission of decisions taken by administrative bodies at the faculty or departmental level.

The university council consists of a maximum of 25 members. At least one third of the seats are occupied by members of the academic staff, with no more than one third by members of the administrative and support staff, and no more than one third by students. To become a member of the university council one has to be elected by members of the university group to which he or she belongs (academic staff, administrative and support staff or students). The university council elects its chairman from among its members. The main duties and powers of the university council concern the determination of the university's budget, the introduction and closure of study programmes, as well as the establishment of the institution's plan, regulations governing administration and organisation, and guidelines on the organisation and coordination of teaching and research. The university council can call the executive board to account. It has the general power of controlling the performance of the executive board, although it cannot discharge board members.

4 Middle level

At the faculty level (middle level) there are also two governing bodies with general powers and duties: the faculty board and faculty council. The faculty board comprises a maximum of five members, the majority of whom are members of the academic teaching staff. Faculty board members are elected by the faculty council. The chairman, who has to be a full professor, is the dean of the faculty. The main duties and powers of the faculty board concern the organisation and coordination of teaching and research in the faculty, and the supervision of the implementation of teaching and examination regulations and research programmes. Furthermore, the faculty board contributes to university administration by consulting with and advising the executive board on several matters that concern faculty interests, such as the institution's plan, faculty teaching and research, and requirements to be imposed on buildings, and other equipment needed for teaching and research. The faculty board also plays an important role in the process of advising the executive board on the appointment of professors, through its power to appoint a committee on this matter. The faculty board is accountable to the faculty council. It is also accountable to the executive board.

The faculty council comprises a maximum of 15 members, that are elected according to the same principles as those of the university council. At least one half of the seats are occupied by members of the academic staff, the remainder are occupied by members of the administrative and support staff and students within the faculty. The dean is the chairman of the faculty council. The powers and duties of the faculty council concern the establishment of faculty regulations governing faculty administration and organisation, the establishment and regular assessment of teaching and examination regulations, the formation of research guidelines and a budget plan, the approval of research programmes, the creation of departments, the appointment of members of the permanent committee for research, and advising of the executive board on the appointment of professors.

5 Basic level

At the basic level there is one governing body, the departmental board. A department is created by the faculty council for the purpose of organising, coordinating and integrating the activities of education and research of those whose activities fall within the same subject area. Through decisions taken by the faculty council or the executive board, there may also be working groups between departments, research institutes and research schools that are charged with powers and duties which have exclusively belonged to the departments.

The departmental board comprises the members of the academic teaching staff of the department, i.e. professors, senior university lecturers and university lecturers. They constitute the majority of the board. The chairman of the board is elected by the board from among the professors of the department. The powers and duties of the departmental board cover the drawing up of a research programme, the (further) regulation of teaching and examinations, and the allocation of departmental duties among its members. With regard to the latter, it determines, in agreement with those concerned, with which professor each of the other members of the academic teaching staff will organise their teaching and research, and under whose supervision other members of the department will work. If agreement cannot be reached, the dispute may be submitted to the departmental board for a decision in the matter. Although a professor within a department has no individual powers in the fields of education and research, but only shared powers with the other members of the academic staff on the departmental board, the Higher Education and Research Act stipulates that professors "shall be primarily responsible for the academic development of the subject area assigned to them and for teaching in that field". In practice, it is not always clear in what way this principle relates to the powers of the departmental board. Although the departmental board exercises the formal powers of the chairholder, it does not mean that the position of the professor has been fully brought into line with that of the other members of the academic teaching staff. According to a sentence of 30 March, 1995 (AW 1994/206) of the *Centrale Raad van Beroep*, the highest civil service court, this principle of professorial academic responsibility seems to be violated, in that the decision by the departmental board to allocate the duties of education and research amongst departmental members means that there is not an effective leading responsibility left for professors in matters of education and research.

6 Administrative organisation criticised

Since the preparation and consolidation of the Higher Education and Research Act in the late 1980s, discussions have been held about the shortcomings of this detailed legal structure of university organisation. In 1995 these discussions peaked mainly because of the plans for higher education as laid down in the coalition agreement of August 1994. The general opinion has been negative, and during analysis some significant problems have been pointed out:

- There is not one person or body to whom, or which, the responsibility for education can be exclusively attributed. The arrangement of curricula is strongly dependant on the cooperation of the departments. The departments, however, are strongly self-reliant, forming an "archipelago" in a faculty.
- The lack of a clear point of address in matters of education makes it difficult for students to hold the institution responsible for the quality of education.
- The separation of powers between management, and education and research has been proved not to be effective. With the execution of management powers it is necessary that there are institutional guarantees for feed-back to education and research.

7 Recent developments

In April 1996, the government presented a bill to parliament regarding the modernisation of university administrative organisation. In this bill, the principle of participation in decision-making, as practised at the hogescholen, was introduced to the universities. According to this principle, the democratically composed councils within the university will have the right of consent or of advice on what the executive board announces as its decision-making intentions. Also, the university council and faculty council will not be able to exercise decision-making powers. Their role will be to advise, to control, or support the decisions of the administrative organs. Furthermore, as a result of these modernisation plans, the administrative organisation will be changed fundamentally.

The following are some important elements of the bill. The institution's administrative powers will be exercised by an executive board and a supervisory board. The executive board will be the institution's representative body, and will have powers that are currently held by the university council, i.e. determining the institution's budget and plan, the introduction and closure of study programmes, etc. As a consequence the university council will change from being an administrative body to a participative body. The supervisory board will be charged with the supervision of the institution's overall administration and management. For public universities, it will be placed in a relationship with the Minister, on the one hand, and the executive board on the other. It will have the power to approve certain decisions of the executive board that are of great importance to the strategic policy and internal organisation of the institution. The supervisory board will appoint and dismiss members of the executive board. The executive board will be accountable to the supervisory board, and the supervisory board of a public university will be accountable to the Minister. The five members of the supervisory board of a public university will be appointed for a period of four years by the Minister.

Comparable to the executive board's position, the dean will become the sole administrative body at the faculty level. The executive board can decide that, instead of a dean, a faculty board consisting of three to five members, will execute the administrative powers of the faculty. In both cases, the faculty council will remain with participative, not administrative powers, like those of the university council. The dean (or faculty board) can receive mandate from the executive board to exercise certain powers in the field of administration and management. The dean (or faculty board) will decide on education and examination regulations and will supervise the execution of those functions and, furthermore, provide for the administration of every study programme in the faculty. The faculty board will be accountable to the executive board.

According to the new bill, the legal obligation of creating departments within a faculty will disappear. There is no intention, however, to go back to the professor's faculty from the time before 1970. The professor is, and will be, the primus inter pares, primarily responsible for the academic development of the subject area assigned to him or her, and for teaching in that field, as is already laid down in current regulations. The organisational form of the department will be abandoned when the organisation of research is taken care of by institutes or research schools, as often already happens, and when the responsibility for the organisation and execution of study programmes lies with the dean, which is the intention of the new bill.

8 Hogescholen: principles of administrative organisation

At the beginning of 1996, new legal provisions regarding administrative organisation and participation were laid down in the Higher Education and Research Act. Within the hogescholen a distinction is made between the institution's board, the central management board, the executive board, faculties or "organisatory units" and participation (sub)councils. The institution's board decides on the administrative regulations of the institution; it can delegate its powers and duties to the executive board. If it does not do this, the institution is governed by itself and a central management board that are in charge of preparing and implementing the hogeschool's policy and that are accountable to the institution's board. The latter can also provide for the establishment of faculties (or "other organisatory units", hereafter referred to as faculties). If faculties have been created, the administrative regulations of the institution should provide for:

- the number and nature of powers and duties of the faculty board,
- the relationship of the faculty board to the institution's board, the executive board (if present) or the central management board,
- the number and nature of study programmes created within the faculties,
- the composition and method of the faculty board.

For every study programme, a study programme committee is to be established, with at least half the seats on the committee occupied by students. This committee has advisory duties with regard to decisions on, and the judgement of, education and examination regulations. Furthermore, the committee can advise the faculty board on all educational matters in the study programme.

9 Participation in decision-making

The democratic functioning of the hogescholen has more in common with that found in companies than that in universities. The participation council, like a work council in a company, is not an administrative body, but is the counterpart to the functioning administrative bodies within the hogeschool: the institution's or executive board, the faculty board, etc.. The participation council has the right of consent, or of advice, on what the board announces as its decision-making intentions. It has no power to make decisions of its own, but, as mentioned above, it advises, controls or supports decisions of the administrative organs within the institution. Depending on the circumstances, participation councils can be installed at three levels:

1 If several hogescholen come under the same governing board, this board has the legal obligation to install a common participation council, as its counterpart. The members of this common council are chosen from and by the members of the participation councils in the hogescholen.

2 At each hogeschool a participation council will be installed. The participation council is the counterpart to the institution's or executive board. One half of the seats should be occupied by personnel members, the other by students. To become a member of the council one has to be elected by the members of the group to which he or she belongs.

3 If faculties have been created, then every faculty should have a sub-participation council. This sub-council exercises the powers of the institution's participation council at the level of the faculty, and it is the counterpart to the faculty board. Its composition and membership conditions are like that of the institution's participation council.

10 Conclusions

In 1996 institutional governance of universities and hogescholen came under review. New legal provisions have modernised the system of participation at hogescholen, and a new bill, will completely change and modernise the administrative organisation of universities. With these developments, the principal distinction between the administrative organisation of hogescholen and universities will disappear. In this respect, the universities will move in the direction of the hogescholen. There is a general consensus about the necessity of these changes: the market needs strong and decisive institutions that are responsive to their environments. These general tendencies can be summarised as follows:

- hierarchisation: strengthening the administration at the middle and central level at the cost of the basic level,
- centralisation: moving the core of the administration to the executive organs,
- professionalisation: the core of the administration is coming under the control of professionals at the central and middle level, e.g. dean,
- disengagement of education and research: the modernisation of university organisation will make it possible to institutionally separate education and research,
- liberalisation: the institutions will have more freedom in the future, to arrange their administrative organisation.

10.22

NORWAY

Rolf Kåre Jenssen & Gro Beate Vige

1 Introduction

In February 1992, the government set up a commission to propose a new law for higher education. Based on the proposals put forward by the commission in June 1993, the government presented a bill to the Storting (National Assembly) in June 1994. The resulting Act no. 22 of 12 May, 1995 on Universities and Colleges is applicable as of 1 January, 1996.

There are two crucial legal provisions. The first is found in paras. 2 no. 3 and concerns academic freedom at higher education institutions: "The institutions cannot be instructed as to the content of their teaching, their research, or their artistic or scientific development work."

The second provision found in chapter 2 of this Act concerns the principle of democracy in the governing bodies of the institutions, and more particularly those concerning the elections of rector, pro-rector, board and council in paras. 10 and 11.

Para. 10.2: "Holders of at least half-time permanent academic posts at the institution are eligible to become rector and pro-rector. No-one can be re-elected rector or pro-rector who will have served in that position for a continuous period of six years at the beginning of the new election period."

Para. 11.1: "Members of the Board and Council who hold posts at the institutions, and their deputies, are elected for three years. Elections are held separately for the two groups of permanently and temporarily appointed staff, cf. para. 8, and technical or administrative staff, cf. para. 6 subsections 1, 2 and 3.

Para. 11.2: Student members of the Board and Council, and their deputies, are elected for one year."

The Ministry of Education, Research and Church Affairs determines the division of the institutions into departments (faculties) on the basis of a recommendation by the institution's board. The university/college board can freely establish basic units under individual departments. 'Basic unit' is a legal term; in practice, basic units are often called 'institutes', but other terms are also in use.

Following decisions by the departmental steering committee, the responsibility for teaching, research, scientific development and other academic activities in particular subject areas can be delegated to the basic units. The Universities and Colleges Act also regulates what kinds of decisions may be delegated to the various levels of the institutions.

This country report focuses on the state (i.e. government funded) higher education institutions, and more particularly on those institutions to which the 1995 Universities and Colleges Act applies. These include the 4 universities, the 6 specialised national colleges (university colleges), and the 26 state colleges. Since the overwhelming majority of students attend these institutions, approximately 149,000 out of around 164,000 registered students in 1995, the detailed descriptions of this report will concentrate on the legal and governance systems that are applicable to these institutions. In order to convey a more complete picture of Norwegian higher education the categories of higher education to which the Universities and Colleges Act does not apply will also be briefly mentioned. They encompass (state) higher education in the arts, with 800 students in all, and private higher education, with about 14,000 students.

The state art colleges are presently undergoing a process of reorganisation and merging. Before 1 August, 1996, there were seven relatively small arts and crafts colleges, but since that date, these institutions have merged into two 'new' colleges, one in Oslo, and one in Bergen. Much of the legislation and the procedures concerning monitoring and control referred to in this country report is equally valid for these colleges, for instance those procedures concerning avenues of appeal for administrative decisions and appointments of staff at state institutions. In addition, the rules applicable for the elections of rector and pro-rector at the new institutions, as well as for the elections of board members, decided through ordinance by the Ministry of Education, Research and Church Affairs, generally follow the pattern laid down in the Universities and Colleges Act and pertaining regulations. The main difference is that for the art colleges, external board members are appointed by the Norwegian Council for Cultural Affairs instead of by the local county council.

At present, the two state art colleges are brought under the 1995 Universities and Colleges Act through an amendment to the law in June 1997.

Private higher education is regulated by special legislation. The Act of 11 June, 1986 no.53, on the recognition of study programmes and state (i.e. government) funding of private colleges, is entirely administered by the Ministry of Education, Research and Church Affairs. Private higher education institutions may only receive state funding for recognised study programmes, but they are not automatically entitled to such support. In 1996, there were 19 private higher education institutions which received state funding for (or part of) their activities, and 3 institutions with recognised study programmes without such funding. All of these institutions have to send budget proposals, as well as yearly accounts and reports on exam procedures, numbers of registered students and graduates, etc., to the Ministry. In 1994, there were 13,598 registered students in private higher education.

In order to receive government funding for specific study programmes, a private higher education institution must:

a) have been established for religious purposes e.g. private nursing colleges and theological colleges,
b) have been established for the purpose of creating a pedagogical alternative e.g. teacher and eurhythmics training for anthroposophical schools (Rudolf Steiner),
c) to supplement the education and training of public institutions in areas where this is needed.

The private higher education institutions cover a wide spectrum of study programmes, from theology and religious studies, teacher training, nursing and social work education, to ballet, music, engineering, computer technology, business administration and marketing. Recognition is given for one or more specified study programmes, and not to an institution as such. Though most of the private higher education institutions offer programmes for the lower degree (undergraduate level), some have programmes for higher degrees, and one, the Free Faculty of Theology, can confer doctoral degrees. Private higher education institutions with programmes in nursing, teacher education, etc., follow the relevant national curricula.

For purposes of national co-ordination of academic and budgetary resources at state institutions (Network Norway), the Universities and Colleges Act lays down that the degrees an institution can award and the professional training programmes or other educational programmes it can offer must all be decided through Royal Decree. This includes the breadth and depth of study required, the length of time in which it should be possible to complete the course of study, and the title conferred by each degree, professional training course or educational programme. Following applications according to specific procedures, from the institution concerned, it is the Ministry that decides on new courses of at least one semester's duration (1/2 academic year) which form part(s) of a degree.

In order to adapt the legislation concerning private higher education to the provisions of the 1995 Universities and Colleges Act, new proposals are under way for amendments to the 1986 Private Higher Education Act.

The Ministry of Education, Research and Church Affairs has the overall responsibility for the monitoring and control of all the higher education institutions, whether public or private.

2 The legal framework: principles and structures

An important principle in the preparation of the 1995 Universities and Colleges Act, was the introduction of a common legal basis for the university and non-university sectors, and a common framework for the regulation of conditions relating to the students, as well as for the management and organisation of all the institutions to which it applies.

The Act also formally established and secured 'Network Norway', a national higher education and research network based on the principles of specialisation, co-operation and communication. The network's governing principle is to ensure that new study programmes are planned and viewed in relation to an overall national plan.

Another very important principle underlying the Act is the administrative freedom of the institutions. The power of decision-making has been delegated to the institutions as far as possible, after due consideration had been given to the need for overall national governance and co-ordination of the sector.

Academic freedom is fundamental to a sound system of education and research, and the Universities and Colleges Act clearly states that the higher education institutions cannot be instructed as to the content of their teaching, research, or of their artistic or scientific work.

A relatively new notion in Norwegian educational policy is that of a 'national access' to higher education institutions, in a large number of subject areas. This means that all qualified applicants (i.e. applicants fulfilling the minimum entrance requirements) should be admitted to the type of study they want, though not necessarily at an institution they applied to, although the applicant's priorities are adhered to as far as possible. Consequently admission capacity is kept at a maximum level, after due consideration has been made of the quality of study and the capacity of the institutions concerned.

Finally, the principle of democracy underlying all the provisions of the Act on the governance of the institutions implies that all the various categories of staff, as well as the students, have the right to be consulted and to participate in decision-making.

In the Act the lists of duties of the board (para. 4) and of the director (para. 15) explicitly provide for discretionary decisions in strategic policy, general management, daily administration, and the management of teaching and research – provided laws, regulations, and national policies are adhered to. The higher education institutions appoint their own staff and, following central (i.e. national level) negotiations between the Ministry of Education, Research and Church Affairs and the relevant trade unions, the right to negotiate salaries in so-called 'local negotiations' was delegated to the institutions as of 1 May, 1996. It should be noted however, that such local negotiations must be in accordance with the centrally negotiated framework of wage agreements for the various categories of employees, and that they only concern the distribution of funds obtained through national level negotiations between the Ministry of Government Administration and the trade unions.

The most important changes in the governance since 1985 are:

- that the management of the universities and colleges are defined by a common legal framework, implying that more decision-making power has been delegated to the institutions of the non-university sector,
- the establishment of the academic 'Network Norway',
- the abolition of the intermediate level between the Ministry and the colleges of the non-university sector, represented by the Regional Boards of Higher Education until the 1994 reorganisation and merger of colleges. (On 1 August, 1994, 98 regional colleges were merged into 26 new ones.)

3 Democracy

The universities and colleges are governed by a board, and, as a rule, also by a university or college council. The Ministry may, however, exempt an institution from the obligation of having a council. In such cases, the role of the council must be taken care of by other bodies at the institution.

The university or college board is the highest governing body of the institution. It is responsible for maintaining a high standard of academic activity, and for seeing that the institution is run efficiently and in accordance with the applicable laws and regulations, and within the limits and targets laid down by the national authorities.

The board should draw up the strategy for the institution's educational, research and other academic activities, and make plans for its scientific development in accordance with the goals established by the authorities for the sector and for the institution.

The university or college council advises the board on matters relating to the overall development of the institution's activities, or raise important questions of principle relating to them. Such questions are for example the long-term planning of activities, the guidelines and principles for the use of the institution's resources, the long-term and annual budget proposals to be submitted by the institution to the Ministry, the principles underlying the development of new study programmes, and major organisational changes.

The council is also intended as a forum for exchange of information and for contacts between the board and the various academic and professional entities (groups). In addition, the board, the rector, and the pro-rector may ask for advice from the council. The council can also have any matter submitted to it for comment, except for appointments and other specific questions concerning individuals.

The intention of the legislator was that the council, being proportionately representative of the various groups of students and professionals (academic, technical, administrative) at the institutions, should have an important function as a meeting place and forum for discussing principles, especially at the newly reorganised and merged institutions. The importance of the council lies in its representativity of the institution as a whole.

The board may delegate decision-making powers, for instance concerning appointments, to the level of the departments (usually called 'faculties' at the universities), which again may delegate such power to the 'basic units'.

The Universities and Colleges Act regulates the kind of decisions that may be delegated to the various levels. Departments are governed by departmental steering committees, and the basic units by basic unit steering committees. The Act also provides for the participation of students and of all categories of employees in all the governing bodies of the higher education institutions.

The board has 9, 11, or 13 members, i.e. the rector, the pro-rector, between 2 and 5 members elected from among the academic staff, 1 or 2 members elected from among the technical and administrative staff, 2 or 3 members elected from among the students, and 2 to 4 external members. The rector is the chairman of the board and on its behalf has the overall responsibility for, and manages and supervises the institution's activities.

External board members and their deputies are nominated in equal numbers by the institution's own council and by the county council of the county in which the institution is located. The Ministry appoints the members and their deputies.

The university or college council must have at least 15 members, coming from the following categories:

- permanently appointed academic staff (51-60%),
- temporarily appointed academic staff (0-10%),
- technical and administrative staff (5-25%),
- students (15-30%).

In the same way, the departmental (faculty) steering committees must also be constituted from representatives of the corresponding groups at their level: permanently appointed academic staff, temporarily appointed academic staff, technical and administrative staff, and students. In addition, it is obligatory to have practical training representatives and external members included in the departmental committees.

It is worth noting that the students must have at least two representatives on all collegiate bodies that have decision-making powers, unless the delegating body unanimously, i.e. including the student representatives, decides otherwise. The students of an institution can establish a student body to safeguard student interests, and to present their views to the board and to the council. Similarly, the students can also establish student bodies at department (faculty) and/or basic unit (institute) level, if deemed necessary. The student bodies are legally entitled to be heard on all questions relating to students at the level concerned.

In addition, the governing bodies can appoint special committees and/or steering committees for special areas or questions, like for instance international co-operation.

On 21 June, 1996 the Ministry issued a set of general rules concerning the elections of the rector, the pro-rector, the board and of the council at the universities and colleges. Included in these rules are provisions concerning the election of election committees responsible for the preparation and administration of the elections. Such committees have either 3, 5, or 7 members. Ordinary academic staff are all eligible to be elected as rector and pro-rector. Elections for these two posts are held separately; the election of the pro-rector is only held after the results of the election of the rector are known.

Elections of student representatives to the board and the council are always done by ballot from among all the students to be represented. The student members of these bodies, and their deputies, are elected for a period of one year.

The remaining representatives of the institution's board and council come from among academic, administrative and technical staff. Members of the board and council who hold posts at the institution, and their deputies, are elected for a period of three years. Elections are held separately for the two groups of academic staff (permanently and temporarily appointed), and technical and administrative staff.

For rector, for pro-rector, and for ordinary staff representatives of the board and council, elections may be done by ballot, take place at election meetings, i.e. meetings where all eligible staff are present, or through electoral colleges, i.e. meetings of electors and according to specific rules.

For all these elections, the board can draw up more detailed rules, supplementary to those issued by the Ministry. The board is also responsible for making rules for elections to governing bodies at other levels of the institution, i.e. departments and basic units, as well as to other elective assignments or posts.

4 External influence

Most of the decision-making taking place at the institutions is done without 'external influence' other than the laws, directives, and other provisions laid down by national authorities. It should be noted however, that all higher education institutions have 2, 3, or 4 external board members. These are appointed by the Ministry after nomination by the institution's council, and by the governing bodies of the county where the institution is located.

On some issues, like those concerning curriculum development and/or administration of study programmes for which there are national curricula (e.g. teacher education, nursing, etc.), the relevant national board often gives advice to the institution, and may even assist in control functions, particular in areas where it is responsible for making recommendations to the Ministry.

All higher education institutions report directly to the Ministry of Education, Research, and Church Affairs for the totality of their activities. All control in the first instance is therefore done by the Ministry. In addition, as for all state institutions, the Office of the Auditor General, and the Ombudsman for public administration of the Storting (National Assembly), also have important in-depth control functions.

Questions relating to staff working conditions for staff (wages, working hours, etc.) are regulated through agreements following negotiations between trade unions and the employer at the various levels.

Overall framework agreements valid for all state institutions are always made between the Ministry of Government Administration and the trade unions at the national level. Agreements specifically concerning the (higher) education sector are negotiated between the Ministry of Education, Research and Church Affairs and the trade unions concerned at the national level. Only negotiations on matters of relevance to one institution have institutional level trade union and employer representatives.

The trade unions and the Ministry of Government Administration in fact play important roles in advising and, especially indirectly, in forming the basis for decision-making in various fields at the institutions. Moreover, as the national authority for the interpretation of laws, regulations and national level agreements (the latter together with trade unions) concerning personnel at state institutions, this Ministry has second instance control functions at higher education institutions, after the Ministry of Education etc..

In addition, the Gender Equality Ombudsman Office can also be consulted. It is the national authority controlling matters concerning discrimination between the sexes, notably those pertaining to the Gender Equality Act.

5 Hidden or indirect governance

It is difficult to detect hidden state governance in regulations and requirements relating to higher education in Norway. Most of the government funding of state higher education institutions, for instance, covers a budget for salaries and other ordinary costs necessary for the running of the institution, with the possibility of additions for increased levels of activity, and a budget for investments and new equipment.

A few of the allocations to the sector are results oriented, the basis being that incentive is a means of governing. One of these is that the universities have to compete for their share of a reserved lump sum – 200 million NOK in 1996 – which is allocated on the basis of (study unit) credits obtained by the students at each of the universities. Another consists of special funds allocated to the universities on the basis of the number of students obtaining higher university degrees, i.e. completed study programmes of between 5 and 7 years' duration, as well as on the number of doctoral degrees obtained. These incentives to obtain certain results have hitherto been linked to openly stated national policies, as stated in two of the aims of the 1996 budget proposal to the Storting:

- a better use of the sector's resources,
- to reduce the time needed by students before graduation, i.e. completion of their studies, so that the length of the study periods needed will correspond more closely to the formal study periods, i.e. as stated in Royal Decrees.

All the state higher education institutions can earn complementary funds for research and development activities conducted in co-operation with, or for, national or local research institutes, or gain private or public funding for special projects or activities, or earn money from the sale of publications etc., provided the relevant national regulations for the sector are adhered to. For the University of Oslo, such income constituted approximately 250 million NOK in 1995, out of a total budget of 1,800 million NOK (i.e. 14%). The proportion of such income is approximately the same for the other universities, whereas it is inferior, between 6-7% of the total budget for the non-university sector (the state colleges). It is quite likely that the possibility of securing extra income of this order of importance could influence decision-making at the institutions.

6 Legal protection

The state higher education institutions, like all state institutions, have to follow the administrative provisions and procedures laid down in the Act of 10 February, 1967 relating to Procedure in Cases concerning Public Administration (short title: the Public Administration Act). According to this Act, any individual decision, meaning any administrative decision applying to the rights or duties of one or more specified persons, may be appealed. The appeals instance is the administrative agency immediately superior to the administrative agency which rendered the decision concerned (the subordinate instance). The administrative decision of the appeals instance in an appeal case may not be made the subject of further appeal.

In addition, the Act on Universities and Colleges contains more specific rules, and according to this Act, the board can appoint an appeals committee to rule on appeals on its behalf. The matters to be dealt with by the appeals committee, should be defined in general instructions issued by the board.

The appeals committee has five members with personal deputies. Two of the members are students. The chairman and the chairman's deputy must satisfy the statutory qualification requirements for judges. The chairman and the chairman's deputy cannot be members of the institution's staff.

As a rule, the decisions by the appeals committee are final. Exceptions are decisions on the exclusion of a student, which can be appealed to the Ministry. In such cases, the student is entitled to seek the assistance of a solicitor or other spokesman from the time when the question of exclusion is raised, or, alternatively, from the time when the first written warning was given. The cost of such assistance is met by the institution.

The Ministry's decision is final, and the internal avenue of appeal is thus exhausted. There are external avenues of appeal, however, and the student in question can then have the exclusion decision tried before the district or city court of the jurisdiction in which the institution's head office is located.

There are also special provisions in the law concerning complaints relating to examinations. A student is entitled to an explanation of the marks awarded for his or her performance at any examination. The demand must be made immediately after the announcement of the results for oral examinations/tests, and within one week of the announcement for written examinations/tests. Students can also complain of procedural errors in connection with any sort of examination or test, and such complaints are ruled on by the board's appeals committee on behalf of the board.

For written examinations, a student can in addition appeal in writing against a mark awarded for his or her performance within three weeks of the announcement of the examination results, and the performance then has to be reassessed. For oral examinations and tests for which the performance cannot be reviewed, there is no avenue of appeal related to the mark awarded.

7 Conclusion

Overall the system is such that all fields of activity of the higher education institutions are regulated, either through legislation, royal decrees or regulations, or through agreements between the trade unions and national authorities. The trend has been that the texts of such documents have gradually become less detailed, they generally outline a framework for the scope of decision-making, thereby building up a system of checks and balances in which, after due consideration for the needs of national policy and national governance, there is always some room for the use of discretionary decisions by the institutions. In the field of economic management, for instance, the institutions are free to transfer allocated government funds between budget items (for example between those for salaries and for other ordinary running costs), within the limits laid down in relevant general regulations for all state institutions. As for provisions concerning the working hours of the staff, the Ministry of Education, Research and Church Affairs has negotiated a framework agreement for the whole sector, on the basis of the Working Environment Act. Local adaptations to this agreement can be negotiated at each of the higher education institutions.

10.23

POLAND

Julita Jablecka

1 Introduction

Specific legislation concerning institutional governance of state higher education institutions is contained, inter alia, in the Higher Education Act of 12 September, 1990, and in the Establishment of the Committee of Scientific Research Act of 12, January 1991. Statutes of higher education institutions must comply with these Acts.

The current system of governance for higher education institutions is the result of considerable modernisation which pursues a policy of autonomy, decentralisation and a competitive system of funding, all of which is in sharp contrast with the system in force prior to 1990. Art. 2 para. 1 of the Higher Education Act states: "Schools of higher education (...) are founded and operated on the principle of freedom of scientific research, freedom of artistic activity, and freedom of education and teaching." The whole system of higher education is guided by the principles of collegial autonomy of the academic community, which is reflected in:

- the domination of collegial governing bodies over individual administrators,
- election of all individual bodies,
- decision-making procedures based on voting within collegial bodies.

These principles apply to each level of governance of higher education and research, including the central level, e.g. to the Central Council of Higher Education and the Committee of Scientific Research.

For the first time non-state institutions may be founded. The Higher Education Act, Art. 15, para. 1, states that they can be established "by any natural or legal person, (...) upon permission granted by the Minister of National Education after having considered the opinion of the Central Council of Higher Education."

2 Governance

Higher education institutions have obtained far-reaching institutional autonomy which covers various aspects of their governance. One may distinguish between fully and partly autonomous institutions. The former have the right to adopt their own statutes. Art. 12, para. 1 of the Act: "In the state school of higher education which employs by nomination at least sixty academic teachers holding academic titles and where at least half of its basic organisational units are licensed to award the academic degree of doctor habilitate, the statute shall come into force from the date specified in a resolution of the senate." The state schools which do not comply with these requirements are partly independent, and must submit their statutes for approval to the Minister.

Statutes of non-state (private) institutions must also be approved by the Minister: Art. 16, par. 2 states that: "The first statute of a non-state school of higher education to be valid for a period of one year shall be provided by its founder, or upon his application, by the Minister of National Education"; Art. 18, para. 2 states that: "The Minister of National Education shall approve the statute of the non-state school upon assuring its compliance with the statutory law and the permission granted."

Most of the provisions for the functioning of higher education institutions, general priniciples of their organisation, governing bodies, their responsibility, employees of school, minimum and maximum teaching load are determined by the Higher Education Act. Those which are not determined by the Act are inclosed in the schools' statutes. However, as Art. 74 and Art. 138 of the Higher Education Act state, the provisions in respective sections of the Act "shall apply to non-state schools of higher education in areas not already regulated by the schools' statute." This means that the statutes of non-state schools may determine its organisational structure, governing bodies, posts and qualifications required by postholders as well as the right and duties of employees, in a manner different from that within the framework given by the Higher Education Act.

Art. 31 of the Act states that: "The Minister of National Education shall exercise supervision over the school of higher education to assure that its bodies act in conformity with statutory provisions and the school statute (...)". The Minister coordinates the cooperation within the framework of international agreements. The Minister issues rules and sets limits regarding the employment of professors, sets maximum and minimum salaries for academics in various positions, grants permission for the establishment and operation of non-state institutions after consultation with the Central Council of Higher Education.

As a result of the changes introduced by the legal regulations, the power of the Minister of Higher Education has been considerably restricted, compared with the period before 1990.

On the other hand the Central Council of Higher Education which is an elective, representative body of the schools of higher education, has gained considerable power *vis à vis* the Minister. The Central Council's term of office is three years; it is composed of 50 elected representatives of professors and habilitated doctors (35), other academic teachers holding academic degrees (10) and students (5).

The Central Council shall – according to Art. 42, para. 1, 2, and 3:

- determine conditions to be met by a school of higher education in order to organise and run studies in a given field,
- set minimum programme requirements for particular fields of study and determine the names for such fields,
- lay down criteria setting the number of posts of professors (ordinary or extraordinary, full or associate) for each field of study, for which subsidies are provided to support the schools' teaching activity,
- determine conditions to be met by the school to be able to award professional titles.

The Council also presents opinions on all regulations concerning higher education, academic titles and the organisation of research funding.

The second important change introduced by the new legislation is the principle of competition which applies both to research and recruitment of academic staff. Recruitment and promotion of academic staff at all levels is conducted through open competition. The legislation also envisages periodic appraisal of academic staff.

The system of research funding introduced by the Committee of Scientific Research Act (CSR), and supplemented by executive regulations, separates research funding from funding for teaching. It introduces a separate source of research funding from the state budget, namely the CSR. State higher education institutions compete for block research grants. The basic units of higher education institutions are the faculties, unless the school statutes provide otherwise. The faculties compete for so-called statutory research funds, while individual scholars and research teams apply for project grants, which are peer reviewed at the CSR.

The legal framework provides for discretionary decisions in strategic policy, general management, daily administration, and supervision of teaching and research. According to the Higher Education Act every state university is governed by:

- a rector,
- a university senate,
- faculties,
- faculty councils.

The university senate devises the university statutes and study regulations. All decisions concerned with the development of the university, such as financial matters, international cooperation, and the introduction of new fields of study by faculty must be referred to the senate for approval. Faculty councils decide about the kinds of studies offered (day-time, evening, extramural), admission requirements, programme of studies and curricula. The faculties determine the number of students to be enrolled and tuition fees on extramural and evening studies. They adopt their material and financial plan, and further they decide on the use of financial revenues received from the state subsidies and external sources for instruction, research and other activities.

As mentioned above, at non-state higher education institutions the relationships between collective bodies and individual competences may be subject to statute regulations which may differ from the organs established for public institutions (the latter must comply with the Act regulations). As a result, a diversity of solutions concerning internal governance has emerged in that sector.

At public higher education institutions the collective bodies are the senate, faculty councils, and the councils of institutes and other organisational units. As stated in Art. 47 of the Higher Education Act:

> The senate is composed of:
> 1 the rector and
> 2 pro-rector(s)
> 3 the deans
> 4 the elected representatives, comprising, as specified in the statutes of the school:
>   a) academic teachers employed in positions of ordinary or extraordinary professor, or holding a degree of doctor habilitate
>   b) remaining academic teachers
>   c) student self-governments
>   d) employees of the school who are not academic teachers
> 5 and also, if the school's statutes provides for it, an administrative director, a bursar, a director of the main library, and a director of the centre of scientific documentation and information.

Further, Art. 47, para. 2 states that the elected representatives should be elected according to the procedure determined by the statutes of the school. The number of elected representatives referred to in categories b) and c) should not be lower than 10% of the membership of the senate, and the number of elected representatives referred to in category d) should not be higher than 10% of the senate membership.

The faculty councils consist of:

- the dean,
- deputy dean(s),
- academic teachers holding posts of ordinary or extraordinary professor,
- other academic teachers holding a degree of doctor habilitate,
- elected representatives of the remaining academic teachers, student self-government and employees who are not academic teachers.

The proportion of the different kinds of elected representatives is similar to the composition in the senate.

Rectors' and deans' terms of office are three years. The rector is elected from among applicants holding the academic title of professor, or degree of doctor habilitate, including persons not employed at the institution.

According to Art. 60, para. 1, "The rector shall be elected from among the board of electors, or by the senate." The deans are elected by the faculty councils or by the board of electors. The composition of the board of electors is specified by the school statute. The boards are usually set up in bigger schools but there is no general rule.

For non-public institutions there exists a diversity of governing bodies determined by their statutes. The rector may be elected by the senate, or be appointed by the board of the institution. The board may also be involved in governance itself; and there may also be the position of chancellor to supervise the director and the bursar.

3 External and hidden influences

At public higher education institutions external stakeholders are not formally represented nor take part in the decision-making process since there are no provisions for this mentioned in the Act. In this respect the public institutions are closed systems of governance. There are also no legal provisions for the involvement of external stakeholders in the governing processes as such. In non-public institutions the representatives of local government or business organisations may be members of boards, or advise the rector or collegial bodies.

Although the law protects the institutional autonomy of higher education institutions, financial regulations in particular permit hidden forms of governance. Until the end of 1990, patterns of public funding of higher education institutions were based on an historical pattern and the number of students. Research funds included in such general university funds constituted a small percentage of these monies, since the majority of research funding was channelled through centrally planned research programmes.

Since then the financing of higher education and research has been based on quasi-market competition and various formulae for funding. Public funding for higher education is currently distributed separately to research and to education. The costs of teaching activities, capital investments, maintenance and operating costs, including salaries and financial aid, are covered by different sources of money from the Minister of Education. Money for research is allocated, again through various funding channels, by the Committee of Scientific Research. The subsidies for investments and teaching activities are distributed according to algorithms; the latter taking into account not only the value of the subsidy given the previous year, but also elements such as the number of students per subject category, and staff graded according to their qualifications (degrees and titles).

The influence of the algorithm has been seen in the gradual increase in the employment of highly qualified scholars and workers, and in the increase of the number of doctoral studies. In addition, many public higher education institutions apply the algorithm internally to allocate subsidies among faculties. That along with the delegation of power by the central university level to the faculty level regarding financial management has resulted in new mechanisms of financing, such as the possibility of raising money from external sources by faculties and individual scholars, as well as augmenting faculty revenues with tuition fees.

The system of project funding and statutory research funding in faculties has increased their financial autonomy within the school. As it is based on performance evaluations, it influences the research output. For example, since one of the evaluative criteria is the number of publications, so the frequency and pattern of publishing has changed.

In Poland there are no internal or external avenues of appeal of decisions and actions taken by academic institutions.

4 Conclusions

New legal regulations create a new framework for the functioning of higher education. However, as a result of budgetary constraints, and correspondingly low salaries in higher education, some rules and regulations may not realistically be implemented. For instance, because of scholars' low salaries, open competition for positions is often a fiction: there may very well be only a single applicant for a given position. Also, the detailed regulations on governing bodies and internal structures of public higher education institutions, as well as the autonomy given to the faculty, inhibit interdisciplinary programmes cutting across the faculty structure. Further, these characteristics obstruct the reform of educational programmes. For instance, the introduction of a credit system for the more conservative faculties is hampered by their competency for curricula. The power given by the Higher Education Act to the collective bodies having decision-making procedures and the lack of external stakeholder representation in the decision-making structures of these institutions, are other obstacles to their effective management in the current socio-political and market orientated environment.

10.24

RUSSIAN FEDERATION

Evgueni I. Popov, Yury A. Kudryavstev,
Stanislav S. Ivanov & Irina E. Volkova

1 Introduction

Changes in the political and socio-economic system in Russia have created a new situation in the field of higher education. New goals should be achieved in its organisation as well as in the structure and functioning of its institutions. This has been reflected in the laws concerning the education system which include higher education and institutional governance. The qualitative changes to the whole of Russian legislation began with the adoption of the Declaration of State Sovereignty of the Russian Soviet Federative Socialist Republic in 1990, and the Presidential Decree No. 1 on "The Immediate Measures concerning the Development of Education in the RSFSR" on 11 July, 1991, which introduced considerable changes in educational legislation. Laws and regulations for building a new social system have been or are being approved. They provide regulations for all members of an academic community and conform to world trends and Russia's needs.

2 Mechanisms of institutional governance

In the mechanisms of institutional governance the following changes are of importance:

- broadening the autonomy of higher education institutions, and aiming for total academic self-management,
- implementation of the new state regional policy of the Russian Federation in higher professional education,

- repudiation of the centralised planned management of higher education (for example, state imposed tasks and assignment of specialists) and liquidation of the state monopoly and the selected public organisations that may establish higher education institutions; foundation and support of the non-state sector of higher education,
- elimination of ideology from higher education institutions, the prohibition of political organisations' activities in these institutions, and the liberation of teaching staff and students from ideological control.

The changes in legislation aim to eliminate the main defects in the former educational system and include higher education. These defects are:

- the bureaucratic regulation of both the activity of the higher education institution and of each member of the academic community,
- the suppression of free thinking in the field of ideology, in teaching and research,
- the command, administrative, and technocratic approaches to higher education development,
- isolation from the international research networks.

The necessity to transfer from a mainly branch to a mainly regional development of the professional education system, and from branch federal management to joint federal regional management of higher education institutions located on territories of the Russian Federation is also the reason for changes.

3 Legal framework: principles and structures

The new legal basis for education incorporates laws of the Russian Federation and its component parts, Presidential decrees and orders, decisions and instructions of the government and the central education management bodies. The following items should be distinguished: Art. 43 of the Constitution of the Russian Federation (1993), the "Law On Education" of the Russian Federation (1996), and the Standard Statute for an Educational Establishment of Higher Professional Education of the Russian Federation (1993). Thus a higher education institution's foundation and functions are based on legislation; it is a legal entity and it implements programmes in accordance with its licence. However, these institutions may have different organisational legal forms. They can be established under state, municipal and non-state authority and they can be of three types: university, academy or institute.

Article 2 of the Law entitled "Principles of the State Policy in the Field of Education", states principles such as "freedom and pluralism in education; the democratic and public nature of management; the autonomous status of educational establishments." On this basis, Art. 32, para. 1 of the Law provides that a higher education institution "shall be independent in carrying out the educational process, in selecting and placing personnel and in conducting financial, economic and other activities within the limits stipulated" by the legislation, its bye-laws and its charter.

In accordance with Art. 35, para. 2 of the Law, management of state and municipal educational establishments is based on principles of self-management and individual management. The organisational forms of self-management for an educational establishment are: the council of an educational establishment, for a higher education institution this is the academic council, the board of trustees, the general meeting (conference) of employees and other bodies. The election procedure of the academic council is determined by the general meeting. The rector and vice-rectors are members of the academic council. The other members of the council are elected in the general meeting by secret ballot.

Art. 36, para. 1 of the Law states that management of a non-state educational establishment shall be carried out directly by its founders, or upon instruction by the board of trustees formed by the founder. The founder is the State Committee of the Russian Federation for Higher Education. In accordance with educational laws and regulations the founder and a higher education institution under its jurisdiction conclude an agreement determining the relationship between the aforesaid State Committee and that institution, which clearly defines the rights, duties and responsibilities of the parties. Decisions of the Committee are of a general regulating nature.

4 Governance

According to Sections 7 and 12 of the Standard Statute a higher education institution can have all or some of the following structural units: branches, faculties, chairs, preparatory departments, research laboratories, a post-graduate research course, doctoral studies, units of recurrent professional education, experimental production units, and instructional theatres. Enterprises, establishments and organisations may be part of a higher education institution.

A *filial vuza*, a division of a higher education institution, offers training in various fields of interest to enterprises, offices and agencies situated in the institution's locality. The *fakultet*, i.e. faculty, is a structural educational, research and administrative unit within a higher education institution. It trains undergraduate and post-graduate students in one or several related disciplines, supervises instruction and research, recruits staff for its departments and laboratories, and arranges advanced training for them. The *kafedra*, i.e. department, is an academic unit within a branch or faculty of a higher education institution, and is responsible for planning and conducting teaching and research in one or several related disciplines.

Individual management is regulated by Art. 35, para. 3 of the Law which provides that "direct guidance of a state and municipal educational establishment shall be carried out by a manager who has passed proper certification". In a higher education institution such a manager is the rector, elected by the general meeting of academic staff, representatives of other categories of staff and students, for a term up to 5 years. His appointment is confirmed by the education management body supervising the activity of that institution, e.g. the State Committee of the Russian Federation for Higher Education. A higher education institution can also be represented by a group elected body such as the academic council. The rector and the academic council act on the basis of the charter adopted by the general meeting of the teaching and research staff and representatives of other categories of staff and students.

In some cases, the rector is appointed by the appropriate education management body by contract, for a maximum of 5 years or minimum of 1 year. If this occurs then the members of the academic council are appointed by the founder of the higher education institution or by the authorised education management body upon the rector's presentation. The term of office for the academic council headed by the rector should not exceed 5 years. Pre-term elections of the academic council are conducted upon request of no less than half of its members.

In state higher education institutions the Law provides for positions for teaching, research, engineering, and for administrative staff, production workers, support staff and other personnel.

According to Art. 50, para. 4 and Art. 55, para. 1 of the Law, and by order of the rector, students and institutional staff can participate in the institution's management. Moreover, the Standard Statute provides in Section 78 that "Staff of a higher education institution shall have the right: to elect and be elected in the institutional management bodies; to participate in the discussion and solution of the most important questions of institutional functioning including that through public organisations and education management bodies"; Section 67 provides that "students shall have the right to participate in the discussion and solution of the most important questions of institutional functioning including that through public organisations and education management bodies"; and Section 57 provides that "representatives of all categories of institutional staff and students, public and other organisations can be elected as members of the academic council of a higher education institution".

5 External influence

In their activity, higher education institutions are subjected to direct and indirect external influence mainly through operational decisions, consulting, control and other types of influence concerning managerial decisions. Such influence is exerted by: government bodies (federal-central and regional); education management bodies (federal-central, departmental branches and regional); organisations (associations, unions); and legal entities and public organisations with or without legal personality. Their influence is regulated by the Law, the Standard Statute, and other laws concerned with government activity, and the Statute for the State Committee of the Russian Federation for Higher Education (1993), etc.. Their activity will also be regulated by the Russian Federation Law "On Higher and Post University Professional Education" now in its final stage of approval.

For example, the Statute of the State Committee of the Russian Federation for Higher Education (1993) which is a state central education management body, has assigned 40 functions and 10 rights to this Committee. It is a legal entity and it accomplishes the following functions: it determines admission quotas for all categories of students in the educational establishments under its jurisdiction; it determines the organisation of the educational process of specialists under professional education programmes in state institutions irrespective of their departmental affiliation; it establishes general admissions regulations to state establishments of secondary and higher education, post-graduate research courses and doctoral studies; it organises the participation of the educational and research institutions in scientific and technical programmes, and projects; it reconciles and approves the charters of educational and other establishments under its jurisdiction; it allots direct finances to the establishments under its jurisdiction from the federal budget and other sources; it conducts inspections of the educational establishments and education management bodies within their competence (or delegates its power to other state education management bodies); it controls the efficient allocation of the federal budget for research and other activities under its jurisdiction.

About 90 associations and organisations, e.g. the Union of Rectors of the Russian Federation, the Consortium for Curriculum Development and the Execution Methodology are involved with the enforcement of the Law and other regulations on higher and post-university education; elaborating regional programmes and programmes for particular fields of study; examining applicable educational legislation; forecasting specialists' training; working with gifted young people; participating in the licensure, attestation and accreditation of educational institutions; and participating in drafting state educational standards, etc..

6 Conclusion

The legislation on higher education is in a constant state of development *vis à vis* the correlation between international and national legislation as well as that between federal and regional legislation. The main problem occurs as a result of variable competencies between federal and regional bodies and the need to preserve a single education space and ensure a common state education policy under the principles formulated in Art. 2 of the Law.

10.25

SLOVAKIA

Peter Plavčan

1 Legal framework: principles and structures

The basic legal framework for governance of higher education is represented by the Higher Education Act No.172/1990. Its content and main principles for governing higher education concerns concepts of higher education development and it represents the basic document approved and developed in the Programme Declaration of the government.

The main trends in higher education development are defined in the Programme Declaration and are drawn from higher education development concepts discussed and approved during deliberations of the government. The documents approved at government sessions become the principal documents defining government priorities in the field of higher education. They determine the annual implementation of the state preferences for higher education, particularly, concerning its overall development as well as that of selected fields, e.g. support of regionalisation, application of Bachelor degrees, or, the development of study programmes not found in Slovakian higher education institutions, such as textiles and clothing which before the split up of the Czech and Slovak Federal Republic in 1993 was concentrated in Liberec, which is now in the Czech Republic.

After 1990, a few principles of higher education development were worked out on the basis of approved government programmes. During 1992-1993, a "Concept of Higher Education Development" in the regions of western, central and eastern Slovakia was formulated to define the main principles of higher education institution development in relation to the decision-making and entrepreneurial sectors in the regions where the institutions operate. In 1994, a document was prepared entitled "The National Programme of Education and Training in the Slovakian Republic – Constantine", a part of which focuses on higher education. The higher education section was discussed and approved separately by the government and produced in a document entitled "The Concept of Higher Education Development by 2010". This represents the basic document setting out the higher education development priorities in Slovakia. After the 1994 elections the new government completed the Constantine material 1995-1996, incorporating new material on the development of the school system.

All of the above concepts were prepared by expert groups made up of specialists from the academic community such as outstanding professors, other university teachers, academic officials and representatives of departmental research, as well as the top employees of the Ministry of Education, and administered by the state secretaries of the Ministry of Education.

The individual higher education institutions are working out their development guidelines to be submitted by their rectors to their academic senates. These guidelines are concerned with internal questions such as the organisation of educational and research activities.

According to government policy documents in the field of higher education, one of the main goals is the outstanding improvement in the level of higher education science research and teaching, the involvement of higher education institutions with the broader European academic scene, and by 2010-2015, a 30% share of the students admitted to higher education institutions from the school leaving population. This process of transformation in the economic, social and political areas as well as the financing of higher education institutions from the national budget underline the necessity of a functional intervention by the state, and the strengthening of supervisory functions preserved under the academic rights and freedoms of higher education institutions.

In the field of higher education management, the basic principle of higher education institution governance is autonomy and self-governance oriented towards responsibility for the institution's scientific level, its educational efficiency, international cooperation, and the optimum use of allotted and acquired funds, including the responsibility for entrepreneurial activities. This self-governance is based upon the interaction between three aspects of governing:

- the self-governing bodies: the Higher Education Council, the Slovak Rectors Conference, the academic senates of higher education institutions and faculties, and the scientific councils of higher education institutions and faculties,
- the academic officials: rectors and pro-rectors of higher education institutions, and the deans and subdeans of higher education institutions,
- the Ministry of Education: governance at the state level.

During the next administrative period the following issues will come under legislative scrutiny:

- the establishment and dissolution of higher education institutions, and the establishment and dissolution of non-state higher education institutions,
- the functioning of foreign higher education institutions on the territory of the Slovak Republic,
- the functioning of higher education institutions in Slovakia from a regional perspective,
- the possibilities of the existence of professional higher education institutions,
- the problems associated with a teaching basis for medical, pharmaceutical and nursing faculties, and teacher training faculties,
- the strengthening of the integration tasks of the academic bodies of higher education institutions (academic senates and scientific councils),
- the codification of the Higher Education Student Council,
- the course and finalisation of higher education study, including the recognition of degrees and academic degrees, and problems with credentials,
- PhD study (scientific preparation),
- the employment arrangements of assistant lecturers, senior lecturers, lecturers and scientific workers.

One of the basic tasks of Slovakian higher education is its accommodation to international conventions, standards and habits. It is also necessary to promote the direct cooperation of Slovakian higher education institutions with those abroad, their participation in international organisations and associations of higher education institutions, and in existing international programmes such as Tempus, Phare, etc.. A significant step will be the involvement of Slovakian higher education institutions in the new international programmes of Socrates and Leonardo.

The basic legal framework of higher education in the area of higher education governance is the Higher Education Act No.172/1990 of the Law Code, developed under the move to democratisation, and which confirms the academic rights and freedoms of higher education institutions. The Act came into force on 1 July, 1990. Among the most significant changes it set up was a new definition of the position of higher education institutions as the top educational, scientific and art institutions. The Act simultaneously set up the fundamental academic rights and freedoms of higher education institutions, namely, the freedom of scientific exploration and the publishing of results, the freedom of artistic creation, the right to teach and learn, the right to elect self-governing bodies, and the right to hold diverse philosophical opinions and religious creeds. In contrast to previous amendments on higher education, this Act permitted higher education institutions to independently, and without the intervention of a superior body, to decide about their internal structure, the content and organisation of studies, the filling of governing posts, the numbers of students admitted and criteria for their selection, and the allocation of finances from the national budget. The Act defined the Higher Education Council which is composed of representatives of the self-governing bodies of higher education institutions and faculties and the Accreditation Commission, the government's advisory body which evaluates the level of the quality of higher education activities in the fields of science, art and education. In accordance with this Act, the task of the Ministry rests in the creation of conditions for higher education development, coordination of higher education institutions, allotment and control of the use of finances from the national budget and the registration of higher education institution statutes. During the implementation of the Higher Education Act, it appeared that, first of all, these competencies in the field of financing have substantial influence upon activities of higher education institutions in all aspects, similarly so does the statute registration. The Act defines the legal status of higher education institutions and faculties; some are of the opinion that an amendment to the Act is needed in this area. At present, the leadership of higher education institutions and faculties have found a natural degree of mutual relationship between themselves and government over the distribution of authority in keeping with the Act.

2 Governance

Higher education institutions in Slovakia are self-governing; in keeping with the 1990 Act, their organisation and activities are decided upon by the academic bodies. The academic bodies of a higher education institution are the academic senate, the scientific council and, at art academies, the artistic council. Faculty bodies are also represented by the academic senate, the scientific council and, at art academy faculties, the artistic council. Faculty bodies are also represented by the academic senate, the scientific council, and at academy faculties, the artistic council. The academic community of a higher education institution elects from among their members the academic senate in such a way that each faculty is represented by the same number of members. The members of the academic senate are answerable to the academic community for their activities. The academic senate of a faculty is elected by the academic community of the faculty from among its members. Members of the faculty academic senate are answerable to the faculty academic community. The academic community of the higher education institution/faculty comprises teachers, scientific workers, students and, if set up by the statute of the institution/faculty, includes the professionals of the higher education institution/faculty. The academic senate of a higher education institution establishes, merges, splits and dissolves the faculties, approves the higher education statute, proposes a candidate for rector of the institution, negotiates the establishment of scientific, pedagogical, developmental, economic and information institutes of the institution, and approves the rector's proposal for the annual distribution of finances to the faculties and institutes, pronounces agreement with the rector's proposal to nominate a scientific council, approves the statutes of the faculties, and fulfils additional tasks. The academic senates of the faculties have similar authority. The academic officials of a higher education institution/faculty are represented by the rector/dean and pro-rectors/subdeans. The rector is a representative of the higher education institution, he administers the institution, answers to the academic senate and, in some instances, also to the Ministry of Education.

3 External influence

Other professionals who are not members of the academic community also take part in the decision-making process and any additional professional orientation of the higher education institution. This occurs via the scientific council of the higher education institution/faculty. The members of the scientific council are appointed, with agreement from the academic senate, by the rector from among the teachers, scientific workers and other significant specialists, the number of which must not exceed one third of the total number of scientific council members. This number also includes practical specialists who participate in the work of the scientific council of the faculty. The scientific council of a higher education institution/faculty negotiates questions concerning teaching activities, scientific research or artistic activities of the institution/faculty.

4 Hidden or indirect governance

In accordance with the Higher Education Act, the Ministry of Education has, in addition to its coordinating functions, other tasks, the most important of which is the allocation of funds to the individual higher education institutions as well as checking upon their use. The distribution of the finances from the national budget is managed with consultation from the Higher Education Council. The Ministry of Education annually allocates, upon approval by the Higher Education Council, a few percentage points from the total budget for the extra financing of developmental tasks in keeping with the overall goals of higher education development and the Ministry's intentions. These tasks and their priorities are substantiated by the Ministry's representatives at joint sessions with the Higher Education Council; their fulfilment means the opportunity for higher education institutions to obtain more financing. Therefore, the Ministry indirectly influences higher education institutions to develop on the basis of financial stimuli. The Ministry of Education submits to higher education institutions recommendations for them to fulfil. This procedure is based upon the mutual trust between the Ministry and the representatives of the academic community.

5 Legal protection

The higher education institutions are autonomous and self-governing. The decisions of academic bodies and academic officials cannot be revised on the part of the Ministry with the exception of expulsion from study or decisions concerning scholarships. Since the decisions according to the Higher Education Act are not related to general rules for administrative procedures, the decisions of higher education institution are final; they may, however, be appealed at the appropriate court.

In the event of finding an abrogation of the law on the part of a higher education institution, the Ministry warns the higher education institution concerning the identified wrongs. The higher education institution as a self-governing and autonomous institution is obliged to remove the wrongs and the academic officials are responsible for additional procedures.

10.26

SLOVENIA

Alenka Šelih & Majda Širok

1 Introduction

Art. 10 Higher Education Act 1993, the Legal Status of Universities and Their Members

A university is a legal entity. Faculties and academies of art and possibly also professional higher education institutions and other institutions, members of the university (hereinafter referred to as members of the university), shall be established within a university. Members of a university have the rights and obligations stipulated by this Act, a university charter and university constitution. When executing the National Plan for Higher Education, which shall be funded by the Republic of Slovenia, members of the university, subject to the stipulations of the university charter and constitution, act for and on behalf of the university; in other cases, members of the university act for and on behalf of themselves in accordance with the university charter and constitution.

Art. 20 of the Higher Education Act Organs establishes that:

- the organs of a university shall be: the rector, senate, administrative board and student council,
- the organs of a university member shall be: the dean, senate and student council,
- the organs of other university institutions shall be: a director and possibly a council of experts,

- the organs of a non-university higher education institution shall be: the senate, administrative board, student council and dean,
- higher education institutions and other university institutions may have other bodies in accordance with their charter or constitutions.

2 The legal framework: principles and structures

The most important principle for higher education institutions' governance is that of autonomy, and this is enshrined in the Constitution (Art. 58). From this principle are derived 2 further rules concerning governance: that of autonomous internal organisational structure, and that of autonomous decision-making in the sphere of teaching and research. As higher education institutions in general, and universities in particular, were previously part of a decentralised system, the principle that has had most effect on the organisation of higher education institutions has been the one dealt with by Art. 10 of the Higher Education Act. It defines the "legal status of universities and their members" and provides for the status of a legal person for universities only, and not for other higher education institutions who have so far enjoyed such a status. It is this principle, giving fully fledged legal personality to universities, has been seen as the most important new legislation by the higher education institutions themselves.

The legal framework provides for strategic policy decisions to be taken within the higher education institutions by the senate and board of administration, and outside these institutions by parliament as stipulated in Art. 43-46 of the Act, and by the Council for Higher Education, an advisory body stipulated by Art. 49 of the Act. General management is secured through the functions of a rector at university level and that of a dean at faculty level. They are responsible for the preparation of the strategic policy decisions and for management of teaching and research. Daily administration is organised within the administration which is divided into university level and faculty level administration, Art. 290-292.

The reasons for these changes are evident; efforts to achieve these changes had started in the late 1980s but the political and social changes after 1989 have enabled them to occur.

3 Democracy

In the following account on the functioning of higher education governing bodies, the faculty will be refered to as a higher education institution. The governing bodies are the senate, the dean and the administrative board.

According to the law and to the statutes, the senate is the decision-making body and the dean is the "manager" of the faculty overseeing its teaching, research, financial and service functions. The dean implements the senate's decrees and at the same time is involved in preparing the senate's work, by formulating strategic policy proposals, representing the faculty, being responsible for the lawfulness of the senate's operation and coordinates the senate's work at the faculty. The administrative board of a higher education institution deals with and decides on financial questions for which the institution acts on its own account and name. At the university level these two functions are carried out by the senate and the rector. The university administrative board, however, deals with a wider range of questions and has broader financial competence.

This system has only been in operation since the end of June 1995, and it is therefore difficult to give any outline of the practice of checks and balances between the governing bodies at this stage. The senate is the body which proposes the dean to the rector who nominates him/her. Proposing the dean seems to be the senate's most powerful function. The dean can be challenged by any body or any individual within the higher education institution on the issue of the lawfulness of his/her work.

Full professors as senior academic staff have a strong role in the internal governance since it is only they who are, as a rule, members of the senate, both at university and faculty levels. This poses a problem of democratic division of power as well as of participation. It may also pose a problem with the possible demotivation of middle and junior academic staff in the process of governing, thus producing rather negative effects. Non-academic staff have a minor role in these processes and the external community has none. This latter point can be explained by the strong influence of the outer community during the whole socialist period and especially after 1975.

Members of academic staff are senate members by their position as full professors; representatives of other groups are either elected to the university administrative council, or nominated by the body defined by the Act. Election procedures have not yet been worked out.

4 External influence and hidden governance

External influence can be exerted in the field of teaching by parliament and the Council for Higher Education. Research activities can be monitored and/or controlled by the Ministry of Science and Technology, and the financial operations of higher education institutions are monitored and controlled by the usual public accountant service controls and also by the Ministry of Finance.

Parliament establishes and decides on the national plan for higher education including all teaching programmes, and through this it is able to influence decision-making processes. The Council of Higher Education carries out a broad range of functions as stipulated in the Act by which it can advise, monitor and/or control higher education institutions. The Ministry of Science and Technology can exercise an influence on these institutions by distributing funds for research projects. Although this is not the only source of funding for the university it is the most important one. Public accountancy services and the Ministry of Finance have control over the spending of public funds in a lawful way.

It would be very improbable if "hidden influences" did not exist and exercise their influence. There are many interest groups within higher education institutions which would like to influence their decisions and many outside interest groups wishing to gain influence within the institutions. The division of academia into humanities and social sciences on one hand and natural sciences and technical sciences on the other provides an obvious example of these interest groups. Another division never admitted to but nevertheless prevalent is the political divide. If Vaclav Havel's assertion is correct that the post-communist states have become to a great extent the "property of parties", then there is no doubt that this is also covertly true of higher education institutions; universities have always been, to a greater or lesser extent, a mirror of social processes within society.

5 Legal protection

There are four main types of internal procedure covering: violations of labour discipline (one for students, and another one for academic and non-academic staff), violations in the election procedure of academic staff, violations in the admission procedures for students, and violations in the grading procedure for students. In principle, and always in a case of serious violation, a collective body takes the decision. In disciplinary proceedings the rules of the Act on Criminal Proceedings are applied in the degree deemed appropriate.

In all of these cases there exist internal appeal procedures and after these have been exhausted a review by a court is secured. In cases of violations of labour law the appeal goes to a specialised Court of Labour disputes; in cases of violations of election procedure and in cases dealing with a student's status such as over exclusion from the university then the appeal goes to the Supreme Court.

6 Conclusion

The new legislation has only been in force for a short time. It has brought about enormous changes some generally regarded as positive, e.g. autonomy, and some which have been met with mistrust, e.g. abolishing the legal entity of faculties. Analysis shows that perhaps the delimitations among decision-making, advising, controlling and monitoring functions and the governing bodies has not been cut sufficiently clearly in all areas; however, overall, the law represents a well balanced piece of legislation.

The structure of the bodies dealing with individual procedures referring to infringements of rights may be seen as satisfactory. What is lacking are procedural norms which are, of course, of crucial importance and promote or block implementation of rights.

It is open to debate whether concentrating all decision-making power in the hands of one group within academia, i.e. full professors, will prove itself to be useful and productive. So far it has resulted in a great part of the academic staff being cut off from decision-making processes, a situation that may become counterproductive, especially since this group is part of the most vital and motivated part of academia.

10.27

SPAIN

Jose Ignacio Cebreiro & Maria Jesús San Segundo

1 The legal framework: principles and structures

There are three clearly differentiated sectors in the field of higher education: university education, non-university education and higher vocational education. The most important is university education, which is focused on in the following discussion.

Spanish universities can be public, private, or run by the Catholic church. The universities enjoy wide-ranging independence that enables them to adopt their own statutes and other rules of internal working. University governing bodies are established under the university statutes, together with the procedures for their election, appointment and removal. The system adopted in its statutes by each university relative to its administration must guarantee representation of the different groups within the university community, as well as the participation of representatives of society's interests.

The financial independence of public universities, or their independence to manage and administer their resources, has been recognised. This allows them to draw up, approve and manage their budgets, as well as administer their assets. These universities receive a total annual subsidy from the self-governing regions to which they are attached, and they also collect fees from their students.

Each university selects its own academic staff as well as its administrative and service personnel, while respecting the principles of merit, job advertising and non-discrimination. The universities draw up and adopt their own curricula, in which they must state the required subjects for earning each degree.

The independence granted to universities with the University Reform Act of 25 August, 1983, makes it possible for the different university governing bodies to take discretionary decisions on a wide range of matters. The social council of each university is empowered to propose to the corresponding self-governing region the setting-up and disbanding of faculties, higher technical schools, university schools and university institutes. The self-governing region takes the appropriate decision bearing in mind the report put out by the *Consejo de Universidades* (universities' council).

The decision-making organ par excellence is the rector. Apart from carrying out the decisions of the most relevant collegiate bodies, he is in charge of running the university and is responsible for taking all the discretionary decisions that are not explicitly vested in other university bodies. The rector is authorised to impose disciplinary sanctions on the academic staff and administrative and service personnel who report to him. S/he applies the general rules applicable within the civil service for this purpose.

Discretionary decision-making powers regarding daily administration are conferred on the university administrator (*Gerente*) who takes decisions bearing in mind the principles of good administration.

When there is a vacant position in the corps of government employed university teaching staff, the university governing board can decide whether or not to abolish the position or whether to change its name or category, taking the university's teaching and research needs into consideration. Even though the scale of remuneration for academic staff in public universities is uniform throughout the country, the social council at each university may decide on the allocation of any additional remuneration that it deems advisable on an individual basis, bearing teaching and research requirements in mind, as well as relevant merits.

The most important change that has taken place in university governance during the past 10 years was that introduced by Act 9/1992, of 23 December 1992, which authorised the transfer of state competencies over universities to 10 regional communities. The other 7 regional communities had previously assumed such competencies, since they had already been governed by special provisions authorising them to exercise state competencies in education.

With the entry into force of Act 9/1992, all the public universities were henceforth attached to the regional communities in which they were located, and from which they now receive the annual general subsidy necessary for the operation of their services; previously they had received this from the state.

2 Democracy

The governing bodies of each university must include at least some of the following:

a) At a collegiate level: social council, university senate, governing board, faculty boards, higher technical school and university school boards, department and university institute councils.

b) At an individual level: rector, vice-rectors, secretary general, administrator, deans of faculties and directors of higher technical schools, university schools, university departments and university institutes.

The social council is responsible for approving the budget and annual university plan, as well as for the supervision of financial activities and the performance of university services. Furthermore, it promotes external sources of funding.

The university senate draws up the statutes, chooses the chancellor and approves the general outlines of the running of the university. The governing board is involved with the university's daily management. The faculty and school boards, as well as the councils of departments and university institutes are the bodies that represent these establishments; they choose their own deans or directors.

The rector represents the university and manages it; he also implements the agreements of the university senate, of the governing board and of the social council.

The secretary general of the university, who must be a member of the academic staff, acts as secretary to the governing board. The university administrator is responsible for managing administrative and financial services, and may not work in a teaching capacity. The deans and directors represent, respectively, the university faculties, and schools, departments or institutes under their responsibility.

Usually the agreements adopted by the social council are based on proposals submitted to them by the university governing board, but the social council may modify or reject these, requiring, in the latter case, that different proposals be formulated. In the event that the university senate is not satisfied with the rector's running of the university, it may revoke his appointment by means of a motion of censure. A similar procedure may be used by the faculty or school boards, as well as the councils of university departments or institutes, in respect of their deans or administrators.

University governing boards are made up of deans of faculties, directors of higher technical schools, directors of departments, heads of university schools, vice-chancellors and the secretary general. Academic staff, students and administrative and service personnel are represented on the university senate, on the boards of faculties, higher technical schools and university schools and on councils of university departments and institutes. The choice of representatives of the 3 aforementioned sectors is made by universal, free, equal, direct and secret suffrage.

The social council is the body through which society participates in the university. Two-fifths of its members are from the governing board, and are elected from among its members, and three-fifths represent external social interests and are figures of recognised prestige in the fields of science, technology, culture, art, the liberal professions, sociology and economics as well as representatives of trade unions and professional associations.

3 External influence and hidden governance

External influence within the university occurs through the workings of the social council, the sole university governing body having external members, as has been mentioned above.

The *Consejo de Universidades* has coordinating and consultative duties and advises the universities on higher education. This body is presided over by the Minister of Education and Science, and comprises those in charge of university education in the governing councils of the self-governing regions, chancellors of the public universities and 15 people of recognised prestige in the fields of university education and research.

The universities' financial activities may be subject to audit by the General State Auditors and control by the Court of Audit.

As stated previously, the public universities receive an annual subsidy to cover their running costs which comes from the self-governing region to which they belong. To establish the amount of this subsidy, the numbers of students and of academic staff, as well as the features of the teaching to be given, are taken into account. The self-governing region may also take other factors into consideration to which it attaches discretionary importance. The self-governing community's decision is crucial for the university as it determines its activities.

In most of the universities the demand for places is greater than their capacity, and therefore the universities decide annually on the maximum number of students that can be admitted to each establishment. The public universities must submit the agreements that they reach on this issue to the *Consejo de Universidades*, and obtain its authorisation regarding the ceilings that they have established for student admission.

The *Consejo de Universidades* examines the universities' reports justifying the limitation of places, and, bearing in mind the foreseeable overall demand for university education, it reaches an agreement whereby it accepts, modifies or rejects the proposals received from the universities.

The decisions taken on this issue by the *Consejo de Universidades* have a decisive influence on the universities' teaching activities, and are the culmination of a long process of negotiation between each university and the *Consejo de Universidades*.

4 Legal protection

Decisions by university chancellors and agreements reached by university senates constitute final stages in administrative procedures. Therefore these decisions can only be contested in courts of appeal against acts of government.

Decisions and agreements by the other governing bodies can be appealed to university chancellors, who are the competent authorities for deciding on appeals lodged by these bodies. After a decision has been taken by a chancellor, it can be contested in a court of appeal against acts of government.

5 Conclusion

The independence granted to universities with the 1983 University Reform Act has enabled them to draw up their own statutes and other rules for internal operation, as well as the election, appointment and removal of their governing and administrative bodies, with the participation of the different groups within the university community.

Thus the universities have an organisational independence that is not interfered with through outside intervention. Nevertheless, the necessary coordination between universities is carried out by the *Consejo de Universidades* which, moreover, offers advice and planning.

The public universities' financial independence enables them to approve their budgets and allocate the resources at their disposal in the way they consider most advisable in order to meet their needs. However, as their major source of income is the annual subsidy that they receive from the self-governing region to which they are attached, this link determines their freedom of action to a certain extent. In view of this there is a need to increase the volume of the universities' alternative sources of income, in order to give them greater freedom in administering their available resources.

10.28

SWITZERLAND

Christine Lenzen & Monique Stress-Sulser

1 Introduction

The most important legal provisions are found in the Federal Constitution.

Article 3 stipulates:

> The cantons are sovereign insofar as their sovereignty is not limited by the Federal Constitution and, as such, they exercise all rights which are not entrusted to the federal power.

Article 27, paragraph 1 specifies:

> The Confederation is entitled to set up, in addition to the existing institutes of technology, a federal university and other establishments for higher education or to subsidise such institutions.

Article 27, paragraph 1 provides:

> The Confederation shall encourage scientific research. The provision of finance may be conditional on co-ordination being guaranteed.

Federal Law on Assistance to Universities (LAU) of 22 March, 1991, Article 1, paragraphs 1 and 2 provides that:

> Jointly with the cantons, the Confederation shall encourage the implementation of a co-ordinated university policy which also takes international co-operation into consideration.

> The Confederation shall encourage through financial aid, the running and development of cantonal universities and recognised university institutes.

The Federal Law on Research of 7 October, 1983 provides in Article 6 that the Confederation shall encourage research in accordance with this law and specific laws:

- by maintaining the federal institutes of technology and research establishments attached to them,
- by allocating subsidies in accordance with the federal law on assistance to universities,
- by allocating subsidies to institutions responsible for promoting research (in particular the Swiss Science National Foundation),
- by allocating direct subsidies and other forms of support through the intermediary of the federal government.

The majority of university laws have been amended (Federal Institutes of Technology, 1991; St-Gallen, 1988; Geneva, 1994; Basel, 1995; Bern, 1996; Neuchâtel, 1996). For others, e.g. Bern, Fribourg, Neuchâtel, Lausanne, Zürich, legislative review is under way. Generally, they are all moving in the same direction; however differences will remain regarding the role and composition of the university council and the powers of the rector.

2 Federal issues

Under the Swiss federal system, in principle, educational establishments come under the exclusive jurisdiction of the cantons (educational sovereignty). In the field of higher education, the Confederation has parallel powers to those of the cantons: it can establish, take over and subsidise institutes of tecnology, universities and other higher education establishments. For its own establishments (federal institutes of technology), it has exclusive jurisdiction; for the cantonal universities, it has no real regulatory powers; it only allocates subsidies. There is no framework federal law in Switzerland on higher education.

The Law on Federal Institutes of Technology (EPF) governs the Federal Institutes of Technology in Zürich and Lausanne and the research establishments attached to the FIT. These establishments come under the jurisdiction of the Confederation.

The eight cantonal universities of Zürich, Basel, Bern, Fribourg, St-Gallen, Lausanne, Neuchâtel and Geneva are each governed by a cantonal law. For Zürich part of the general law on education is devoted to the university.

On 6 October, 1995 the federal parliament adopted a new Law on Specialised Higher Education Establishments. Through this law, the Confederation wants to encourage the creation and development of such specialised establishments in the fields of industry, arts and crafts, services, as well as agriculture and forest management. The Confederation will regulate their activities, recognise their diplomas and provide financial support. The Confederation's powers are derived from the Federal Constitution: Article 27 and Article 34, which gives powers to regulate vocational training in the aforementioned fields. These new specialised higher education establishments are currently being set up and should be operational in 1997.

In order to involve those cantons which do not have universities in the funding of cantonal universities, the 26 Swiss cantons and the Principality of Liechtenstein have signed an agreement on contribution to the funding of the universities. Pursuant to the agreement, which continues to be in force until the end of 1998, the cantons operating universities receive an annual contribution to the running expenses from those cantons not having universities; in 1996 amounting to 8750 Swiss francs (CHF) per student enrolled, and payable by the canton in which the student is legally domiciled at the time of graduation from secondary school. A new agreement has been elaborated which will come into force in 1999. It foresees that the annual contributions per student will be substantially higher than at present, and, they will differ according to the discipline: 9500 CHF for students of humanities, 23000 CHF for students of natural and technical sciences and 46000 for students of clinical medicine. The agreement aims at contributions which would cover running costs occasioned by students not-residents of the University's home canton. The procedure of adhering to the agreement is underway in the cantons.

3 Institutional governance

The following are some principles applicable to the management of almost all universities and higher education establishments.

- Universities and higher education establishments are state public law institutions (e.g. Art. 5, para. 1, Law on FIT; Art. 1, Law on the University of Lausanne).

- They enjoy legal personality; they administer and conduct their affairs autonomously (e.g. Art. 5, para. 2, Law on FIT; Art. 1, 5 and 7, Law on the University of Lausanne).

- The budget is decided upon by the competent parliament, on a proposal from the government. According to the circumstances of each case, all or part of the funds may be granted as a budget package (e.g. Art. 35, Law on FIT; Art. 49, Law on the University of St-Gallen; Art. 26, Law on the University of Basel).

- The operational management of the universities and higher education establishments is the responsibility of the rector/president. The strategic management (university statutes, general policy directives, approval of development plans, distribution of financial resources, creation and abolition of teaching and research units, etc.) is carried out by the University Council/the Board of FIT (e.g. Art. 25 and 28, Law on FIT; Art. 8,9 and 16, Law on the University of St-Gallen). In the cantons where such a body does not exist, the cantonal government carries out many of the tasks of a University Council. Freedom of teaching and research is guaranteed (e.g. Art. 5, para. 3, Law on FIT; Art. 59, Law on the University of Lausanne).

- The cantonal universities are made up of faculties (sections at the University of St-Gallen). The EPFs are made up of departments for research and sections for teaching.

- Members of the universities (teaching staff, scientific assistants and students) participate in the preparation of decisions of superior authorities and decision-making within the faculties insofar as they are concerned (e.g. Art. 32, Law on EPFs; Art. 11, Law on the University of St-Gallen).

- Switzerland has no central research body, such as exists in France and Italy for example; as a result, scientific research is almost completely integrated into university programmes. Through the Swiss Science National Foundation, the Confederation pays grants directly to lecturers and institutes for high quality research projects. The procedures are regulated by the federal law on research.

The tasks of the different bodies have been described in broad terms. As in all public authority activities, the bodies must obey the general principles of administrative law: the requirements to act on a legal basis, and for the public interest, to observe equal treatment, proportionality, good faith and nonretroactivity.

10.29

TURKEY

Kemal Gürüz

1 The legal framework: principles and structures

Prior to 1981, higher education in Turkey was a ternary system, comprising universities, academies, which were roughly the equivalent of polytechnics, teacher colleges and 2-year vocational schools. The latter two were affiliated to various Ministries. Following the enactment of the Higher Education Law in 1981, the system was unified and 8 new universities were formed, mainly from the existing academies, bringing the number of universities to 27. Teacher colleges were converted into faculties, and, together with the vocational schools, were made parts of the universities. Along with this reorganisation, the Council of Higher Education was established as an intermediary body, and provisions were made that allowed non-profit foundations to found private universities.

The following period was one of rapid expansion of the system. Total enrolment which was 237,369 in the 1980-1981 academic year increased to 1,150,137 in 1995-1996, the total academic staff increased from 20,816 to 49,234 in the same period. The number of universities is now 61, and 8 of these are private. The gross enrolment ratio is presently 22.4%, when all undergraduate students are included, and 13.5% when students in distance education programmes are excluded.

The Council of Higher Education is a 24-member corporate public body responsible for the planning, coordination and supervision of higher education within the provisions set forth in the law. Seven of its members are academics elected by the Interuniversity Council, seven are appointed directly by the President of the Republic with priority given to former rectors, and ten are appointed by the government, mostly from among senior civil servants, all for a renewable term of four years. The president of the Council is directly appointed by the President of the Republic from among the members. The day-to-day functions of the Council are carried out by a 9 member executive committee, elected from among its members.

The Interuniversity Council is an academic advisory body, comprising the rector and one member elected by the senate of each university.

The Minister of National Education represents higher education in the parliament and can chair the meetings of the Council but has no voting powers. Decisions of neither the Council nor the universities are subject to ratification by the Ministry.

Each university consists of faculties and 4-year schools, offering bachelor level programmes the latter having a vocational emphasis, and 2-year vocational schools offering pre-licence level programmes of a strictly vocational nature.

Graduate level programmes consist of masters and doctoral programmes which are coordinated by the institutes for graduate studies. Medical specialty training programmes equivalent to doctoral level programmes are, however, carried out within the faculties of medicine and the training hospitals owned by the universities.

Universities, faculties, institutes and 4-year schools are founded by law, while 2-year vocational schools, departments, and divisions are established by the Council of Higher Education. Likewise, the start of a degree programme at any level is subject to ratification by the Council. Universities are free to determine the number of students to be admitted to graduate-level programmes, as well as admission requirements to the curricula and degree requirements of such programmes, in line with the general rules and regulations adopted by the Interuniversity Council.

Students admitted to bachelors and pre-licence level programmes are determined annually by the Council of Higher Education upon the recommendations of universities. Students are admitted to such programmes through a central competitive entrance examination, organised and administered by the Student Selection and Placement Centre, affiliated to the Council. Common course requirements of such programmes are determined by the Council upon the recommendation of the Interuniversity Council. Universities are completely free to determine the rest of the curricula, all course contents, grading systems and degree requirements, while teaching methods and grading are prerogatives of individual instructors.

Both academic and administrative staff in state universities have civil servant status, and, except for research assistants and assistant professors, have tenure. The numbers of academic and administrative staff posts allocated to each state university are determined by acts of parliament. Staff appointments at all levels are, however, made exclusively by the universities themselves, and are subject to ratification by no outside authority. The law only sets forth the minimum requirements for academic promotions, and the procedures to be followed in making appointments.

At all levels, the chairperson of a council, senate or board, such as the president of the Council of Higher Education, rector, faculty dean, institute and school director and department chairperson, is responsible for the implementation of the policies adopted by the various boards. At the university level, however, the rector is both the academic leader and the chief executive officer of the university, and so are the deans, directors and department chairpersons in their respective units.

Each unit head referred to above, with whom the final decision making power rests, is assisted by an academic board with a broad membership, and an administrative board of a relatively narrower membership, such as the senate and the university administrative board, in the case of the university as a whole, and the faculty board and the faculty administrative board, in the case of a faculty. The academic boards make general policy decisions, while the administrative boards are responsible for the day-to-day implementation of such policies. Institutes and schools have similar structures.

The election, nomination and appointment procedures of rectors, deans, directors and chairpersons and requirements thereof, as well as the compositions of boards, together with the responsibilities and authorities of each are stipulated in the law.

Universities are completely free to accept gifts and donations and to enter into research contracts and service provision agreements with outside bodies, both national and foreign. Academic staff have complete freedom in choosing research topics and methods. To obtain financial support for such activities, other than the infrastructure provided by the university free of charge, individual academic staff must submit a proposal which must be approved by the outside body concerned, or the research fund of the university administered by the university itself.

Private universities have only to conform to the basic academic requirements and structures set forth in the law. Other than this, they are completely free to manage their own affairs according to rules and regulations adopted by their boards of trustees, in which lay members in most cases make up the majority.

2 Democracy

The Higher Education Law of 1981 has undergone a number of relatively minor changes since its enactment. The most important of which occurred in 1992, and brought in a new nomination and appointment procedure for rectors. According to this, six candidates who are full professors are elected by the assembly of faculty members, which includes all full, associate and assistant professors at the university. From among these six, the Council of Higher Education elects three nominees by secret ballot, and submits them to the President of the Republic, who appoints one of them as the rector for a period of four years, renewable only once.

Deans are appointed by the Council from among three full professors nominated by the rector, while institute and school directors are directly appointed by the rector.

Each department within a faculty is made up of scientific divisions. Division heads are elected by faculty members in that division, who in turn advise the dean for the appointment of the department chairperson.

All boards in a university consist of elected and ex officio members. The senate, for example, consists of all faculty deans and a faculty member elected by each faculty board plus the vice-rectors, directly appointed by the rector from among full professors, institute and school directors. The university administrative board, on the other hand, consists of all faculty deans plus three faculty members elected by the senate. Both the senate and the board are chaired by the rector, and in general are advisory in nature, except concerning academic staff appointments at the full and associate professor levels, which are finalised by the university administrative board.

In a similar manner, the faculty board consists of three full and two associate professors, and one assistant professor elected by all the faculty members in these respective ranks plus all department chairpersons in the faculty. The faculty administrative board, on the other hand, consists of three full and two associate professors plus one assistant professor elected by the faculty board. Both boards are chaired by the dean. Institutes and schools have two similar boards each.

At the department level, the departmental assembly consists of all faculty members, while the department board consists of division heads, and both are chaired by the chairperson of the department.

The term of office of elected members in the senate and all boards is three years, and is renewable. Although the senate and the various boards are general advisory in nature, rectors and deans usually use discretion in delegating decision making powers to these bodies in most, and especially in academic, matters.

All expenditures are subject to the approval of the rector, who, in turn, may delegate this authority to the vice-rectors, deans, directors and the secretary general to the extent he or she deems fit. Students and administrative staff have no representatives in any of the boards.

3 External influence

There are no lay members, i.e. other stakeholders, in either the senate or the various boards of state universities. The only potential source of external influence comes from the lay members of the Council of Higher Education in the case of state universities.

4 Hidden or indirect governance

Hidden or indirect governance stems from the public finance laws which stipulate in cumbersome detail the procedures to be followed in the preparation of annual budgets, procurement, including construction contracts, and auditing of expenditures, to which all public agencies are subject.

The recurrent budget of each state university is negotiated jointly by the Council of Higher Education and the university concerned with the Ministry of Finance, and the investment budget with the State Planning Organisation. The Council transmits these budgets, together with its own budget to the Ministry of National Education and the Minister defends them in the parliament. The president of the Council is also given the floor at the beginning and the end of the debate in the parliamentary commission. The result is a line-item budget with very specific earmarked budget figures.

In addition to the state budget, a university has three more funds. Income from the services provided by a university, such as from patient care in university hospitals and contract research are collected in a revolving fund. Student contributions towards highly subsidised services are collected in a separate fund. The research fund is made up of a lump sum grant from the state budget plus a portion of the income from the revolving fund and earmarked projects given by the State Planning Organisation.

The above mentioned three funds are also subject to laws, rules and regulations similar to those of the state budget, which leave little room to manoeuvre. The major difference between these three funds and the state budget is that any money left in the former is carried over to the next fiscal year while that left unspent in the state budget reverts back to the treasury.

The Scientific and Technical Research Council of Turkey also supports research projects by evaluating proposals submitted by faculty members. However, such grants are directly given to faculty members, and are thus not included in university income.

5 Legal protection

The right of all Turkish citizens to petition and to appeal all matters concerning themselves is under constitutional guarantee. Furthermore, the Constitution also subjects all administrative and executive decisions and actions to the scrutiny of courts.

Thus all staff and students can petition and appeal matters concerning themselves, such as academic promotions, disciplinary actions and grades. The process generally starts at the departmental level, with the right of appeal to a board at the next level, and can eventually end up in the Supreme Court of Appeals, a constitutional body that protects the rights of citizens *vis à vis* the state.

6 Conclusion

By far the major source of income of state universities are the funds allocated through the annual state budget. In fiscal 1995, such funds accounted for 69%, income generated by state universities themselves, mainly from university hospitals was 27.5%, and that from "student contributions" was 3.5% of the total income of state universities. Only 7% of the income from student contributions was spent on education, the rest, 93%, went towards the very highly subsidised meals, lodging and medical services provided to the students and to financing extracurricular activities. Thus, there are no real tuition fees in Turkey.

The scarcity of public resources allocated to higher education is one negative aspect of the system, the other important negative aspect is the line-item budgeting system, essentially prepared by negotiations on the basis of past years allocations, which allows insufficient discretionary powers to state universities and is based on neither input nor output parameters.

The view held by the Council of Higher Education is that higher education is a semi-public service with an associated cost, which must be partly borne by those benefiting from it. To reconcile quantity with quality, a healthy competitive environment must be created in the provision of this service, whereby state universities and private universities will compete not only among themselves, but also with universities abroad.

Two prerequisites are considered to be *sine quo non* for fair competition: a) state universities must be equipped with the same financial and administrative decision making powers as those of their competitors; b) academic assessment and evaluation mechanisms, eventually leading to a full accreditation system, must be established so that funding can be linked to performance, and that potential consumers can be properly informed about the alternatives.

Draft legislation to encourage these prerequisites was prepared and submitted to the government in 1996. In the interim, the Council of Higher Education has established the Academic Assessment Board as an advisory body. Rules and regulations governing the operation of this board have been published in the Official Gazette. Attempts are also underway to incorporate certain incentive mechanisms into the existing budgeting system.

Shortage of qualified academic staff is the major hurdle that must be overcome before the system can be further expanded. Since 1987, universities have been sending research assistants abroad for graduate studies and to be trained as future faculty members. The number of such assistants presently studying abroad is 1,923. Until the year 2000, 700 students will be sent abroad annually. In order to coordinate this ambitious and costly programme, the Council of Higher Education established the Board for Training Faculty Members and Researchers. Rules and regulations governing the operations of this board have also been published in the Official Gazette. In addition, in 1996 construction of graduate student housing complexes were started at eight of the major universities so that the existing scientific research potential within the country can be fully exploited while at the same time increasing the quantity and quality of university research within the country.

10.30

UKRAINE

Mikhail Stepko & Georgy Kryuchkov

Examination of a draft law is undertaken by the Ministry of Finance, Ministry of the Economy, Ministry of Education, Ministry of Justice, and the Cabinet of Ministers. This can take up to 12 months to complete and may involve other interested parties such as regional educational bodies, trade unions, associations of rectors, teachers etc..

The law is then submitted by the Cabinet of Ministers to the Supreme Rada (the Parliament) where it is looked at by the Supreme Rada's Commission for Education and Science. This can take up to 2 months to complete and may also include other interested parties. After that it is considered by a plenary session of the Supreme Rada for a period of up to 2 months, which then passes a resolution to adopt the law and states the procedure for its implementation. The law is signed by the President after which it comes into force.

A draft law is also examined by higher education institutions' collectives, such as the associations of rectors, teachers, etc., and also by regional bodies concerned with higher education administration. The draft law is also published in the press and is discussed by representatives of the general public. It is also discussed in the meetings of the board of the Ministry of Education and at the meetings of the Presidium of the Supreme Rada. It may also be examined by expert representatives of international organisations.

The legal services of the Ministry of Justice and the Cabinet of Ministers provide the first assessment to see whether a draft law is in compliance with the constitution. Subsequent assessments are made by regular Commissions of the Supreme Rada. The final decision to adopt the draft law is taken in the plenary session of the Supreme Rada. The current Education Law was adopted when the new Ukrainian constitution was not in existence.

The compliance of a draft law to international law is checked during all phases of its development by the experts working on it as well as by the Supreme Rada's Commission for Education and Science. The current Education Law was examined by the Council of Europe's Legislative Reform Programme mission members.

There have been no cases of revision to provisions of the Education Law by a Constitutional Court, since such a court does not exist in the Ukraine.

There is a lack of correspondence between the active Education Law and the new social and economic realities of the Ukraine and with the international normative documents that were signed by the Ukraine. As a result there have been negative consequences for the practical application of some articles of the active law.

Any political conflicts that arise while preparing education legislation are resolved by Parliament and its political factions, the Supreme Rada's Regular Commissions and, in certain cases, by the administration of the President or the Cabinet of Ministers. The scope of the legislation's contents are monitored by the Regular Commissions of the Supreme Rada, the Cabinet of Ministers, the Ministry of Education, particularly for questions of competence, and the committees of trade-unions and teachers associations. The procedure of the legislation is regulated by the heads of higher education establishments, the Supreme Rada and its Presidium.

In the preamble to the Education Law adopted in May 1996, the importance of education to the all-round development of the state is underlined and the objectives of education are formulated. These are identified as the development of a person and his/her personality, talents and mental faculties to produce citizens capable of making conscious social decisions, and providing the national economy with qualified specialists. The preamble also states that education in the Ukraine is based on the principles of humanism, democracy, national self-consciousness, and the harmonious relations between people and nations.

Higher education and research are not regarded as highly politicised issues. However, there are certain problems associated with the introduction of new sources of financing in addition to state budget funding; with relations between educational establishments and the church; and over the property relations between the educational establishments and the state, particularly with respect to the question of property rights.

The signing of the Vienna Convention and the Ukraine's membership of the Council of Europe promoted a deeper legislative awareness particularly within education legislation. Broad contacts with representatives from European countries as part of the activities of the Council of Europe's Higher Education and Research Committee have allowed for the development of the educational system while drawing on the experiences of European countries, initially Germany, and then that of the USA, and incorporating these with domestic experiences acquired during the time when the Ukraine was a member of the USSR. For example, in 1991 the idea of broadening the scope of preparation during the first years of study was drawn from the American-Canadian higher education system; at the same time earlier specialisation typical of Germany and the countries of the former USSR was preserved. These trends were reflected in the Education Law adopted in 1996. The education models typical of France, Great Britain, and some Scandinavian countries have not been introduced.

Anticipating implementation of a draft law is not admitted. Before a new law comes into force, the active law as well as other normative documents such as presidential decrees, Cabinet Minister resolutions etc., are used. They will have also passed legal expert examination.

Each type of legislative document has its jurisdiction according to the following hierarchy: law, presidential decree, Cabinet Minister resolution, normative order of the Ministry of Education (which is registered in the Ministry of Justice), and statutes of educational establishments. To settle outstanding issues efficiently presidential decrees and Cabinet Minister resolutions are mostly used. For educational issues orders of the Ministry of Education are used. Statutes of educational establishments regulate its external and internal relations and must correspond to the main legislative normative documents as mentioned above.

Legal provisions which require the government to evaluate a law's impact on higher education development or policy are in proxy of the Cabinet Ministers.

At the institutional level implementation of state policy is assessed and controlled by local checks and in the hearings of the following bodies responsible for assessment, the Supreme Rada's Commission for Education and Science, the Cabinet Ministers and the board of the Ministry of Education.

Development of the Ukraine's legal system is one of the most important aspects of the country's transfer to a market economy. Legislative work is currently in the stage of formation and the efficiency of the new legislative-normative base greatly depends on the state of the Ukrainian economy, which is now undergoing a process of transformation.

10.31

UNITED KINGDOM

Chris Kempson

1 Introduction

The publicly funded higher education sector in England consists of 72 universities, 49 colleges of higher education and 16 directly funded institutions of the University of London. The Further and Higher Education Act 1992 (FHE Act 1992) abolished the previous distinctions between the universities and polytechnics. It also created the Higher Education Funding Council for England (HEFCE), which superseded the Universities Funding Council (a Great Britain-wide body) and the Polytechnics and Colleges Funding Council, to distribute public funds to the institutions, account for their use, promote value for money and the proper use of public funds, and advise the Secretary of State on higher education's funding needs. There is a long tradition of independence in universities and in HE colleges with a voluntary foundation: this covers both issues of governance and academic autonomy. The variety in the constitution and historical background of the various higher education institutions means that a prescriptive approach in matters of governance would not be appropriate.

2 Legal framework

Governing bodies of most of the pre-1992 universities are bound, either by the institutions' Royal Charter together with an associated set of statutes, or by Act of Parliament. The Privy Council grants Royal Charters and, in the case of higher education institutions established by the Education Reform Act 1988 (ERA), it now approves their instruments and articles of government under the provisions of the FHE Act 1992. Some pre-1992 universities were also established as companies limited by guarantee. Some higher education colleges have been established by churches as charitable trusts operating under a trust deed or through a scheme made by the Charity Commissioners. Institutions administered as charitable trusts and designated for funding by the HEFCE under section 129 of the ERA 1988, are required to have an instrument and articles of government approved by the Privy Council. Institutions administered as companies limited by guarantee and similarly designated for funding by the HEFCE are founded on a memorandum and articles of association which incorporate the provisions of the instruments and articles of government also requiring approval by the Privy Council.

3 Decision-making

Institutions of higher education are legally independent corporate institutions. The council or board of governors as the executive body of the institution is responsible for ensuring the effective management of the institution and for planning its future development. It has ultimate responsibility for all the affairs of the institution. The council or board's role is one of overall responsibility, and not of detailed day-to-day management. The latter is properly the responsibility of the head of the institution and his/her senior colleagues. The division of these responsibilities stems from:

- the charter and statutes in the case of pre-1992 universities,
- the ERA 1988 (as amended by the FHE Act 1992) together with the instruments and articles of government in the case of the post-1992 universities and colleges of higher education.

In the pre-1992 universities the council is the executive governing body of the university. It is responsible for the university's finances and investments and for the management of the university estate and buildings. It has the authority to make contracts on behalf of the university and to enter into loans and mortgage agreements. In many cases it also has responsibility for the oversight of the powers of teaching and research. University statutes will normally state that, subject to the powers of the senate, the council has responsibility for the conduct of all the affairs of the university. The council will carry out many of its functions through committees; in particular it will often have, jointly with the senate, a resources or strategy committee which is responsible for planning the development of the university bringing together academic priorities, financial considerations and building needs.

The senate is responsible for regulating and directing the academic work of the university. The senate's specific responsibilities normally include: academic strategy, promotion of research, approval of content of curriculum and new programmes, academic standards, procedures for the award of qualifications, appointment of internal and external examiners, policies and procedures on examinations, criteria for admission, and student discipline.

In the post-1992 universities and colleges of HE the board of governors is responsible for:

- the determination of the educational character and mission of the institution and for oversight of its activities,
- the effective and efficient use of resources, the solvency of the institution and safeguarding its assets,
- approving annual estimates of income and expenditure,
- the appointment, grading, suspension, dismissal and determination of the pay and conditions of service of holders of senior posts,
- setting a framework for the pay and conditions of service of all other staff,
- the appointment of external auditors.

In practice the governing bodies delegate many of their functions to committees.

The academic board which is the equivalent of the senate in the post-1992 universities and colleges of higher education, is responsible for academic affairs, including academic standards, research, scholarship, teaching and courses at the institution, and for considering the development of the academic activities of the institution, subject to the overall responsibilities of the governing body and the head of the institution. The academic board and the senate in the pre-1992 universities delegate many of their functions to committees.

4 Important changes in governance since 1985

There have been a number of significant changes in the governance arrangements of higher education institutions since 1985. Two of the most significant are: (a) the establishment under the ERA 1988 as Higher Education Corporations (i.e. legally-independent corporate institutions) certain higher education institutions previously maintained by, and as part of local education authorities (LEAs) and (b) the FHE Act 1992 which abolished the previous distinctions between the universities and polytechnics and also empowered the new post-1992 universities to award their own degrees. The 1992 Act also requires the Privy Council's approval for the governance arrangements of the post-1992 universities and colleges of higher education as it does for the governance arrangements of their pre-1992 counterparts.

5 Democracy

The structure of governance in higher education institutions in England follows this general pattern. In many of the older pre-1992 universities the court is defined as the supreme governing body, even though the charter and statutes of many of these universities place severe limitations on its powers. In the charters of some of the universities established in the 1960s the court has an entirely advisory status. However, in all cases the role of the court is in practice largely formal and it does not take part in the day-to-day oversight of the university's affairs.

The court is typically a large body, often in the region of 200 members with newer universities tending to have smaller courts. Its constitution is specified in the university's statutes, and it typically includes representatives of local authorities, MPs, representatives of other universities, colleges, schools and the professions, members of the council and university officers, elected staff and students, representatives and graduates of the university. The court is thus a means whereby representatives of the community can be associated with the university. It also provides a public forum where members of court can raise any matters of concern about the university.

The court is required by statute to meet at least once a year and its powers typically include consideration of the university's annual report, approving the annual accounts, approving amendments to the institution's governance arrangements, prior to submission to the Privy Council; and in many cases appointing the chancellor.

However, the council is the executive governing body of the university. It is responsible for the university's finances and investments and for the management of the university estate and buildings. Its membership is specified in the statutes by class of appointment. At least half the members of the council are called 'lay' members (i.e. they are not staff or students of the university). They may be selected by virtue of the links between the university and the local authority, industry or commerce, from former graduates, or distinguished men and women in their own right who are seen to be both willing and able to contribute to the governance of the university. The others are largely academic. Typically they include students and sometimes non-academic staff. An example of such a council's membership is as follows. Uniquely the governing bodies of the Universities of Oxford and Cambridge do not contain a lay element.

Appointment of Governors
Pre-1992 Universities

(a) The chancellor, the pro-chancellors, the vice-chancellor, the treasurer, the deputy treasurer and the pro-vice chancellors.

(b) Members not being students or members of staff are appointed by the court.

(c) Members are appointed by the local civic authority (where there is one) and also by LEAs.

(d) Members of the senate are appointed by the senate.

(e) Members are appointed by the council who are not students or members of staff.

(f) Members are appointed by convocation who are not students or members of staff

(g) The president of the university's students union and another students are appointed by the student union.

Terms of office vary, often along the following lines, for those in category (a) above it is for the time that they occupy their position, for those in categories (b) to (f) it is often for three to five years or shorter depending on what the appointing body determines, and for those in category (g) it is for the university year for which they are appointed.

All retiring members are normally eligible for re-appointment.

For the post-1992 universities and colleges of higher education, the board of governors is the executive governing body of the institution.

The FHE Act 1992 and the instrument of government state that it must consist of not less than 12 and not more than 24 members, plus the principal unless he or she chooses not be a member. It is a requirement that at least half and up to 13 members shall be independent members with experience in industrial, commercial or employment matters or the practice of any profession. No specific guidance has been given on particular areas from which membership should be drawn.

Up to two may be teachers at the institution, who are nominated by the academic board, and up to two may be students at the institution nominated by the students. At least one, and not more than 9, are co-opted members nominated by the members of the board of governors who are not co-opted members. The co-opted membership may include members of staff, whether teachers or not, and students and at least one of the co-opted members must have experience in the provision of education. Elected members of any local authority may only serve on the board of governors as co-opted members.

Before the initial members of boards of governors of higher education corporations were appointed by the Secretary of State under the ERA 1988, guidance was given that independent governors for each institution should show a reasonable spread in terms of age, sex and field of expertise. Independent members were also to have high standing in local or regional industry, business or a profession. Once the initial appointments had been made by the

Secretary of State, future appointments were for the boards of governors themselves to determine.

Terms of office of the members are determined by the board of governors. They are usually for between 3-4 years, but students normally serve for one year. All retiring members are normally eligible for re-appointment.

The board of governors are responsible for:

- the determination of the educational character and mission of the institution and for oversight of its activities,
- the effective and efficient use of resources, the solvency of the institution and safeguarding its assets,
- approving annual estimates of income and expenditure,
- the appointment, grading, suspension, dismissal and determination of the pay and conditions of service of holders of senior posts,
- setting a framework for the pay and conditions of service of all other staff,
- the appointment of external auditors.

6 Hidden or indirect governance

Higher education institutions are legally-independent corporate institutions having charitable status, accountable through a governing body which carries ultimate responsibility for all aspects of the institution. Higher education institutions are not subject to "hidden influence". There is openness and transparency in the operation of their governing bodies especially with regard to their financial responsibilities to the HEFCE. Higher education institutions' books and accounts are open to inspection by the Controller and Auditor General. In practice National Audit Office (NAO) are selective in their use of inspection rights. The HEFCE is responsible for both quality assessment of individual subjects taught within its institutions and institutions' research output. The new Quality Assurance Agency for Higher Education (QAA) undertakes quality audit of institutions' quality assurance mechanisms and also quality assessment on behalf of the HEFCE. As autonomous institutions, higher education institutions are responsible for establishing their own entry requirements. The Universities and Colleges Admissions Service (UCAS) is an independent body established by the universities and institutions of higher education in the United Kingdom to administer admissions arrangements for individual students to gain entry to various courses of higher education.

7 Legal protection

Ministers have no powers to intervene in the internal affairs of higher education institutions. All higher education institutions have their own internal appeals and grievance procedures. Ultimately, it is open to individuals (i.e. staff and students) to pursue their case through the courts or tribunals if they choose to do so.

The statutes of the pre-1992 universities specify procedures covering the suspension or dismissal of academic staff for misconduct or other good cause and arrangements for academic staff to seek redress for any reason relating to their employment.

Their governing bodies are responsible for appointing individuals or bodies, as specified in the governance arrangements, to hear disciplinary charges which could result in dismissal of academic staff, and appeals and grievances from academic staff.

The articles of government of the higher education colleges and the post-1992 universities require the governing body to make rules relating to the conduct of staff and procedures according to which staff may seek redress of any grievances relating to their employment. The articles also specify procedures for the suspension and dismissal of staff and rights of appeal against suspension or dismissal.

In the pre-1992 universities, rules and procedures concerning student discipline (both academic matters and instances of misconduct) are normally prescribed in the university's ordinances. Responsibility for overseeing the implementation of these procedures normally rests with the senate. Students have the right of appeal to the governing body (i.e. council) and/or to a specially constituted appeal body.

The articles of government of the post-1992 universities and colleges of higher education state that responsibility for student disciplinary procedures relating to academic procedures rests with the academic board, although a student has the right to appeal to the governing body if he/she considers that these procedures have not been properly followed.

The articles of government of the post-1992 universities and colleges of higher education also provide for the governing body, after consultation with the academic board and student representatives, to make rules relating to the suspension and expulsion of students on disciplinary grounds. The rules should include procedures for students to make representations to the board of governors against expulsion or suspension.

The office of visitor exists in most pre-1992 universities. The visitor has power to inspect the university and to hear appeals from members of the university (including the staff and students). Although the post-1992 universities and colleges of higher education are not precluded from establishing the office of visitor, it appears that relatively few have done so.

If a student considers that there is misleading information in an institution's prospectus, he/she can contact the Quality Assurance Agency for Higher Education (QAA), who will look into the matter if the student is not satisfied with the outcome of the internal complaints system within the institution.[1]

8 Conclusion

Institutions of higher education in England have diverse backgrounds and traditions, but are united in the common purpose of the provision of teaching and the pursuit of knowledge and research. The internal organisation, procedures and governance arrangements of individual institutions vary considerably and higher education has experienced an unprecedented period of

1 The National Committee of Inquiry into Higher Education, chaired by Sir Ron Dearing CB, published its report entitled "Higher Education in the learning society" on 23 July 1997. The report addresses a number of recommendations on the management and governance of higher education institutions to the government, to the institutions themselves and to their representative bodies, which they will need to consider carefully.

change and expansion in the 1980s and the early part of this decade. Governing bodies have responded well to those changes and will need to continue to do so as we move towards the next millennium to help ensure that higher education continues to be the success story of the UK's education system.

ACKNOWLEDGEMENTS

Albania

Ylly Gjançi
Inspector of Higher Education Department, Ministry of Education, Tirana

Armenia

Avetik Kalantaryan
Specialist, Education and Social Programmes Desk, Foreign Aid Co-ordination Centre, Ministry of Economy, Yerevan

Austria

Gerald Bast
Head of Department for University Refonn and Legal Affairs, Federal Ministry for Science, Transport and Arts, Vienna

Belarus

Boris Kopyssky
Head of the Analytical Department, Ministry of Education and Science, Minsk

Nikolai Listopad
Director of the Computer Analytical Centre, Ministry of Education and Science, Minsk

Belgium (Fl)	*Marie-Anne Persoons* Assistant Director at the Directorate-General of Higher Education and Scientific Research, Ministry of the Flemish Community of BelgiuM, Department of Education, Brussels
Bulgaria	*Ivan Rangelov Atanassov* Senior Expert, Department of Higher Education State Policy, Sofia
	Ervant Rafy Stepanyan Head of Department, Department of Higher Education State Policy, Sofia
Cyprus	*Cristodoulos Cleopas* Director of Higher and Tertiary Education, Ministry of Education and Culture, Nicosia
Denmark	*Ulrik Jørgensen* Associate professor, Danish Technical University, Lyngby
	Jane Planck Head of Section, Department of Higher Education, Ministry of Education, Copenhagen
Estonia	*Ain Heinaru* Ministry of Education, Department of Research and Universities, Tallinn
France	*Sophie Decker* Deputy to the Head of the Office for Institution Regulations and Statutes, General Directorate of Higher Education, Ministry of Education, Higher Education and Research, Paris

Georgia	*Georgi Machabeli* Chief of Foreign Departinent, Ministry of Education, Tbilisi
	Irakli Machabeli Vice-President, Intemational Black Sea University, Tbilisi
Germany	*Kornelia Haugg* Federal Ministry of Education, Science, Research and Technology, Bonn
	Werner von Trützschler Thüringen Ministry of Scienee, Research and Culture, Erfurt
	Michael Daxner President, Oldenburg University, Oldenburg
Greece	*Frida Meropouli* Head of the Section, Ministry of National Education and Religion, Athens
Holy See	*Mgr. Walter Edyvean* Head of the Office for Universities, Congregation for Catholic Education, Vatican City
Iceland	*Thordur Kristinsson* Director of Academie Affairs, University of lceland, Reykjavik
	Arnór Gudmundsson Head of Section, Ministry of Culture and Education, Reykjavik
Italy	*Wladimiro Gasparri* Departinent of Public Law, Universita'degli Studi di Firenze, Rome

Latvia

Andrejs Rauhvargers
Head, Academie Infonnation Centre (ENIC), Riga

Jánis Čakste
Director, Departinent of Higher Education and Research, Ministry of Education and Science, Riga

Lithuania

Gediminas Dubauskas
Former Programme Specialist, Ministry of Education and Science of Lithuania, Vilnius

Malta

Paul Heywood
Pro-Chancellor, University of Malta, Malta

Moldova

Stefan Tiron
Adviser to the Minister, Ministry of Education, Youth and Sport, Chisinau

Dimitrie Ungureanu
Ministry of Education, Youth and Sport, Chisinau

The Netherlands

Ernst M.H. Hirsch Ballin
Professor of International Law and General Theory of Legislation, Catholic University of Brabant, Tilburg

Paul J.J. Zoontjens
Staff member at the Department of Legislation and Legal Affairs, Ministry of Education, Culture and Sciences, Zoetermeer

Norway

Rolf Kåre Jenssen
Executive Officer, Department of Higher Education, Royal Norwegian Ministry of Education, Research and Church Affairs

Gro Beate Vige
Executive Officer, Department of Higher Education, Royal Norwegian Ministry of Education, Research and Church Affairs

Poland

Julita Jablecka
Assistant Professor, Centre for Science Policy and Higher Education, Warsaw University

Russia

Evgueni I. Popov
Head of the Division, Division of Information and Methodical Provisions, Libraries, Publishing Houses and Editorial Boards of the Ministry of General and Professional Education, Moscow

Yury A. Kudryavstev
Research Centre for Problems of Quality in Specialists' Training, Deputy Director, Moscow

Stanislav S. Ivanov
Research Centre for Problems of Quality in Specialists' Training, Head of Department, Department for International Co-operation in Education, Moscow

Irina E. Volkova
Research Centre for Problems of Quality in Specialists' Training, Department for International Co-operation in Education, Moscow

Slovakia

Peter Plavčan
Director of Higher Education Department, Ministry of Education, Bratislava

Slovenia

Alenka Šelih
Professor of Law, University of Ljubljana, Ljubljana

	Majda Širok State Under-secretary, Ministry of Education and Sport, Ljubljana
Spain	*Jose Ignacio Cebreiro* Legal Adviser, Ministry of Education and Culture, Madrid
	Maria Jesús San Segundo Professor of Economics, University Carlos III, Madrid
Switzerland	*Christine Lenzen* Research Officer, Swiss University Conference, Bern
	Monique Stress-Sulser Lawyer, Research Assistant, Institute of Federalism, University of Fribourg, Fribourg
Turkey	*Kemal Gürüz* President, Council of Higher Education, Ankara
Ukraine	*Mikhail Stepko* Head of Department, Department of Higher Education, Ministry of Education, Kiev
	Georgy Kryuchkov Ministry of Education, Kiev
United Kingdom	*Chris Kempson* Department for Education and Employment, Higher Education Quality Division, London

INDEX

LRP Publications

The Council of Europe's Legislative Reform Programme (LRP) was established in 1992 by the Higher Education and Research Committee (CC-HER), a specialised committee under the European Cultural Convention. The LRP publishes the series "Legislating for Higher Education in Europe" as part of its continuing assistance to reforms in European higher education.

Each volume of the series presents a comparative discussion on a topic of particular relevance to the development of higher education legislation in Europe. Surveys from participating countries provide the basis of fact of the discussions and conclude each volume.

"Legislating for Higher Education in Europe" has been made possible by generous financial support from Denmark, Germany, Greece, Ireland, Italy, the Holy See, The Netherlands, Norway, Sweden, and Switzerland. The graphic design of the series is sponsored by Slovenia.